how to garden

how to garden

A practical encyclopedia of gardening techniques
with step-by-step photographs

Jonathan Edwards

HH
HERMES
HOUSE

This edition published byHermes House in 2003

© Anness Publishing Limited 2003

Hermes House is an imprint of Anness Publishing Limited
Hermes House, 88–89 Blackfriars Road, London SE1 8HA

A CIP catalogue record for this book is available from the British Library.

Publisher: Joanna Lorenz
Managing Editor: Linda Fraser
Project Editor: Rebecca Clunes
Copy Editor: Lydia Darbyshire
Designer: Michael Morey
Editorial Reader: Penelope Goodare
Picture Research: Gary Murphy, Joanna Skordis, Nansong Lue
Production Controller: Steve Lang

1 3 5 7 9 10 8 6 4 2

Bracketed terms are intended for American readers

Previously published as *The Practical Encyclopedia of Gardening Techniques*

Contents

Introduction

Most people find a garden a relaxing place, but for the gardener the pleasure is immeasurably increased. Firstly, there is the fun of deciding on a design, then the satisfaction of preparing the ground and planting, followed by the sense of achievement from the careful maintenance that keeps plants looking their best.

The appeal of gardening

In recent years, interest in gardening has mushroomed, and there has been an increasing demand for advice and information. Garden designs are becoming more imaginative, although one of the most appealing things about gardening is that you don't need any special skills or experience to start you off. Basic gardening is not only fulfilling and great fun, but is so easy to achieve that nobody is excluded. Perhaps even more important is that everyone can garden to their own level and in their own way, investing as much time and money as their own particular circumstances will allow.

This sunny border has been planted with a range of hot-coloured perennials, creating a bright, cheerful atmosphere.

Getting it right

To be an efficient gardener you need to master a few basic but very important skills, so that you avoid mistakes and get the most from the plants in your care. Many techniques are common sense, such as choosing the right plant for a particular position and knowing when to water, but other skills such as sowing, planting and pruning require knowledge and a bit of practice to get right. In this book, we guide you step-by-step through all the essential garden tasks you will need, whether creating a garden from scratch or taking care of an existing one.

How to use this book

The key to successful gardening is careful planning so that it meets both your needs and aspirations. The first section of this book helps you to design and plan a garden, whether you have a new, empty plot or are converting an existing design. Each step is explained, from assessing what you have and its potential to making new plans and turning them into reality.

Any garden is only as good as the soil that sustains it. For this reason, this book includes a dedicated chapter that explains exactly how to assess the soil in your garden, the various steps you can take to improve it, and how to prepare the ground ready for planting.

A stone urn planted with white and soft purples creates a lovely calm effect. Containers require a lot of watering but they do add an extra dimension to the garden.

Magnolia x *soulangeana* 'Amabilis' is a magnificent sight in mid-spring.

Columbines can be grown in the open border, but are frequently found in open woodland in the wild. Follow nature and grow them in shady borders or under a tree.

You will find plenty of practical growing techniques, arranged according to the types of plants: trees and shrubs; climbers; and flowers. In addition, this book looks in depth at particular areas of the garden that have techniques specific to them, including lawns; patios and containers; water and rock gardens; and greenhouse gardening.

There is an extensive section on the kitchen garden, explaining how to grow the most popular vegetables, herbs and fruit, whether in a dedicated plot or integrated into the rest of the garden.

The chapter on propagation runs through all the main methods of sowing, taking cuttings and layering to make increasing your stock of plants straightforward.

Many fundamental techniques apply to most if not all the areas of the garden. They are brought together in one section covering all the basics from choosing an essential tool kit, to weeding, mulching, feeding, watering as well as pest and disease control.

Finally, there is a seasonal checklist, to remind you to carry out the essential tasks in all areas of the garden at the right time.

This book contains over 150 step-by-step sequences to guide you through many of the more complicated gardening techniques. Throughout, there is information to help you choose the right plants for a specific situation or purpose, and green tip boxes that give simple suggestions on how to incorporate environmentally-friendly techniques into your gardening. Both beginners and experienced gardeners will find this book the ideal reference guide to achieve the garden they want.

Busy herbaceous borders full of strongly growing plants help to keep the weeds down, and so require less maintenance. A planting scheme like this is unbeatable in midsummer.

Planning your garden

Gardening is much more than just growing plants. To make a garden appealing, it is just as important that the setting in which the plants are placed is right. You can have your garden designed and constructed by professionals, but it will cost a great deal and the chances are that it won't give you as much satisfaction as creating a garden by your own efforts.

Only you can decide what is best for your garden. Tastes in gardens vary enormously, and the best test of a new design is whether it pleases you. Use the planning techniques suggested to experiment on paper – you will soon develop the skills that will enable you to design your garden with confidence. A well-thought-out design will ensure you make the best use of your space, and planning it is an enjoyable challenge in itself.

A well-planned garden will have points of interest all year round. Here, a border of brightly coloured tulips is a welcome sight in spring.

Assessing your garden

Whether you have the blank canvas of a new garden or are trying to make improvements to an existing design, the first step is to decide exactly what you want as well as what changes you will have to make to achieve your ideal garden.

What do you want?

This may seem a simple question, but in practice it can prove problematic, especially if there are two gardeners in the house. The easiest way to decide what you really want is to make several lists. Write down all the things in the existing garden that cannot be changed, such as the position of an established tree or a pond, as well as other features you want to keep. Then make a list of everything you really

A greenhouse takes up a lot of space in a small garden, so consider whether the use you make of it would make it worthwhile.

Garden priorities

Wish list	Essential	Desirable
Structural features		
1. Paving/decking	[ ]	[ ]
2. Gravel area	[ ]	[ ]
3. Lawn	[ ]	[ ]
4. Pond/water course	[ ]	[ ]
5. Summerhouse	[ ]	[ ]
6. Tool shed	[ ]	[ ]
7. Greenhouse	[ ]	[ ]
8. Vegetable garden	[ ]	[ ]
Utility features		
1. Washing line	[ ]	[ ]
2. Compost heap	[ ]	[ ]
3. Cold frame	[ ]	[ ]
4. Dustbin (trash) area	[ ]	[ ]
5. Built-in barbecue	[ ]	[ ]
6. Sandpit	[ ]	[ ]
7. Garden store	[ ]	[ ]
Decorative features		
1. Raised bed	[ ]	[ ]
2. Shrubbery	[ ]	[ ]
3. Herbaceous border	[ ]	[ ]
4. Wildlife area	[ ]	[ ]
5. Arch/pergola	[ ]	[ ]
6. Rock garden	[ ]	[ ]
7. Small water feature	[ ]	[ ]

want in the new design. Invariably, you will have to prioritize this "wish list" to establish which items are most important. Remember to include utility items, such as a rotary washing line or compost heap. If you find prioritizing difficult, then score each feature as either essential or desirable. In this way you can be sure to include all the essential features as well as some of the desirable ones if there is the space.

HOW TO MEASURE

Use a 3m (10ft) retractable tape measure and pegs to measure a small area. For larger areas, it would be easier to hire or buy a 30m (100ft) surveyors' tape.

Measure the plot

The next step in planning a new garden or making alterations to an existing design is to assess what the current garden has to offer and to consider its limitations. The best way to do this is to draw a rough plan of the existing plot, by eye at first, on a piece of paper and record its overall dimensions.

Small rectangular gardens are very easy to measure, and sometimes the boundary can be calculated simply by counting fence panels and multiplying by the length of a fence panel and a post. In most cases, however, you will need to measure the plot with a tape measure. A long surveyors' tape measure is extremely useful. Having someone else to hold the other end of the tape will make measuring a lot easier. Note down any changes in level from side to side or down the length of the plot. Hammer in pegs at 1m (3ft) intervals, and then work out the direction and extent of the gradient, using a piece of straight timber and a spirit (carpenter's) level.

Triangulation

Sometimes it may be difficult to measure the position of a feature, such as a tree or a pond, using right angles. Triangulation is a way of fixing the position of an object in relation to the things around it.

Find two points already fixed on your plan: the corners of the house are often used. Measure the distance from each of the two points to the object. Transfer these measurements into the scale you are using on your plan. Set a pair of compasses (a compass) to each of the scale distances in turn and scribe an arc in the approximate position. When the second arc intersects the first one your point is established.

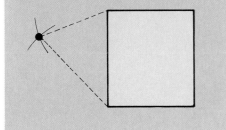

It is important to plan out a formal garden quite accurately before you start any practical work in order to get the proportions right.

HOW TO MAKE A SKETCH

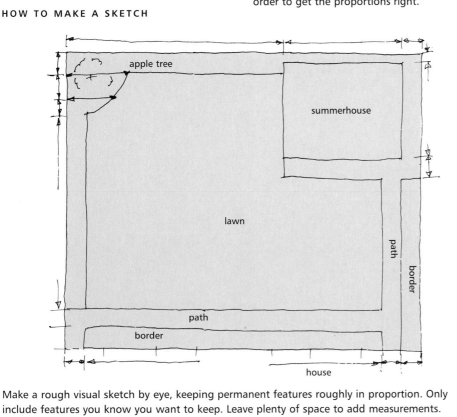

Make a rough visual sketch by eye, keeping permanent features roughly in proportion. Only include features you know you want to keep. Leave plenty of space to add measurements.

Plot the position of fixed features

Next turn your attention to the positions of permanent features, such as trees as well as other structural elements that you wish to keep in the new design. Most objects can be measured in right angles from a base line, such as the wall of the house, on your plan. If an object does not fall in a straight line from this point you will need to use triangulation (see box above left) in order to fix its position, so that it can be placed accurately on your rough sketch.

If your garden is small, sketch the whole plot in one go. If it is too big to do this, sketch it in sections that you can join together later when you draw up a scale plan.

Making plans

Drawing up an accurate plan is the best way to avoid making expensive mistakes later on. Once you have a basic plan that is drawn to scale, you can try out new ideas and see how the different elements fit together.

Draw a scale plan

Using the measurements noted down on your rough sketch of the garden, draw up a scale plan of the area being designed on graph paper, indicating the position of all the permanent features. A scale of 1:50 is suitable for most gardens (that's 2cm in the plan for every 1m in the garden, or ¼in to 1ft). However, if you are planning a large area, a scale of 1:100 (1cm per 1m or ⅛in to 1ft) may be more practical. Drawing your plan to scale will also make it easier to estimate quantities of materials, such as paving. Once you are sure they are accurate, ink the main lines in so that they show up clearly. Then, on an overlay

of acetate or tracing paper, use cross-hatching in a variety of colours to indicate areas of sun and shade at different times of the day. This information will be invaluable when you come to thinking about planting plans.

Try out new ideas

Cut out shapes from another piece of graph paper to represent the different features you want in your new garden design. You can then move the features around or alter the sizes of different elements without having to redraw the plan each time. When you are satisfied with the arrangement, draw them in position on an overlay.

Practical planning

Before ordering materials and beginning work, mark out as much of the design as possible in your existing garden. Mock up the overall shape of larger features to help you

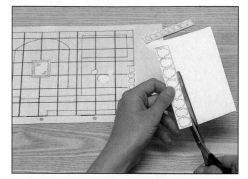

It's helpful to draw and cut out scale features that you want to include in your finished design, such as a raised pond, summerhouse or raised beds. These can be moved around until they look right, but use them as aids only. If you try to design around them, your garden will almost certainly lack coherence.

visualize the impact they will have on the rest of the garden. You could use bamboo canes as an arch or trellis, a piece of garden hose for the edge of a lawn or planks of wood to indicate the edge of a patio or path. Tall canes indicating the position of important features or key plants will

HOW TO DESIGN YOUR GARDEN

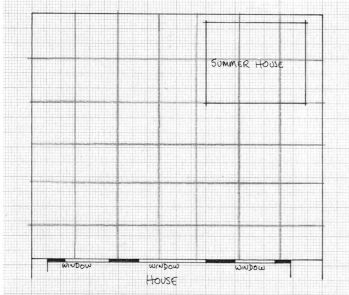

1 The basic grid Transfer all of the measurements of features you wish to retain from your first sketch on to graph paper. Superimpose on to this grid the type of design you have in mind: based on circles, diagonals or rectangles. Most gardens work best with the grid lines about 2m (7ft) apart. Using overlays or photocopies, try out features that you would like to include in their approximate positions. Moving around scale features, cut out of paper, is helpful.

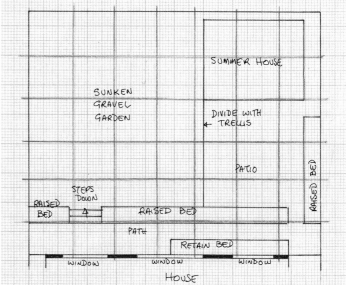

2 The rough Using an overlay or photocopies, sketch in your plan. If you can visualize an overall design, sketch this in first, then move around the cut-out features to fit. If you have not reached this stage, sketch in the features you have provisionally positioned but adjust them as the big design evolves. Make many attempts – the best plan will emerge once you have tried out lots of options. Don't worry about planning details at this stage apart from the important focal points in the design.

Getting inspired

If you are short of inspiration or cannot find a solution to a particular problem in your garden, don't be shy of being inspired by others and adapting their ideas to fit your circumstances. After all, it's what the professionals do all the time. Look at magazines and books to help decide which style appeals to you most. Also collect pictures of features that you like when you are reading magazines, and take pictures of your own when you visit other people's gardens and gardening shows. Note down any plant combinations that catch your eye; they may well come in useful later on.

show how much screening they are likely to offer. By observing the shadow at different times of day you'll also know whether shade is likely to be a problem for other plants or in a sitting-out area.

DECIDING ON A PATTERN

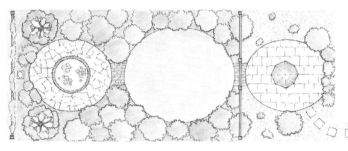

CIRCLES
A circular pattern is good at disguising the sometimes predictable shape of a rectangular garden. The circles can be overlapped, if necessary.

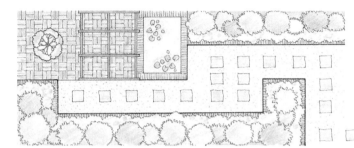

RECTANGLES
A rectangular theme is a popular choice and is effective if you want to create a formal look, or divide up a long narrow garden into smaller sections.

DIAGONALS
A diagonal grid pattern will create a sense of space by taking the eye along and across the garden. It is best to use a grid that is at 45° to the house.

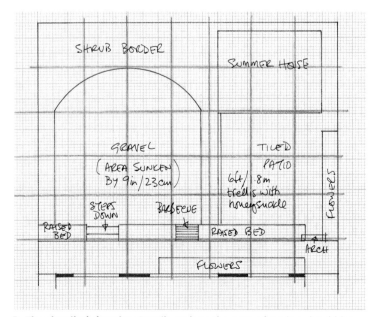

3 The detailed drawing Details such as the type of paving should be decided now – not only because it will help you see the final effect, but also because you need to work to a plan that uses multiples of full blocks, slabs or bricks if necessary. It will also help you to budget for your plan. Draw in key plants, especially large trees and shrubs, but omit detailed planting plans at this stage.

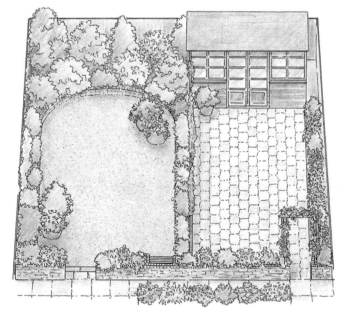

4 Visualize the finished result Before starting construction it is worth being absolutely sure what the end result will look like. If you can draw, sketch out how you plan your garden to look. You may wish to make a 3-D model of your garden, using coloured card, wooden matches and other household items, such as straw, cotton wool (cotton balls) and lentils or rice, to represent the texture of different materials. Think about the garden as it will appear at different times of the year.

Lawns and alternatives

Grass lawns have been the main feature of most domestic gardens for many years, but recent trends in garden design have provided a range of other options to consider for covering the ground.

Why choose a lawn?

A lawn is quick and easy to lay, requires little skill to maintain and looks good when it is well cared for. It is perhaps the best all-round surface and is one of the cheapest methods of covering large areas of ground. When regularly mown and trimmed, a lawn provides an attractive open space that sets off all the surrounding features and provides cohesion to the overall design. There are two main grades of domestic lawn. High quality putting- or bowling-green lawn is the most ornamental, but it requires a lot of attention and fairly frequent mowing to keep it in tip-top condition. For most people, though, a standard lawn, also called a family or utility lawn, is perfectly adequate. It is harder wearing and requires cutting less often, so it takes a lot less time to maintain. Although there are special lawn grass mixes for difficult situations, such as shade, a lawn requires more maintenance if the growing conditions are not ideal.

A lawn is one of the most important elements in a garden for many people, creating a sense of open space that lets the garden "breathe".

Lawn alternatives

In some situations such as deep shade a ground covering of shade-loving plants may be a better option. Also consider alternative coverings where mowing would be difficult or dangerous, such as on a steep slope. If you don't want a grass lawn but still require an open space in the middle of the garden, there are a number of other options you can use to cover the ground.

Herb lawns In a sunny, well-drained site a few herbs, such as camomile, thyme and comfrey, are sufficiently low growing to create a lush lawn effect. Although they are tough enough to be walked on occasionally, these plants are not hard-wearing so are not suitable for children's play areas or high-traffic walkways. Try *Thymus serpyllum* or choose the non-flowering camomile variety *Chamaemelum nobile* 'Treneague'.

HOW TO PLANT GROUND COVER PLANTS

1 Dig over the area and clear the ground of weeds at least a month before planting. Hoe off any seedlings that appear in the meantime. Rake the ground level before planting.

2 Water the plants in their pots, then set them out about 15–20cm (6–8in) apart, in staggered rows to work out the positions and to check you have sufficient plants.

3 Tease out the roots and plant to the original depth. Firm in the soil around the roots. Water thoroughly and keep well watered for the first season.

HOW TO LAY GRAVEL

1 Excavate the area to the required depth – about 5cm (2in) of gravel is sufficient in most cases. Don't disturb the soil to a greater depth than you need to.

2 Level the ground. Lay punctured, heavy-duty black polythene or a semi-permeable membrane over the area to suppress weed growth. Overlap strips by about 5cm (2in).

3 Tip the gravel on top of the base sheet and spread it evenly over the surface, making sure it is about 5cm (2in) thick. Use a rake to get the gravel level.

Ground cover plants Choose easy-care plants – low-growing conifers and heathers as well as the rose of Sharon (*Hypericum calycinum*), for example – to cover difficult or dangerous areas, such as steep slopes where you do not intend to walk. They will quickly smother the ground with a knee-high, weed-suppressing thicket of foliage. Apart from a once-a-year tidy up, they don't need any maintenance.

Flowering carpet Under trees and shrubs a flowering carpet of bulbs can be particularly effective. If you plant early varieties they will bloom before the overhead foliage emerges and then be hidden from view at other times. Choose shade-tolerant species that are suited to the impoverished conditions and mulch the soil well to conserve moisture and prevent weeds.

Gravel A popular option with many designers, gravel, pebbles and other aggregates are versatile and easy to lay. There are now many attractive grades and mixes to choose from including coloured glass chippings. If laid over a semi-permeable landscape fabric these surfaces are practically maintenance free. They are also easy to combine with plants to create a natural-looking effect.

Paving and decking These permanent ground coverings are maintenance-free, and there is a wide range of materials available to suit any garden design. Paving requires a lot of work before laying, particularly on a sloping site, and is an expensive option, requiring some skill. Decking is more versatile as it can be cut to fit any space and can be raised so that the ground does not have to be levelled beforehand. Decking requires basic do-it-yourself skills and costs about the same as paving.

PLANTING THROUGH GRAVEL

Draw back the gravel and make a cross-shaped slit in the base sheet. Plant normally, then firm in the plant, water well, and replace the flaps of the base sheet before re-covering with gravel.

Lawns are not the best option for every garden. In a small courtyard other coverings, such as gravel, might be a more sympathetic or appropriate material.

Patios

Paving requires careful thought and planning because, once laid, it is difficult and expensive to alter. First, consider what you want your paved area for and then identify the ideal position for a patio or paved area.

The purpose of the patio

A patio provides a smooth, level, hard surface on which to sit and relax and entertain. For these reasons patios are usually best sited in a spot that is not overlooked by neighbours and that is in a convenient position near to the house. If you want to use your patio for sunbathing it will

need to catch the sun for much of the day, and if you want it for entertaining a site close to the kitchen would be most convenient.

In a north-facing garden, the best place to site a patio may be at the bottom of the garden to catch the maximum amount of sun. It may be more convenient to have two smaller areas of paving: one for sunbathing and one near to the house for entertaining. Wherever you decide to site your patio, make sure that the outlook is pleasing and that it is well screened; the privacy will create a relaxing atmosphere.

Deciding on a size

The size of the patio should also be determined by what you want to use it for. To accommodate a standard patio set of table and four chairs, you would need a paved area at least 3 x 3m (10 x 10ft) but preferably larger, about 4 x 4m (13 x 13ft), so that there is room to walk around the furniture comfortably while it is in use. However, in a small garden, the patio can dominate the garden and create an unbalanced effect in the overall design. In this situation you may be better off paving the whole garden and using planting

HOW TO LAY PAVING

1 Excavate the area to a depth that will allow for about 5cm (2in) of compacted hardcore topped with about 3–5cm (1–2in) of ballast, plus the thickness of the paving and mortar.

2 On top of the layers of hardcore and ballast, put five blobs of mortar where the slab is to be placed – one at each corner, and the other in the middle.

3 Position the slab carefully, bedding it down on the mortar. Over a large area of paving, create a slight slope to allow rainwater to run off freely.

4 Use a spirit (carpenter's) level placed over more than one slab to ensure that the slab is as close to horizontal as you want. Use a small wedge of wood under one end of the level to create a slight slope over the whole area if necessary. Tap the slab down further, or raise it by lifting and packing in more mortar.

5 Use spacers of an even thickness to ensure regular spacing between the paving slabs. Remove these later, before the joints are filled with mortar.

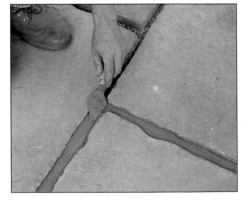

6 A day or two after laying the paving, go over it again to fill in the joints. Use a small pointing trowel and a dryish mortar mix. Finish off with a smooth stroke that leaves the mortar slightly recessed. This produces an attractive, crisp look. Brush any surplus mortar off the slabs before it dries.

pockets, raised beds and plenty of containers to provide visual interest in the garden.

Even in a large garden, expanses of paving can appear austere. You can break up this appearance by combining styles of paving as well as planting up the patio itself. Don't be tempted to overdo it because the effect will look too fussy and undermine the calm atmosphere.

Soften the boundary between the patio and lawn, perhaps with a low wall, designed with a planting cavity.

Check the depth of the foundation before you lay the paving. If it adjoins the house, make sure that the paving will end up at least 15cm (6in) below the damp-proof course.

Choosing materials

There is an incredibly wide range of materials suitable for garden paving. Which you choose is largely a matter of personal preference, although each type does have its own advantages and disadvantages. Try to choose a paving material that is sympathetic to the overall design and to the style of your house. Using materials that are already used elsewhere in the garden will help create a co-ordinated effect. Regularly shaped paving works well in a formal setting, whereas paving that consists of smaller units or a range of paving sizes is often a better choice if you are trying to create a more relaxed feel. If you are combining different materials, make sure they are the same thickness to make laying easier.

RIGHT

The top row shows (from left to right) natural stone sett, clay paver, brick, artificial sett.

The centre row shows a range of the different shapes of concrete paving blocks available.

The bottom row shows some of the colours and sizes of concrete paving slabs available.

Grouping containers together presents an attractive display to brighten up the patio. Here, *Clematis* 'Prince Charles' is planted in a chimney pot next to some potted chives.

Decking

Garden decking is a popular choice these days and in many situations is often the best option. It can be cheaper and easier to construct than paving, especially on a sloping site, and provides a hard, flat surface that is functional and looks good too.

Designing with decking

Decking can be tailor-made to suit any garden design. Its essentially natural appearance makes it ideal for informal gardens where you can make the most of the warm tones of the timber. Decking also looks good in a bold, contemporary garden design. Indeed, it can be made the main focal point by choosing an eye-catching design and colouring it with woodstain. In a formal setting, emphasize the clean lines of a deck by using stepped edges.

Different designs can be achieved by fixing planks in different ways (see opposite), but on the whole, it is best to keep any pattern fairly simple. In some countries there are building codes that may have to be met. If in doubt, seek professional help with the design, even if you intend to construct it yourself.

Timber decking provides a durable, practical and easy-to-care-for floor surface. It makes a refreshing change from a patio made of paving slabs or bricks. Adding containers will help to make the deck a pleasant place to sit in summer.

HOW TO MAKE A DECK

1 Level the area, then use bricks or building blocks to support your decking. Calculate the position of each row. Each timber bearer should be supported in the middle as well as the ends. Excavate the soil and position the brick.

2 Position each block so that about half of it sits in the soil – it is important that air circulates beneath the bearers. Tap down each block to ensure it is level, adding or removing soil if necessary.

3 Use a spirit (carpenter's) level to ensure that the blocks are level. If the ground is unstable, set the bricks or blocks on pads of concrete. Make sure that they are level, or the final decking will not be stable.

Which timber?

Decking can be made from hardwood, pressure-treated softwood or plain softwood. Hardwood decks made from white oak or western red cedar are durable and practically maintenance free, but they cost a lot more to construct. Decking made from pressure-treated (tanalized) softwood is less expensive and reasonably durable, but requires seasonal maintenance, while plain softwood decking needs regular maintenance and is prone to rotting, so it is not very durable. Clad the deck with non-slip grooved planks spaced about 6mm (¼in) apart to allow for expansion and to allow water to drain away freely. Attach them with galvanized nails or screws. All decks should also be laid on a sheet of semi-permeable material such as landscaping fabric.

Choosing a deck

The easiest way to create a deck is to use ready-made decking tiles that can be laid straight on to a firm, flat surface, such an old patio, roof terrace or firmed hardcore. For a better result, lay the tiles on top of a

DECKING PATTERNS

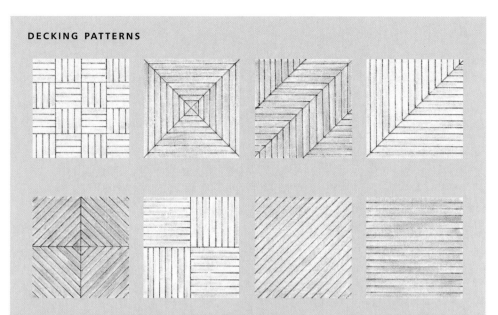

Wooden decking can be laid in a number of decorative patterns. Each style will give your garden a subtly different effect, so consider the pattern carefully before you start. If in doubt, ask a professional designer for help.

framework of pressure-treated timber and treat any cut ends or joints with wood preservative. You can also get decks in kit form, and these are very easy to put together and a good choice where the deck isn't fitted into a particular space, such as an island deck part-way down the garden.

Custom-made decking, supplied and fitted by a professional supplier, is the most convenient but most expensive option. Specialist suppliers will take on the whole process, from planning, checking local planning regulations and getting the permissions necessary to constructing the deck. With custom-made decking you can be more ambitious with split levels, walkways and even raised decks to give the perfect view of the garden.

4 Use wood preservative on the bearers if necessary. Space out the bearers on the block supports. Add extra bearers near the ends and sides of the decking, where planks (boards) will need extra support.

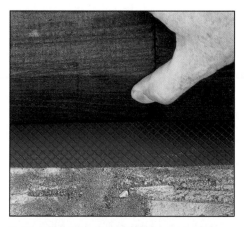

5 Your bearers may not be long enough to stretch the whole length of the deck, in which case make sure joints are made above a block. Use a damp-proofing strip between each block and bearer to prevent water seeping up.

6 Add a plastic sheet to suppress weeds, then saw the decking planks to size and treat with a preservative. Nail in position with galvanized nails leaving gaps of about 6mm (¼in) between planks to allow for expansion.

Beds and borders

The position, size and shape of beds and borders should be considered at the outset of a new garden design, as they have an enormous influence on the way the garden is viewed.

Changing the perspective

Most gardeners consider beds and borders essential, both to grow specific plants and to add interest to the shape of the garden. It is quite easy to change the shape of a border, so consider whether the existing design is making the most effective use of perspective. For example, narrow borders that simply follow the boundary lines will make a narrow garden seem narrower and a short garden shorter.

Create the illusion of space in a small garden by disguising the boundary. Wider borders provide the opportunity to combine a range of plants that together will either hide the boundary from view or break up its outline, effectively camouflaging it. Dividing the garden horizontally will also make the garden more intriguing because at least part of the design is hidden from view, encouraging the casual visitor to explore. In a short garden, use a long, curving border cutting across the garden to make it seem longer, emphasizing the longest dimension, the diagonal.

Breaking up a lawn

A large area of grass can make a garden look plain, and you may want to add a feature such as an island bed or a border alongside a path.

HOW TO CREATE A CIRCULAR BED

1 Insert a post in the centre of the proposed bed. Attach one end of a piece of string to the post and the other end to a bottle filled with sand or soil.

2 Walk slowly around the post, keeping the string taut and the bottle tilted, so that the sand or soil trickles out and marks the outline of the circle.

HOW TO CREATE AN OVAL BED

Place two posts in the ground and loosely tie a piece of string around them. Experiment with the distance between the posts and the length of the piece of string to get the size and shape of bed you require. Place a bottle filled with sand or soil inside the loop of string and walk around the posts, keeping the string taut. The sand or soil will trickle out, creating the outline of a perfect oval.

HOW TO CREATE AN IRREGULAR BED

Use a flexible garden hose to work out the size and shape of an irregular bed. Once you are happy with the shape of the bed, remove a line of turf around the inside edge of the hose to mark it out.

3 Once the circle is complete, the turf can be cut from within the marked area in order to produce a perfectly circular bed.

This will break up the garden visually, and also give you the chance to grow more flowers and shrubs. It can sometimes be more effective to cut a bed towards one end of the lawn rather than in a central position. This can make the most of your lawn by taking the eye across it to the flower bed.

It is important to keep an island bed looking neat as it is a key focal point. However, by choosing low-maintenance plants such as alpines, and mulching with an attractive layer of gravel, an island bed doesn't need to be time-consuming.

Choosing plants

It is essential to choose the right combination of plants for each part of the site. First, consider what you want the plants to do. If you want year-round cover you will need a high proportion of evergreens to provide the screen. But a garden made from evergreens alone becomes very static and lacking in interest. In this situation, make the key plants that block the sight lines evergreen, but fill in and around them with a range of deciduous plants, bulbs and herbaceous plants to add seasonal variety and excitement.

Beds of lavender flank a narrow path. It's a good choice of plant: brushing past the lavender will release its delicious scent.

HOW TO PREPARE THE GROUND

1 Since flowerbeds and borders are likely to be undisturbed for many years it is important to clear the area of weeds first. There are three ways of doing this: spray with weedkiller, skim off the surface with a hoe, or cover with polythene for several months.

2 Dig the first trench to one spade's depth across the plot, and transfer the soil you have removed to the other end of the plot using a barrow where it will be used to fill in the final trench.

3 Fork a layer of well-rotted compost or manure into the bottom of the trench to improve the soil structure and to provide nutrients for the plants.

4 Dig the next trench across the plot, turning the soil on to the compost in the first trench. Add compost to the new trench and then dig the next.

5 Continue down the border until the whole of the surface has been turned. Add some compost to the final trench and then fill with the soil taken from the first.

6 If possible, dig in the autumn and allow the winter weather to break down the soil. In spring, take out any new weeds and rake over the bed.

Raised beds

Although they are time consuming and expensive to build, raised beds can solve a range of gardening problems, such as poor soil or bad drainage, but they are also useful for adding interest to flat plots or for providing level ground in sloping gardens.

Designing with raised beds

Raised beds offer so many advantages that it is surprising they do not feature in more gardens. They are ideal for adding height and interest to otherwise boringly flat gardens, but equally they are a practical solution to providing level areas on sloping ground. In small gardens they can be combined with paving to produce an intimate courtyard garden. Raised beds can be a functional square or rectangle, or designed to fit a corner in the garden.

Choosing the right soil

Raised beds hold a lot more soil than containers, so they are much easier to look after and you can grow much bigger plants. They also offer the opportunity to grow plants in your garden that otherwise would fail to thrive. For example, if your soil is poor or badly drained, raised beds can be filled with good quality imported loam. Indeed, if you fancy growing plants that like a specific

HOW TO MAKE A RAISED BED USING BRICKS

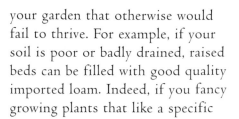

1 Mark out the shape of the bed using short pointed stakes and string. Use a builders' set square (triangle) to ensure the correct angles. Define the lines with a thin stream of fine sand or use line-marker paint.

2 Dig out along the markings to a depth of 30cm (12in) and width of 15cm (6in). Fill with concrete to within 5cm (2in) of the top. Firm down, level and leave for 24 hours to set. For concrete, use 1 part cement to 4 parts ballast.

3 Build up four or five courses of bricks and set each into mortar, checking with a spirit (carpenter's) level at every stage.

4 Clean up the mortar while it is still wet with a pointing trowel. Leave it to harden.

5 Before filling with soil, coat the inside of the wall with a waterproof paint.

6 Put in a layer of rubble topped with gravel for drainage. Fill with topsoil and stir in a layer of a good potting medium.

7 Plant up the raised bed in the usual manner and water in well.

8 The completed bed planted with a selection of culinary herbs and wild strawberries.

type of soil, such as acid-loving rhododendrons, raised beds filled with ericaceous compost (soil mix) will provide that opportunity even if your garden soil is not suitable.

The soil in raised beds warms up more quickly than garden soil so you can start off new plants earlier in spring, which is useful if you grow early vegetables or flowers. For anyone who finds bending difficult, raised beds are particularly welcome.

Which material?

Traditional permanent raised beds made from bricks or blocks are built in much the same way as solid brick retaining walls, the only differences being that the walls in a raised bed are built vertical rather than slightly sloping. They can made from bricks or blocks mortared together, with "weep-holes" (vertical joints free of mortar) every metre (yard) or so along the base of each wall to allow water to drain out. Check the bricks are frostproof; ordinary housebricks may not be suitable. In a cottage-style garden, dry-stone walls also make good raised beds, with cracks and crevices used to grow plants.

Raised beds can also be constructed from wood. Old railway sleepers (railroad ties) were traditionally recommended, but designer mini-sleepers are more readily available from garden centres, either as individual logs that can be nailed together tailored to suit any position, or as part of a raised bed kit, which is easily slotted together. Pressure-treated softwood gravel boards, which will withstand damp, are an economical material for making simple raised beds for the vegetable garden. Alternatively, once the boards have been stained they will make an attractive feature container on the patio.

Growing a mix of fragrant herbs in a raised bed will bring the scents, colours and textures closer to you, making a feature of this attractive part of the garden.

HOW TO MAKE A RAISED BED USING WOOD

1 Set the log edging in position and tap it into place. Check with a spirit (carpenter's) level. If you are using flexible edging, drive in stakes to which you nail the edging.

2 On geometric shapes, as shown here, nail the corners together with rust-proof nails.

3 Fill with soil, ensuring that you create the correct conditions for the types of plant you are intending to grow. Heathers will need an acid soil to grow well.

4 Plant up the raised bed and water the plants in well. Mulch the ground with shredded bark or gravel to retain moisture.

Paths

Paths exert a strong influence on the design and sense of movement in a garden, so consider the effect during the planning process. It is also essential to match the construction to the type of use a path will receive.

Designing with paths

A path's design should reflect the overall theme of the garden. In a formal setting straight paths with clean lines will reinforce the formality of the design, whereas in an informal garden gently meandering paths will be more appropriate. Try to avoid straight paths that lead the eye directly to the bottom of the garden, because they will be less inviting and make the plot seem smaller. Calm the feeling of movement by adding changes in direction along the path and create a sense of mystery by allowing the path to disappear from view – behind a garden structure or border, for example.

Temporary paths

Roll-up plastic paths are useful for protecting areas of the garden when heavy one-off construction projects or seasonal heavy maintenance tasks are being carried out. They are particularly useful for protecting lawns during the autumn and winter months. Builders' planks (boards) are another option.

Which path?

There are three main types of path: functional paths that are constantly used come rain or come shine; occasional paths that are largely ornamental and are used infrequently or not at all; and temporary paths that are rolled out for specific jobs. All paths should have a slight slope or camber to prevent puddles forming in wet weather.

Regularly used paths

A well-used path needs to be at least 60cm (2ft) wide and have an all-weather surface. If laid against the side of the house the path needs to be at least 15cm (6in) below the

HOW TO LAY A GRAVEL PATH

1 Excavate the area to a depth of about 15cm (6in), and ram the base firm.

2 Provide a stout edge to retain the gravel. For a straight path, securing battens by pegs about 1m (3ft) apart is an easy and inexpensive method.

3 Place a layer of compacted hardcore. Add a mixture of sand and coarse gravel (you can use sand and gravel mixture sold as ballast). Rake level and tamp or roll until firm.

4 Top up to within 2.5cm (1in) of the edge or battens with the final grade of gravel. In small gardens the size often known as pea gravel looks good and is easy to walk on. Rake the gravel level.

A winding gravel path, bordered with carefully chosen cottage garden plants, is an inviting way to the front door.

damp-proof course and slope gently away from the house to shed water.

The amount and type of traffic a path will carry is one of the main considerations when you decide the type of path to opt for. Paved paths, using concrete slabs set on blobs of mortar on a solid base of rammed hardcore, are the best choice for an all-weather path that's used for regular foot and light wheeled traffic (bikes, wheelbarrows etc). This type of path is expensive, a lot of work to construct and not very adaptable.

Paved paths made from small unit paving blocks bedded into a layer of sharp sand on top of well-firmed soil are less expensive and are easier to construct. They can be adapted to any design, but you do need to have solid edges to the path to keep the paving in place. These can be wooden, concrete or simply a row of blocks set in a foundation of concrete.

Gravel paths are simple to construct on firmed soil with an underlay of membrane. They can be made any shape, including complicated curves. Little maintenance is required apart from removing the odd weed and the occasional rake to keep it looking neat. Unfortunately, the gravel tends to be kicked into nearby borders and may get walked into the house.

Occasionally used paths

Paths constructed for largely ornamental reasons can be made from a wider range of materials. In general, choose a material that is in keeping with its surroundings and will provide a solid footing. Stepping stones made from the paving used elsewhere in the garden can look good set into the lawn to provide access to the washing line. Under trees or through a shrubbery, log stepping stones or a path of chipped bark can be more appropriate.

Neat edging

For a period garden, Victorian-style rope edging looks appropriate. You can use it either to retain a gravel path or as an edging to a paved path.

Wavy edgings such as this are also reminiscent of some of the older styles of garden, but they can also be used in a modern setting to create a formal effect.

HOW TO LAY BRICKS AND BLOCKS

1 Excavate the area and prepare a sub-base of about 5cm (2in) of compacted hardcore or sand-and-gravel mix. Set an edging along one end and side first. Check that it is level, then lay the pavers on a bed of mortar.

2 Once the edging is set, lay a 5cm (2in) bed of sharp sand over the area. Use a straight-edged piece of wood to level the surface. Position the pavers, butting them tightly to the edging and to each other.

3 Brush loose sand into the joints of the pavers with a broom. Hire a flat-plate vibrator to consolidate the sand or tamp the pavers down with a club hammer used over a piece of wood.

4 Brush in more sand and repeat the vibrating process once more for a firm, neat finish. To avoid damage do not go too close to an unsupported edge with the vibrator. The path should be ready to use straight away.

Walls

Although walls are mainly thought of as a structure to provide security and privacy along the boundary, they are also useful within a garden for building terracing on a sloping plot as well as a range of other features, including raised beds, barbecues, garden screens, seats and plinths for containers and ornaments.

Most builders' merchants have a wide range of bricks suitable for garden walls. Bricks come in many colours and finishes and these are just a small selection of the many available.

Designing with walls

Walls can be made from a wide range of materials so can be constructed to suit any style. Substantial or prominent walls, such as those used along the boundary, will fit in more easily with the rest of the garden if they are constructed of the same material used for the house. Smaller walls within the garden can be designed to reflect the overall design of the garden. They can also be combined with other materials, such as wooden trellis, to help soften the overall effect.

Which wall?

There are basically four types of wall: free-standing walls for boundaries and screens; solid retaining walls for terracing; loose dry-stone walls also for terracing; and retaining walls for raised beds. All walls require some skill to construct, so if you are in doubt seek professional advice.

Plants for wall crevices

Aubrieta deltoidea
Campanula portenschlagiana
Dianthus deltoides
Erinus alpinus
Erodium reichardii
Geranium sanguineum var. *striatum*
Mentha requienii
Pratia pedunculata
Saxifraga paniculata
Scabiosa graminifolia
Sedum spathulifolium

Foundations

All walls need a concrete foundation along their entire length. The higher the wall, the wider and deeper the foundations have to be. For walls up to 75cm (30in) high the foundations should be 10cm (4in) deep and about twice as wide as the wall being constructed. For walls over 75cm (30in) high, foundations should be 15cm (6in) deep and about three times as wide as the wall.

Boundary walls

The way a boundary wall is constructed will also depend on how high you want to build it. A small wall at the front of the house could be made from single bricks, 10cm (4in) thick, if it is up to 45cm (18in). Any higher, and you will either have to use a double brick wall, 23cm (9in) thick, or build supporting piers every couple of metres (yards) along a single brick wall. Walls over 1.2m (4ft) need a double-brick construction and supporting piers. Add coping stones on top of the wall to help shed water and to protect the bricks.

BRICK BONDING

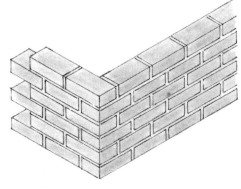

Running bond or stretcher bond The simplest form of bonding used for walls a single brick wide.

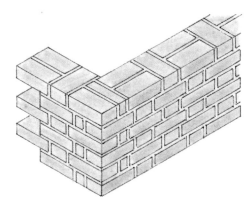

Flemish bond Creates a strong bond in a wall two bricks wide. Bricks are laid lengthways and across the wall in the same course.

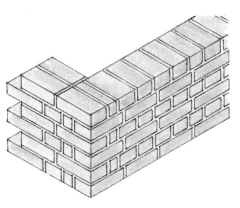

English bond Used for a thick wall where strength is needed. Alternate courses are laid lengthways then across the wall.

Retaining walls

Solid retaining walls are made from bricks or blocks mortared together. The wall will have to be strong enough to hold back the weight of the soil behind it. For this reason, always use the double-brick construction method but this time lay the foundations and build the wall so that it slopes back slightly. Leave weep-holes (vertical joints free of mortar) every metre (yard) or so along the base of the wall to allow water to drain out from the soil. Pack in rubble behind the weep-holes and cover with coarse gravel to prevent soil washing out and to stop the weep-holes from becoming blocked with soil.

Dry-stone walls also make good retaining walls up to 1m (3ft) high. Again the wall needs to be built so that it leans back slightly. The blocks should be selected so that they interlock as much as possible, leaving few gaps. Pack rubble behind the wall as you go to help secure each layer in place. Any large crevices can be planted with suitable plants.

Retaining walls provide an excellent opportunity to experiment with climbers and wall shrubs.

A wall is cloaked in the scented creamy white flowers of *Rosa* 'Climbing Iceberg'.

HOW TO BUILD A WALL

1 All walls require a footing. For a low wall this is one brick wide; for larger and thicker walls the dimensions are increased. Excavate a trench about 30cm (12in) deep and put 13cm (5in) of consolidated hardcore in the bottom. Drive pegs in so that the tops are at the final height of the foundation. Use a spirit (carpenter's) level to check that they are level.

2 To form the foundations, fill the trench with a concrete mix of 2 parts cement, 5 parts sharp sand and 7 parts 2cm (¾in) aggregate, and level it off with the top of the pegs. Use a straight-edged board to tamp the concrete down and remove any air pockets.

3 When the concrete foundation has hardened for a few days, lay the bricks on a bed of mortar, adding a wedge of mortar at one end of each brick as you lay them. For a single brick wall with supporting piers, the piers should be positioned at each end and at 1.8–2.4m (6–8ft) intervals, and can be made by laying two bricks crossways.

4 For subsequent courses, lay a ribbon of mortar on top of the previous row, then "butter" one end of the brick to be laid.

5 Tap level, checking constantly with a spirit (carpenter's) level to make sure that the wall is level and vertical.

6 The top of the wall is best finished off with a coping of suitable bricks or with special coping stones sold for the purpose.

Fences

One of the most popular choices for marking a boundary, fences offer instant privacy and security. They are less expensive to construct than a wall and need less maintenance than a hedge.

Designing with fences

There is a huge selection of fencing styles in a range of different materials, including various woods, metals and plastic, so you should have no problem finding a style that will enhance your garden. In the front garden fences with a more open structure are often used. Examples include picket or post-and-rail fences, ranch-style fences and post-and-chain fences. They do not provide privacy or much security, but they are an attractive way of marking the boundary.

In most back gardens, a boundary fence should recede from view, so choose something robust enough to support climbers and wall shrubs that will help disguise it. However, in certain circumstances you might want to make a feature of a fence. Painting with a woodstain used

A fence has been erected to screen the practical corner of the garden from view. It is strong enough to support a climber.

elsewhere in the garden or to co-ordinate with a nearby planting scheme will emphasize its presence.

Which fence?

The most popular type of fence is the ready-made panel, which comes in various forms, including horizontal lap, vertical lap and interwoven. They are also available in several heights including 1.2m (4ft), 1.5m (5ft) and 1.8m (6ft). Fencing panels are very cheap and easy to put up between regularly spaced, well-anchored posts. Most fencing panels are rather flimsy and have a lifespan of less

HOW TO ERECT A RANCH-STYLE FENCE

1 The posts of a ranch-style fence must be well secured in the ground. Use 10cm (4in) square posts, set at 2m (6½ft) intervals. For additional strength add 8cm (3in) square intermediate posts. Make sure the posts go at least 45cm (18in) into the ground. Concrete the posts into position, then fill in with soil.

2 Screw or nail the planks (boards) in place, making sure that the fixings are galvanized. Use a spirit (carpenter's) level to check that the planks are horizontal. Butt-join the planks in the centre of a post but try to stagger the joints on each row so that there is not a weak point in the fence.

3 Fit a post cap to improve the appearance and also protect the posts. Paint with a good quality paint recommended for outdoor use. Choose the colour of the paint carefully; you will need to keep white paint clean in order for the fence to look good.

than ten years, even when regularly maintained. For a better quality and longer-lasting wooden fence, opt for the close-board fencing. Here, a structure of posts with two or three cross-members, called arris rails, is constructed before cladding with wooden strips. These are sometimes thinner along one edge than the other and are overlapped when nailed to the arris rails. Alternatively the fence can be regular, where the pales are nailed on to the arris rails butted together with no spaces between them and without overlapping.

Posts

With all types of fence, the posts should be durable. For preference choose a naturally rot-resistant hardwood, but pressure-treated softwood is more commonly available. With panel fencing they are set 1.8m (6ft) apart to accommodate the panel, but with close-board fencing they are usually spaced more widely – 2.4–3m (8–10ft). Either buy posts that are long enough for the bottom section to be buried into the ground and held firm with concrete, or buy posts the same height as the fence and secure them with special fencing spikes.

Planning permission

Check with your local planning authority before erecting a new wall or fence to make sure there are no restrictions. In certain circumstances, particularly in front gardens near to a highway or in designated conservation areas, there may be restrictions on the type and height of boundary you are allowed to erect. Normally, you require planning consent for any wall more than 1.8m (6ft) high and for a wall more than 1m (3ft) high that abuts a highway.

HOW TO ERECT A PANEL FENCE

1 Post spikes are an easier option than excavating holes and concreting the post in position. Use a special tool to protect the spike top, then drive it in with a sledge-hammer. Check with a spirit (carpenter's) level to ensure it is absolutely vertical.

2 Insert the post in the spike, checking the vertical again, then lay the panel in position on the ground and mark the position of the next post. Drive in the next spike, testing for the vertical again.

3 There are various ways to fix the panels to the posts, but panel brackets are easy to use. Simply nail the brackets to the posts.

4 Lift the panel and nail in position, through the brackets. Insert the post at the other end and nail the panel in position at that end.

5 Check the horizontal level both before and after nailing, and make any necessary adjustments before moving on to the next panel.

6 Finish off by nailing a post cap to the top of each post. This will keep water out of the end grain of the timber and extend its life.

Other garden structures

Pergolas, trellises and arches are not only quick and easy to construct but, if correctly positioned, can also effectively transform the appearance of a garden. Flatpack kits are now available in a variety of materials and styles to suit both traditional and contemporary gardens.

Designing with arches, trellises and pergolas

Arches can perform several functions in the garden. They look lovely when positioned over a path and festooned with colourful climbing plants. Ideally, the structure should frame a distant object, such as an ornament, or focus the eye on the path as it leads tantalizingly out of sight into the next area of the garden. Arches can also be used to link borders either side of the garden to give the overall design coherence.

Trellises can be used to divide the garden into separate "rooms" and add a strong vertical dimension to an otherwise flat garden scheme. If you are looking for a more subtle application, a trellis can provide a secluded corner for a garden seat, creating a peaceful sitting area or arbour.

A pergola is simply an open structure, often placed over a patio adjacent to the house to create an intimate area for outdoor entertaining. It can be covered in shading materials, such as netting or bamboo screens, or a more natural covering of climbers. Pergolas also can be used away from the house, forming a covered walkway along the sunny side of the garden or a point of focus in the middle of the garden. Being a larger structure means that a pergola lends itself to supporting quite vigorous climbers, such as wisteria, which would swamp an arch or trellis.

Adding a fence or trellis will not only give your garden a strong sense of design, but it also provides a wonderful opportunity to grow climbers.

Choosing materials

In an informal or country-style garden, structures made from rustic poles blend naturally into their surroundings. These can be bought as ready-made structures from fencing suppliers or made from fresh-cut wood. Rustic poles are usually roughly jointed and nailed together with galvanized nails. Rustic structures are not usually as strong as other types and often require more cross-members to improve their rigidity and strength.

If you are using sawn timber for arches and pergolas, choose timber that has been pressure-treated with preservative to prevent it rotting.

HOW TO ASSEMBLE AN ARCH

1 The simplest way to make an arch is to use a kit, which only needs assembling. First, establish the post positions, allowing a gap between the edge of the path and post, so that plants do not obstruct the path.

2 Dig four 60cm (2ft) deep holes to hold the posts. Alternatively, choose a kit with shorter posts for use with fence spikes. Drive the spikes in with a special tool, using a spirit (carpenter's) level to ensure they are vertical.

Scented climbers for garden structures

Akebia quinata
Clematis armandii
Clematis montana
Clematis rehderiana
Jasminum officinale and 'Fiona Sunrise'
Lonicera x *americana*
Lonicera japonica 'Halliana'
Lonicera periclymenum 'Belgica'
    and 'Serotina'
Rosa 'Bobbie James', 'Gloire de Dijon',
    'Madame Alfred Carrière', 'New
    Dawn' and 'Zéphirine Drouhin'
Trachelospermum jasminoides
    and 'Variegatum'
Wisteria sinensis

There are two main styles of wooden pergola: traditional and oriental. The traditional style has fewer, larger roofing timbers with square-cut ends, while oriental-style pergolas have bevelled ends.

You can also get plastic-coated tubular metal arches, arbours and pergolas. These are lightweight and so easier to put up than wooden versions. Their stylish appearance makes them suitable for use in contemporary garden designs.

HOW TO JOIN RUSTIC POLES

If you need to attach a horizontal pole to a vertical one, saw a notch of a suitable size in the top of the vertical one so that the horizontal piece will fit snugly on top.

To join two horizontal pieces of wood, saw two opposing and matching notches so that one sits over the other. Secure the two pieces with galvanized nails or screws.

To fix cross-pieces to horizontals or uprights, remove a V-shaped notch, using a chisel if necessary to achieve a snug fit, then nail into place with galvanized nails.

Use halving joints where two poles cross. Make two saw cuts halfway through the pole, then remove the waste timber with a chisel. Secure the two pieces with galvanized nails or screws.

Bird's mouth joints are useful for connecting horizontal or diagonal pieces to uprights. Cut out a V-shaped notch about 3cm (1in) deep and saw the other piece of timber to match the shape. You may need to use a chisel to achieve a good fit.

Try out the assembly on the ground, then insert the uprights in prepared holes and make sure these are secure before adding any further pieces. Most pieces can be nailed together, but screw any sections subject to stress. Use rust-free screws and nails.

3 Position the legs of the arch in the holes. Backfill with the excavated earth and compact with your heel. Check that the legs are vertical using a spirit level. If using spikes, insert the legs and then tighten any securing bolts.

4 The next stage is to construct the overhead beams of the arch. Lay both halves on a large flat surface and carefully screw the joint together at the correct angle. Use galvanized screws to protect the arch from corrosion.

5 Fit the overhead beams to the posts. In this example they slot into the tops of the posts and are nailed in place.

Preparing the soil

Cultivation is the basis of all good soil husbandry and is the starting point of most gardening activity. Even a garden run on a no-dig system requires thorough cultivation to get it off to a good start.

Digging is the best way of removing weeds and other unwanted debris from the soil, breaking up compacted layers and incorporating organic matter. It also brings pests to the surface so that they can be eaten by birds and introduces air into the soil. However, once planted and mulched with a thick layer of organic matter there may be no need to dig it again provided the soil is not walked on, which will compact it.

Well-rotted garden compost is one of the best soil conditioners. Every garden should have a compost heap, where grass clippings, leaves and other vegetable matter can be left to rot down. Not only is this material absolutely free, but it is an environmentally sound practice.

Look after your soil and it will look after you – requiring less effort and providing reliable bumper harvests.

Know your soil

It is essential that you understand what type of soil you have in your garden and its level of fertility before you can take steps to improve it. Several simple soil-testing kits are available to help you.

Understanding your soil

All soils are made up of the same basic ingredients: clay, silt and sand. It is the proportions of these that determines the type of soil you have.

Clay soil This heavy soil is generally fertile, but is sticky and difficult to work. The tiny clay particles pack together tightly with few air spaces between them, so the soil cannot drain freely and remains wet for longer. This causes problems in spring, because the soil is too wet to be cultivated and remains colder for longer. Soils with a high clay content have a poor structure and compact easily when walked on, further impeding drainage. When clay soils dry out in summer they crack badly and form solid lumps.

Sandy soil The particles in sandy soil are mainly larger and irregularly shaped, which means that water

It is essential that you choose plants that like the prevailing soil conditions in your garden. The rock rose (*Helianthemum*), for example, will thrive in neutral to alkaline soil in a dry, sunny spot.

drains freely and there are plenty of air spaces between the particles. The downside of free-draining, sandy soils is that nutrients are very easily leached (washed) out, which leaves the soil impoverished. Free-draining soils are also more prone to drought during dry spells. However, they are quicker to warm up after winter and easy to work, so are ideal for sowing early crops in spring.

Silt soil In terms of particle size, silt falls roughly between clay and sand. The soil is usually fertile. Silty soils are reasonably free-draining, but like clay soils they are easily compacted.

Loamy soil This type of soil contains both clay and sand particles as well as silt, and in many ways they offer the best of all worlds, being highly fertile and reasonably well drained, but still fairly moisture-

HOW TO TEST THE SOIL FOR NUTRIENTS

1 Collect a soil sample from 10cm (4in) below the surface. Take a number of samples, and mix together for a representative test.

2 Follow the instructions on the kit. Mix one part of soil with five parts of water. Shake well in a jar, then allow the water to settle.

3 Draw off some of the settled liquid from the top few centimetres (about an inch) for your test.

retentive. Loamy soils also warm up quickly in spring so are suitable for growing early crops.

The other essential factor about your soil that will affect the plants you can grow is its acidity or alkalinity. This is measured on a pH scale, of which the mid-point, 7, is neutral. Anything higher than that is increasingly alkaline, anything lower is increasingly acidic. Most plants prefer a neutral to slightly acidic soil (down to pH 5.5), although they will tolerate slightly alkaline conditions (up to pH 7.5). A few plants, such as azaleas, need acidic conditions to thrive; others, such as lilacs, prefer slightly alkaline soils.

Assessing your soil

If you have a new garden or are planting a new area, it is worth finding out what your soil is like so that you can improve it before planting. The first step is to check the drainage by digging holes about 30cm (12in) deep randomly across the area. Fill each with water and see how quickly it drains. If it all disappears within 24 hours all is

Reducing soil acidity

The acidity of your soil can be reduced by adding lime some weeks before planting and working it in thoroughly with a rake. First, check the soil with a soil-testing kit to see how much lime is required.

well. If the hole is still partly full after that time, you may have a drainage problem. In most cases this can be overcome by digging deeply and incorporating plenty of well-rotted organic matter and grit into the soil. Otherwise, you will have to get land drains installed or build raised beds.

Testing your soil

Cheap and reliable soil-testing kits are available from garden retailers that will indicate the nutrient balance in your soil and its pH level. For this to be of value you must test a representative sample of soil. The most reliable way of doing this is to lay four canes on the soil surface in a large W shape, then use a trowel to

Soil-testing kits of various degrees of sophistication are widely available, such as this electronic meter to test the pH level.

dig a small hole, about 15cm (6in) deep, at each point of the W, making a total of five holes. Scoop out some soil from each hole and place it in a garden sieve over a bucket. This will remove any debris and large pieces of organic matter. Mix the soil from the different holes thoroughly before testing. Make sure you do not test contaminated areas, such as where a compost heap has been, otherwise the results will not be representative of the garden as a whole.

4 Use a pipette to transfer the solution to the test chamber in the plastic container supplied with the kit.

5 Select a colour-coded capsule (one for each nutrient). Put the powder in the chamber, replace the cap and shake well.

6 After a few minutes, compare the colour of the liquid with the shade panel shown on the container.

Improving your soil

With the knowledge of what your soil is like, you can take positive steps to improve it through the incorporation of well-rotted manure and compost and thorough digging.

Soil conditioning

Organic matter, such as well-rotted farmyard manure, garden compost or mushroom compost, will improve all but peaty soils, which are already rich in the material. It improves the structure of heavy soils by allowing water and air in, and helps sandy soils by acting as a sponge, holding on to moisture. It also provides food for beneficial soil-borne creatures, such as earthworms, which further aerate the soil.

When well-rotted, organic matter is practically odourless it is ready to add to the soil. Do not use fresh or partly rotted organic material because the micro-organisms will use nitrogen to complete the process and this will be extracted from your soil.

Heavy soils are best dug in late autumn, to allow the large clods to be broken down by frost action. Loamy soils can be dug at any time in winter, as long as the soil conditions allow. Light, sandy soils are best cultivated in spring to avoid loss of nutrients through leaching in winter.

Forking

Light, recently cultivated soils can be simply forked over to the full depth of a garden fork, incorporating organic matter as you work. The soil is roughly turned and placed back in the same position. Remove any weeds and other debris by hand.

Digging

There are three main methods used to dig the garden, simple, single and double digging, although there are variations of each.

HOW TO CARRY OUT DOUBLE DIGGING

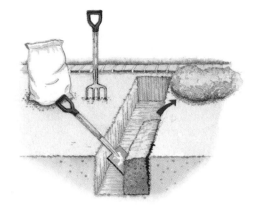

1 Dig a wide trench, placing the topsoil on a plastic sheet to one side to be used later when filling in the final trench.

2 Break up the subsoil at the bottom of the trench, adding well-rotted manure to the soil as you proceed.

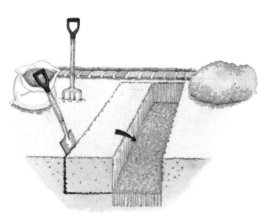

3 Dig the next trench, turning the topsoil over on top of the broken subsoil that is in the first trench.

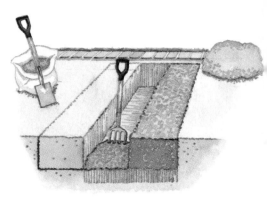

4 Continue down the plot, taking care that subsoil from the lower trench is not mixed with topsoil from the upper.

Simple digging As its name suggests this is the least complicated to do. It is useful for cultivating lighter soils and for removing weeds. The spade is forced vertically into the soil to the full depth of the blade and the handle is eased back to lever the earth up. The spade is turned and the soil deposited in the same place but inverted, burying annual weeds at the bottom of the excavation. Perennial weeds and other debris are removed by hand, and clods of soil are broken up with sharp jabs of the spade. Repeat the technique across the plot. When the other side is reached, step back about 15cm (6in) and repeat the procedure across the plot.

Preparing for planting

You should prepare the soil for planting in the spring, when the surface of the soil is dry. Simply rake level using a soil rake, removing any stones that have made their way to the surface as well as any weed seedlings. Any remaining clods should break down readily to form a breadcrumb-like structure (known as a fine tilth), which is ideal for sowing and planting. If necessary, suitable fertilizers can be added at this point.

Avoid walking on the soil at any time because your weight will cause compaction. Instead, always lay short planks on the surface to spread your weight and work from these.

Single digging Used on heavier soils, this is a very good technique for incorporating organic matter into the upper layer of soil. It follows the same process as simple digging, except a trench about 30cm (12in) wide is excavated across the plot and the soil deposited on one side. A layer of well-rotted garden compost or manure is placed in the bottom of the trench. Moving 15cm (6in) back, the next row is dug, but the excavated soil is thrown forward to fill the first trench. After two passes across the plot the first trench will have been filled and a second trench created. This process is repeated until the entire plot has been dug. The excavated soil from the first trench is moved to the other end of the plot to fill the last trench.

Double digging This goes one step further and is used to break up compacted subsoil or for preparing deep beds for hungry crops. After excavating each trench, use a garden fork to loosen the subsoil at the bottom of the trench and mix in well-rotted organic matter or grit to improve the drainage if required. Then follow the procedure for single digging. It is important not to mix the soils from each layer.

This border was prepared thoroughly before planting. The soil was dug over to remove weeds and stones and to improve the soil structure. Plenty of organic compost was added to improve drainage. The end result is a border full of strong, healthy plants that requires little maintenance.

Using a cultivator

It is worth considering mechanical digging if you have a large plot to cultivate. However, you will need to clear the perennial weeds beforehand, and cultivators are hard work and noisy to operate. If a mechanical digger is used repeatedly on the same plot, the soil structure will suffer and a compacted layer can form just below the maximum depth of penetration of the blades.

HOW TO PREPARE FOR PLANTING

1 Break down the soil into a fine crumbly structure, and level with a rake before sowing.

2 Any large clods that still exist should be broken down with a spade or fork or the back of a rake. Try to avoid walking on the soil as this will cause compaction.

3 Once the soil is reasonably fine, rake it level. At the same time remove any large stones and other debris.

Making compost and leafmould

Composting is good for your garden and good for the environment. It is a convenient way of getting rid of garden waste and will also save you money, so it is well worth making the effort to do it.

Garden compost

Making your own compost is sound sense. It returns organic matter and nutrients to the soil that would otherwise be lost. It is also a very convenient way of getting rid of waste. There are environmental benefits, too, as composting recycles material that would otherwise find its way to landfill sites. Producing your own compost will save you money, because it means you need to buy less organic matter to improve your garden soil.

To compost successfully and efficiently you need the right equipment and an understanding of the principles of the decomposition process. Although you can compost organic waste perfectly well in a loose heap, it looks untidy and tends to decompose unevenly unless carefully managed. In most gardens a compost bin is a far better option.

WHAT TO COMPOST

A wide range of organic material from both the garden and household can be composted including (clockwise, from top left) most kitchen waste, weeds, shredded prunings and grass clippings.

Ideally, a bin should contain at least 1 cubic metre (about 30 cubic feet) of waste to allow it to heat up adequately and compost material quickly. The bin can be a simple structure made from old pallets nailed together to form a box or a neater home-made version fashioned from second-hand, tanalized fencing timber. Do not use untreated timber because it will rot along with the

A bonus crop

After the compost has been turned in the compost bin you can use it to grow a bonus crop of vegetables. Simply cover the top of the compost with about 15cm (6in) of garden soil and plant hungry vegetables, such as marrows (large zucchini), pumpkins or cucumbers. They will benefit from the heat generated by the decomposing compost and the extra nutrients made available.

contents. Alternatively, you can buy a ready-made compost bin, but make sure you choose one that will hold sufficient organic waste. The compost should be easily accessible when it is ready to use.

What can you compost?

Almost all organic waste material from the garden and household can be recycled, but to decompose quickly and form a crumbly, sweet-smelling, fibrous material, the right ingredients must be combined. Ideally, add dry material, such as prunings, old newspapers and straw, with equal quantities of green, wet

HOW TO MAKE COMPOST

1 A simple compost bin, which should be about 1m (3ft) square, can be made using cheap, pressure-treated fencing timber, or by nailing four flat pallets together.

2 Pile the waste into the bin, taking care that there are no thick layers of the same material. Grass clippings, for example, will not rot down if the layer is too thick because the air cannot penetrate.

3 It is important to keep the compost bin covered with an old mat or a sheet of polythene (sheet vinyl or plastic). This will help to keep in the heat generated by the rotting process and will also prevent the compost from getting too wet in bad weather.

organic waste, such as grass clippings. Before adding to the compost heap, make sure that dry and woody material is chopped finely with secateurs (pruners) or a garden shredder. Do not add meat, fish, fat or other cooked foods to the compost bin because they will attract vermin. Also throw away perennial weed roots and annual weeds that are setting seed because these may survive the composting process.

Mix up the material before adding it to the compost bin or add the material in layers no more than 15cm (6in) deep.

Speeding up composting

There are several actions you can take to minimize the time it takes for the composting process to be completed. Give the decomposition process a kick-start by adding a proprietary compost activator or a spadeful of well-rotted compost from a previous bin to each layer of material added. This will provide extra nitrogen and introduce the necessary micro-organisms needed for decomposition. Fill the bin as quickly as you can so that there is

sufficient organic material to heat up and decompose quickly. Make sure that the material is moist enough when it is added. Check after a few weeks to see if it has dried out and water if necessary.

So the material does not get too wet, cover it with a lid, piece of old carpet or sheet of plastic. If the compost does get too wet, turn out the bin and mix in more dry material before refilling the bin. Insulate the bin in winter with bubble polythene or old carpet so that the core of the heap does not cool down. Turn the decomposing organic matter after about a month so that the material on the outside is placed in the centre of the bin. This will introduce air and produce a more uniform compost at the end of the process. After about two months in summer and up to six months in winter the compost should be ready to use.

Making leafmould

Autumn leaves are another source of useful organic matter. If you have a small garden, fill black plastic bags with leaves, add a little water if the leaves are dry and seal by knotting

Chicken wire attached to four wooden posts makes an ideal container for autumn leaves. The leafmould can be used on the garden after about a year.

the top. Puncture a few holes in the sides with a garden fork to allow air in before putting the bags in an out-of-the-way place, such as behind the shed. The leaves take about a year to break down into a rich, crumbly texture, which can then be used on the garden. Speed the process by adding a few handfuls of grass clippings to each bag before sealing.

In a large garden make a special enclosure with chicken wire and corner posts. Cover with carpet to prevent the leaves from blowing away.

4 After about a month, turn the contents of the compost bin with a fork to let in air and to move the outside material, which is slow to rot, into the centre to speed up the rotting process. If you have several bins, it is easier to turn the compost from one bin into another.

5 When the bin is full, you may want to cover the surface with a layer of soil and use it to grow marrows (large zucchini), pumpkins or cucumbers. If you want to use the contents as soon as possible, omit the soil and keep the compost covered with plastic.

Compost

Good garden compost is dark brown, fibrous and crumbly. It has a sweet earthy smell, not a rotting one. Compost can be used straight away or left covered until required.

Choosing and using fertilizers

Plants need a range of essential nutrients to grow well. The amount of fertilizer you use and how often you need to apply it will depend on your soil and the types of crops you are trying to grow.

If they are to flower reliably year after year, perennials and shrubs, such as this camellia, should be given the nutrients they need. Fertilizer rich in potassium encourages good flower production.

Essential nutrients

In nature a nutritional cycle occurs whereby plants take nutrients from the soil as they grow, then eventually die and rot, allowing the nutrients to return to the soil. In the garden you can mimic this process to some extent by recycling all your organic waste in a compost bin and using the compost to return nutrients to the soil. A proportion of the organic matter is not returned, however, so the soil needs replenishment from other sources. Fertilizers are a convenient method of providing the nutrients that are needed for healthy growth. Your choice will depend on the nutrients already available from your soil and the type of growth you want to encourage.

There are three macro- or primary nutrients, nitrogen (N), phosphorus (P) and potassium (K), the proportions of which are expressed as a ratio of N:P:K on the labels of fertilizer packs. Each macro-nutrient promotes a different type of growth.

Nitrogen This nutrient encourages leafy growth, so it is useful for adding to leafy crops such as spinach and cabbages.

Phosphorus An essential nutrient for healthy roots, phosphorus also promotes the ripening of fruit.

Potassium Available in the form of potash, this promotes flowering and good fruit production.

Three other nutrients, calcium, magnesium and sulphur, are needed in smaller quantities and are known as secondary nutrients, and seven more, boron, chlorine, copper, iron, manganese, molybdenum and zinc, are also essential but in very small amounts. These are known as micro-nutrients or trace elements.

Types of fertilizer

Fertilizers are grouped according to their mode of manufacture or origin. Organic fertilizers are derived from naturally occurring organic materials, such as animals and plants. Some of the most widely used are bonemeal (high in phosphorus), fishmeal, fish,

HOW TO ADD ORGANIC MATERIAL

1 Organic material such as well rotted garden compost or farmyard manure is high in nutrients. Fork in when the soil is dug. For heavy soils this is best done in the autumn.

2 If the soil has already been dug, the organic material can be lightly forked in or left on the surface. The worms will complete the task of working it into the soil.

3 In autumn, and again in spring, top-dress established plants with a layer of well-rotted organic material.

INORGANIC FERTILIZERS **ORGANIC FERTILIZERS**

balanced general fertilizer   sulphate of ammonia   blood   bonemeal

potash   superphosphate   seaweed   fish, blood and bone

blood and bone, hoof and horn (high in nitrogen) and seaweed meal (also high in nitrogen). They are slow acting because they have to be broken down by micro-organisms in the soil before the nutrients they contain become available to plants. The rate of breakdown of the fertilizer varies according to the prevailing conditions: if it is warm and moist breakdown speeds up; when it is cold or dry it slows down. Nutrients are thus released when plants need them most and are growing strongly. For these reasons organic fertilizers are acceptable to most organic growers.

Inorganic fertilizers are man-made. Most are manufactured, but a few, such as rock potash, are naturally occurring minerals that are mined. They are concentrated and usually quick acting because they are soluble in water so are immediately available to the plants. Although effects can be immediate, such fertilizers are easily leached from the soil by heavy rains, especially in winter and on well-drained soil.

These fertilizers can be further grouped according to the amount of N, P and K they contain. As the name suggests, balanced fertilizers (also known as complete fertilizers) contain an equal proportion of each macro-nutrient, an N:P:K of 7:7:7 being typical. Specific fertilizers, on the other hand, have different ratios of N:P:K. They are usually sold labelled as beneficial for particular plants, such as lawns or roses. Straight or simple fertilizers are the final group and these supply just one of the macro-nutrients, such as superphosphate (phosphorus), or potassium sulphate (potassium).

To make selection even more complicated, some fertilizers are supplied in combination with other chemicals, such as a fungicide, insecticide or herbicide. They are a convenient but usually an expensive way of buying fertilizer. Slow-release fertilizers are inorganic fertilizers that have been coated in a special resin so that the nutrients are released slowly over time. They

mimic organic fertilizers in that they release more nutrients when the soil is warm and moist, just when the plants need it.

You can buy slow-release fertilizers that will last from a few weeks to the whole season. Because they cannot be washed away they are particularly suited for use in containers that are regularly watered throughout the growing season.

Fertilizers are also available in liquid formulations. Liquid growmore or liquid seaweed extract will promote general plant growth, but a high-potash feed, such as rose or tomato fertilizer, will encourage flowers and the formation of fruit.

Foliar feeds

Dilute fertilizer solutions can be applied to, and absorbed through, the plants' foliage. They are quick acting and useful for giving plants a boost part-way through the growing season or for correcting a deficiency.

Lawns

A lawn has a dramatic effect on the atmosphere of a garden. When it is kept neat and tidy it will greatly enhance the overall appearance as well as act as a calming visual counter-balance to busy and colourful beds and borders. If you have just moved into a new house the best way to get the garden started is to lay a new lawn. You do not have to worry about the size or shape at this stage because it can be easily changed later on when you have formulated your overall garden design.

When you design a new lawn it is important to keep the shape simple to reduce the time you will have to spend mowing and edging. Tight curves and corners might look dramatic, but they are awkward to cut. If the lawn runs right up to the base of a wall or fence consider installing a mowing edge so that you do not have to stop and trim wayward grass stems. An edging strip is also a good idea along borders, reducing maintenance time still further.

A long lawn draws the eye to the end of the garden. Rhododendrons spilling out on to the grass help soften the edges of the lawn.

Creating a new lawn

The decision to create a new lawn is not one to be taken lightly, but it does give you the opportunity to give your garden a top quality surface. A new lawn is best laid in spring or early autumn.

Seed or turf?

The main consideration once you have decided to have a new lawn is whether to grow it from seed or lay turf. Seed is cheaper, costing less than a quarter of the price of turf, and is easier to do. It is also more flexible because you can wait until the weather and soil conditions are just right. Turf, on the other hand, has to be put down almost as soon as it is delivered and is hard work to lay.

Preparing the ground

First dig over the area, clearing the ground of weeds, including the roots of perennials. If sowing seeds, leave for a week or two to allow any weed seeds to germinate. These will need to be killed using a weedkiller spray (choose a type that leaves the area safe for replanting within a few days) or by hoeing.

Creating a level surface

A few days after killing the surface weeds, rake the ground level using a soil rake and remove any stones or other debris that have come to the surface. Then tread the whole area using tiny shuffling steps with the weight on your heels. Repeat this process until an even, level and firm surface has been produced. It is worth investing the time and effort to create a perfectly level bed whether you are sowing seed or laying turf, as this will improve the appearance of your lawn later.

HOW TO SOW A NEW LAWN

1 Dig the ground thoroughly, removing deep-rooted perennial weeds. Rake the soil level. Use pegs marked with lines drawn 5cm (2in) down from the top as a guide, having checked with a spirit (carpenter's) level on a straightedge that the pegs are level.

2 Allow the soil to settle for a week, then consolidate it further by treading it evenly to remove large air pockets. The best way to do this is to shuffle your feet over the area, first in one direction then at right angles.

3 Rake the consolidated soil to produce a fine, crumbly structure suitable for sowing seeds. If you can, leave the area for a couple of weeks to allow weed seeds to germinate. Hoe them off or use a weedkiller that leaves the ground safe for replanting within days.

4 Use string to divide the area into strips a metre (yard) wide and divide the strips into squares with bamboo canes or stakes. Move the canes along the strips as you sow.

5 Use a small container that holds enough seed for a square metre (yard). Make a mark on it if the amount only partly fills the container. Scatter the seeds as evenly as possible with a sweeping motion of the hand.

6 Hire or buy a calibrated granular fertilizer spreader to sow large areas quickly. Check the delivery rate over sheets of paper first and adjust the spreader until the correct amount is being applied per square metre (yard).

HOW TO LAY A LAWN WITH TURFS

1 Dig and consolidate the soil as described for seed, but there is no need to leave it for a few weeks to allow weed seeds to germinate: the turf will prevent them from sprouting. Start by laying the turf along a straight edge.

2 Stand on a plank while you lay the next row, as this will distribute your weight. Stagger the joints between rows to create a bond like brickwork. Turf in a long roll will have fewer joints but again these should not align.

3 Tamp down each row of turf to eliminate air pockets with the head of a rake, then roll the plank forwards to lay the next row. Brush sandy soil, or a mixture of peat and sand, into the joints to help bind the turfs together.

Planting the lawn

A couple of days before laying turf or sowing seed, scatter a general fertilizer at the recommended rate over the area and rake lightly into the surface of the soil. If sowing seed, choose a windless day, preferably when rain is forecast and lightly rake the grass seed into the surface. It is a good idea to protect the area with fine mesh netting to keep off birds and cats.

For both seed and turf, keep the area well watered, if it does not rain heavily, until the grass is well established. For turf this should be about two weeks, for seed it will be considerably longer.

A good-quality lawn invites you into the garden, leading the eye smoothly to beds and borders. If your lawn is in very bad condition it is worth considering starting from scratch and sowing seed or laying turf to get the effect you want.

Looking after your lawn

A lawn needs regular mowing throughout the growing season. Other maintenance tasks such as removing moss and weeds, seasonal feeding and watering and other lawn treatments may also be necessary to keep it in tip-top condition.

Mowing and trimming

From the time the grass starts to grow in early spring it will need to be cut and trimmed regularly until the end of the growing season. The first spring cut should be made when the lawn is dry after the grass reaches about 8cm (3in) long. Brush off any wormcasts before you mow. Make sure the blades of the mower are set high so that they trim off just a couple of centimetres (less than 1in). Gradually lower the cutting height over the next few mows until it is cutting the grass back to 4cm (1½in). Collect lawn clippings from the early cuts. Thereafter, mow the lawn every time the grass has grown about 2cm (¾in). You do not need a grass box to collect the clippings if you mow this often because they can be left on the lawn as a mulch, returning nutrients to the soil.

Controlling moss

A lawn that contains a lot of moss should be treated by applying a specially formulated moss killer to the grass in the autumn or spring. Use a treatment recommended for the season. The mixture known as lawn sand, sometimes used to kill moss, is fine in spring, but it contains too much nitrogen for autumn use. Moss is fairly easy to eliminate using a lawn treatment, but to achieve long-term control you need to tackle the underlying causes that encourage moss. A lawn becomes colonized by moss because the grass is not growing vigorously enough. This could be due to poor drainage, too much shade or soil that is too acidic – if you are unsure, check it using a simple pH kit. Where shade is the problem, thin out any overhanging branches of trees or cut back shrubs.

Killing weeds

Isolated weeds can be removed with an old kitchen knife or treated using a spot weedkiller. You may need to treat areas of established perennial weeds several times to kill them completely. Where the problem is more widespread use an overall lawn treatment. On a small lawn apply a granular weedkiller using a hand shaker pack or apply a liquid weedkiller using a watering can fitted with a weedkiller dribble bar. Large lawns are quicker and easier to treat by applying a granular weedkiller using a calibrated fertilizer spreader. Coarse grass weeds can also spoil the appearance of a lawn and are not affected by lawn weedkillers. You can either dig out the coarse grasses by hand and reseed the bare patch, or weaken the weed grass over time by slashing through the patches with a sharp knife each time you mow.

HOW TO REMOVE WEEDS

1 Use a special weeding tool or a knife to prise up single weeds. Push the tool in next to the root and lift the plant out with a lever action as you pull with the other hand. Even deep-rooted plants can be removed like this.

2 Widespread weeds are best controlled by a selective weedkiller, ideally in spring. They are usually applied as a liquid, using a dribble bar attached to a watering can. Always mix and apply as recommended by the manufacturer.

3 If there are just a few troublesome weeds, spot treatment may be a more economical and quicker method. Brush or dab on a selective weedkiller. Be careful not to kill the grass as well as the weeds.

4 Make any necessary lawn repairs. If you have had to lift a lot of weeds growing close together, leaving a bare patch in your lawn, sprinkle grass seeds over the area.

If your lawn is in poor condition and needs reviving, apply a lawn feed. Choose one formulated for the season: spring and summer feeds have much more nitrogen than autumn feeds.

If you want your lawn to remain green all summer, you will have to water it regularly during dry spells. A water sprinkler takes much of the hard work out of this tedious task.

Feeding and watering

A vigorously growing lawn is less likely to be colonized by weeds and mosses. Keep the grass growing strongly by ensuring it receives plenty of water in long, dry spells. Apply a high-nitrogen lawn feed once a year in spring and use a slow-release formulation feed throughout the growing season. If you also have a problem with moss or weeds use a combined lawn weed and feed, or lawn weed, feed and moss killer.

Clearing the lawn

Where there is no obvious sign of moss but the lawn still feels spongy when you walk on it, the problem is likely to be the build-up of dead grass stems at the base of the lawn, known as thatch. When the thatch gets more than 1cm (½in) thick it starts to suffocate the lawn and must be removed, a technique known as scarifying. Use a spring-tine or wire lawn rake and vigorously rake out the thatch. This is hard work, so if you have a large area to deal with it is worth considering buying or hiring a powered lawn rake to do the job. Scarify your lawn thoroughly once a year in autumn.

Falling leaves also cause a problem and must be removed, otherwise the grass beneath will turn yellow from lack of light and be prone to disease.

HOW TO REMOVE THATCH

Grass clippings, leaves and other debris form a thatch at the base of grasses in your lawn which can stifle them. Remove it with a spring-tine rake. Raking also removes moss.

HOW TO COLLECT LEAVES

1 Don't let autumn leaves lie on your lawn for long or the grass underneath will suffer. Clear the leaves up with a lawn rake.

2 Rake the leaves into piles and scoop them up with a pair of short planks (boards). Choose a still day when the leaves are dry to make the job pleasant.

Repairing your lawn

Many lawns receive a lot of wear, especially during the summer months. Fortunately, the autumn is an ideal time to make repairs. Use the following techniques to tackle humps and hollows, badly draining soil, bare patches, broken edges and areas that are simply worn out.

Bumps and hollows

When an uneven lawn is cut the high points will show up as light green because the grass is being cut too short and the low points as dark green patches. If the problem is widespread, you would be better off topdressing the whole lawn, but if you have just a few isolated bumps or hollows you can cure them using the following technique. Use a sharp spade or half-moon edging tool to make a H-shaped cut in the lawn centred over the bump or hollow. Carefully undercut the turf either side working from the central cut and peel back the turf to expose the soil beneath. Then either remove sufficient soil to level the bump when the turf is relaid, or top up with fine soil if you are levelling a hollow. Fill any gaps with an equal-parts mixture of sieved garden soil and sharp sand.

Repairing any broken edges will give your beds and borders a neat finish, essential when the impact of your garden design relies on straight lines.

Bare patches

Repair any bare patches in the lawn by using a garden fork to scratch the surface and gently loosen the soil. Then incorporate a general fertilizer such as growmore at the rate of 50g (2oz) per square metre (yard), before firming with the back of a soil rake. Sow grass seed over the top at the rate of about 35g (1½oz) per square metre (yard) for really bare patches and about 20g (1oz) per square metre (yard) if over-sowing sparse areas. Cover the seed

Aeration

Surface drainage can be impeded if the grass has become compacted because of excessive wear. You can overcome this by a technique known as aeration. Small areas are best treated with a garden fork. Simply spike it into the grass, pushing the tines into the ground to a depth of about 15cm (6in), spacing the holes about 5cm (2in) apart. For larger areas of lawn consider hiring a powered spiker or slitter instead. Fill the holes with sharp sand or a mixture of soil and sand for poorly drained soils, or use peat or very fine, well-rotted compost if the ground is sandy. Autumn is the best time to aerate your lawn.

1 If the grass growth is poor this could be because the soil is poorly drained. Aerate the lawn by pushing the prongs of a fork into the ground.

2 Gently brush a soil improver, such as sharp sand or a mixture of soil and sand, into the holes made by the fork.

with a light scattering of sieved garden soil and then water with a fine-rosed watering can. Protect the area from birds and cats by covering with a piece of garden fleece, held down with stones. Water again during dry spells until the new grass is well established.

Heavy wear

Areas that receive constant wear, such as under children's play equipment or at the bottom of steps on to a lawn, need to be reinforced if they are going to cope. If the lawn is used as a shortcut to another part of the garden consider incorporating stepping stones to take the impact. Where children's play equipment cannot be moved to spread the wear and tear around, reinforce the grass with heavy-duty plastic mesh. Cut the grass short, then peg the mesh down over the area so that it is held completely flat. Allow the grass to grow up through the mesh over the winter. When you come to mow next spring, the mesh will be hidden from sight, well below mower blade height so that you can mow straight over the top.

HOW TO RECUT AN EDGE

Insert a half-moon edging tool about 8cm (3in) into the soil. Lever the soil forwards to form a gulley with one vertical side against the lawn and one curved side against the border. Remove any grass to prevent it rooting.

HOW TO REPAIR A BROKEN EDGE

1 Use a half-moon edging tool or a spade to cut a rectangle around the affected area.

2 Push a spade under the rectangle, starting from the broken edge. Keep the thickness of the slice of grass as even as possible.

3 Reverse the turf so that the undamaged part of the turf is against the edge of the bed and the broken edge is within the lawn. Fill the hole caused by the damage with sifted soil and firm it down well.

4 Brush soil into the joints to help the grass knit together quickly and water well. Sow grass seed in the patched area, matching the type of grass if possible. Cover until the seed has germinated.

Broken edges

Isolated broken edges on lawns, perhaps caused by a careless heel or spade, are easy to repair. Use a sharp spade or half-moon edging tool to cut out a square at the edge of the lawn that encloses the damaged area. Undercut the turf and then turn it around 180 degrees so that the broken area is within the lawn and the straight part aligns with the edge of the lawn. Top up the damaged area with sieved garden soil if necessary, then level and firm with the back of a soil rake. Reseed as described for bare patches (above).

If the lawn is broken and uneven all along the edge of a border it is worth re-cutting to improve the appearance of your garden. Mark out where you will re-cut, using a board as a guide for straight edges or a length of garden hose for curved ones. Insert a sharp spade or half-moon edging tool into the soil. Lever back the handle and push the soil forwards to form a gulley with one vertical side against the lawn and one curved side against the border. Remove any unwanted grass to prevent it rooting into the border and becoming a weed problem.

Reducing maintenance time

The shape of a lawn – whether square, rectangular or irregular – will have a great influence on the amount of time it takes to keep it neat as well as the style of garden you are trying to create.

Lawn size

Obviously the larger a lawn the more time it will take to mow. This can, however, be offset somewhat by choosing a mower with a cutting width to match the size of your lawn. For a large lawn – more than 250 square metres (300 sq yards) – look for a mower with a cutting width of at least 35cm (14in). If you have a small lawn – less than 50 square metres (60 sq yards) – a mower with a cutting width of 25cm (10in) would be sufficient. A mower with a 30cm (12in) wide cut would be the best option for lawns in between these two extremes.

Wider mowers are usually more expensive, so consider whether the extra cost is worth it. The extra manoeuvrability of a smaller mower might be better in a smaller garden, with fewer straight runs.

Naturalizing bulbs in the lawn gives you a good excuse to leave the grass uncut.

The shape of the lawn

You can reduce the time and effort involved when mowing by keeping the shape of your lawn simple. Simple shapes often look more appealing than complicated fussy ones in any case. If your existing design has obstacles, such as island beds and specimen trees, you could reduce the amount of stopping and starting as well as the length of edge to be trimmed by joining the beds together or extending borders from the sides to incorporate them.

HOW TO CREATE A MOWING EDGE

1 A mowing edge of bricks or paving slab will prevent overhanging flowers smothering the edge of the lawn. Mark out the area of grass to be lifted using the paving as a guide. To keep the new edge straight, use a half-moon edger against the paving. Then lift the grass to be removed by slicing it off with a spade.

2 Remove enough soil to allow for the depth of the slab or brick and make a firm base by compacting gravel or a mixture of sand and gravel where the paving is to be laid. Use a plank of wood to make sure it is level. Allow for the thickness of the paving and a few blobs of mortar.

3 It is best to bed the edging on mortar for stability, but because it will not be taking a heavy weight, just press the slabs on to blobs of mortar and tap level with a mallet. The slabs should be laid evenly and flush with, or very slightly below, the lawn. Use a spirit (carpenter's) level to double-check.

Saving time in repairing your lawn

Lawns on very light, sandy soils can soon lose their sharpness as the edges of beds and borders crumble away. Even on other soils the edges of a lawn may be damaged by an ill-placed foot. Repairing the edges of a lawn can be a time-consuming task – perhaps repeated every spring – but it is necessary if your garden uses formal beds as an integral part of the design. To reduce the need for repairs, you can install a mowing edge or an edging strip. Bear in mind, though, that a raised edging strip will make it difficult to mow right up to the edge of the bed. Weigh up whether a strong, attractive edging is worth the extra mowing time.

If you have more than one lawn in your garden, consider joining them into one. Small lawns in the front garden often take more time to look after than the main one at the back. You may be better off getting rid of the small lawn altogether and replacing it with an area of gravel.

Mowing edges

It is a good idea to create a mowing edge if your garden is bounded by a border. It will mean the grass always has a neat edge and you won't damage overhanging border plants when you mow. On a large lawn the edging can be wide, especially if you have large, trailing plants that are likely to flop over the edge of the bed. If the lawn is small, however, use narrow edging so that it will look in proportion with the rest of the garden.

Cutting to different heights

If you have a large lawn consider leaving part of it to grow longer between cuts so that your workload is reduced. Keep broad "pathways" cut regularly, cut other areas with the blade set higher, and mow only every second or third time. Some areas can remain uncut except for a couple of times a season, which will allow wildflowers to thrive. Do bear in mind that very long grass cannot be cut with a standard mower and you will have to use a nylon-line trimmer or hire a powered sythe.

A mowing edge will lessen your work on a lawn, as the mower can get right up to the edge of the bed. You may have to trim any spreading grass stems, but this will only be necessary occasionally.

HOW TO FIT AN EDGING STRIP

1 Make a slit trench along the lawn edge with a spade, then lay the strip alongside the trench and cut to length. Place the edging strip loosely into the trench.

2 Backfill with soil for a firm fit. Press the strip in gently as you proceed. Finish off by tapping it level with a hammer over a straight-edged piece of wood.

HOW TO FIT WOODEN EDGING

Cut the roll to length using strong pliers to cut the wires and insert the edging in a narrow trench. Join the pieces by wiring them together. Backfill with soil for a firm fit. Use a hammer over a piece of wood to tap it down. Use a spirit (carpenter's) level to check the edging is level.

Planting in and around the lawn

Adding plants to your lawn can transform the appearance of your garden. Bulbs and wildflowers will provide seasonal interest, while trees and shrubs will add height and structure. Bear in mind that the more obstacles you place in the lawn the longer it will take to mow and trim, and you will break up the sweep of an uncluttered lawn.

Naturalized bulbs

In the wild, bulbs naturally form dramatic flowering drifts of colour under trees. This effect can be reproduced in the garden by planting bulbs in a natural-looking style. Early spring bulbs are a particularly good choice because they not only give a spectacular show but will be

out of the way before mowing starts in earnest. You need to wait six weeks after flowering before mowing the naturalized area. If you want to grow later-flowering bulbs this way, you would be better off creating a wildflower meadow, which does not need cutting until late summer.

To get a natural distribution of bulbs, toss them gently on to the lawn and plant them where they land. Clumps of bulbs are best planted by removing a whole turf with a sharp spade, planting at the correct depth, firming the soil and then replacing the turf. If you use this method, make sure you maintain the informal arrangement of the bulbs. Individual bulbs can be planted using a cylindrical bulb planter. If you are

planting many bulbs, choose a model with a long handle and foot bar, which can be used like a spade. Push the planter vertically into the soil and remove a core that is deep enough for the bulb being planted. After positioning the bulb replace the core and carefully tread level. Bulbs susceptible to rot should be planted on gravel to improve drainage.

Bulbs to naturalize in grass	
Camassia	Galanthus
Chionodoxa	Leucojum
Colchicum	Muscari
Crocus	Narcissus
Erythronium	Ornithogalum
Fritillaria	Scilla

HOW TO NATURALIZE BULBS IN A LAWN

1 If you have a lot of small bulbs to plant in a limited area, try lifting an area of turf. Use a spade or half-moon edging tool to make a H-shaped cut.

2 Slice beneath the grass with a spade until you can fold back the turf for planting. Try to keep the spade level so the soil removed is an even thickness.

3 Loosen the ground, as it will be very compacted. If you want to apply a slow-acting fertilizer, such as bonemeal, work it into the soil at the same time.

4 Avoid planting in rows or regimented patterns. You want the bulbs to look natural and informal, so scatter them and plant where they fall.

5 Use a trowel or a bulb planter for large bulbs, making sure the bulb will be covered with twice its own depth of soil when the grass is returned.

6 Firm the soil then return the grass. Firm again if necessary to make sure it is flat, and water well. Water the grass again in dry weather.

7 Special bulb planters can be used for large bulbs. The planters remove a cylindrical core of soil.

8 Place the bulb at the bottom of the hole on a bed of gravel to improve drainage, if necessary, and replace the plug of earth.

Creating wildlife habitats

The number of flowers growing wild is diminishing. One way of helping is to create a wildflower garden. A massed display of native flowers looks wonderful, and provides a haven for native insects such as butterflies.

Wildflower meadow

The easiest way to create a wild-flower meadow is to sow it like a lawn using a special wildflower and grass mix. You can convert an existing lawn by clearing patches and sowing a wildflower seeds mixture, or by planting pot-grown species directly into the grass.

Feed meadows or lawns containing wildflowers in spring, but use an autumn formulation lawn feed which contains less nitrogen than spring formulations, reducing grass growth.

The meadow will need cutting just twice a year: once in early spring and the second time in mid- to late-summer after the flowers have seeded. Small areas can be cut using a nylon-line trimmer, but larger areas are more easily cut with a powered scythe, which can be bought or hired.

1 Mark a circle 60–120cm (2–4ft) in diameter, using a trail of sand. Lift the grass, removing about 15cm (6in) of soil at the same time.

2 Insert a stake on the side of the prevailing wind. Place off-centre in the hole to allow the rootball to occupy the central position.

3 Check that the hole is deep enough for the rootball by placing the potted tree in the hole. After planting, the soil should be level with the original soil-mark on the trunk.

4 Replace the soil in layers, firming carefully with the heel of your boot as you go. Secure the tree to the stake, and then water well. Mulch the bed to suppress weeds.

Trees and shrubs

The grass underneath a tree or shrub in a lawn is often of poor quality. Its leaves block the light while they are on the tree and suffocate the grass when they fall in the autumn. Specimen trees and shrubs are best grown in a bed cut into the grass.

1 The most satisfactory way to create a wildflower meadow is to sow a special mixture of wildflower seeds. Remember to completely clear the ground of all perennial weeds before you start.

2 To bury the seeds, simply rake in one direction and then in the other. It does not matter if some seeds remain on the surface. Keep the area well watered until the seeds germinate. Protect from birds if necessary.

3 For a very small area, wildflower plants may be more convenient. You can raise your own from seed or buy them. Plant into bare ground or in an existing lawn. Keep the plants well watered until established.

Trees and shrubs

An essential element in most gardens, trees and shrubs provide structure and height as well as acting as foils for other plants. Attractive specimens are eye-catching focal points, while others can be used for specific purposes, such as creating a living boundary or smothering the ground with a carpet of foliage. It is essential to choose the right plant for the function and position you have in mind.

Trees and shrubs should be regarded as permanent additions to the garden and so soil preparation and planting are critical to success. If you get these right, most good garden varieties will establish quickly and thereafter largely look after themselves. In a mature garden, you will need to master techniques to help you keep your plants within bounds or even to move an overcrowded specimen to a new position where it has the space to grow and fulfil its potential.

Trees and shrubs form a vital part of the garden, with a surprising variety of colours and shapes giving structure and, in the case of evergreens, interest throughout the year.

Buying trees and shrubs

Trees and shrubs are permanent additions to the garden and so need to be chosen with care. Many grow into large specimens, taking up a lot of garden space, so make sure you choose varieties that offer more than one season of interest to ensure they offer real value for money.

Buying plants

Trees and shrubs can be bought as container grown, containerized (grown in the field; potted for sale), rootballed or root wrapped (grown in the field; lifted with soil around the roots) or bare root (grown in the field; lifted without soil around the roots) depending on the type of plant and the supplier. Generally, container-grown plants will establish more quickly but are more expensive. Rootballed and bare-root plants are usually available in the autumn or early spring, while container-grown plants are available all year round.

Choosing trees

Most gardens can accommodate just one or two fully grown trees, which will take up a large proportion of the available planting space. It is vital, therefore, to make the correct choice. There is quite a wide range of trees available from garden centres and an even wider choice from specialist nurseries and by mail-order or on the Internet.

To make choosing easier, the first thing you should do is disregard those types of trees that are simply not suitable. Unless you have a very large garden, most can be rejected on the basis of their ultimate size. But other criteria, such as the preferred position (sun or shade) and the soil type in your garden, can also be used to narrow down the choice available. Plant labels, plant catalogues and websites will give this information, or you can check your selections in a reliable plant encyclopedia.

With a much-reduced list of possible candidates, the next step is to consider what features you want the tree to have. Should it be evergreen? When should it bear flowers or fruits? Is scent important? Would your garden benefit from autumn colour or winter interest such as attractive stems or bark? Again, use the information at the point of sale to help you decide.

Once you have made a choice, the next decision is the size of tree you buy (see right). Large trees make an instant impact and might be the best option if your garden is newly laid out and would benefit from the added height and structure a large tree would offer. However, younger specimens – three to five years old, say – generally establish more quickly than older trees. After a few years young trees will often catch up with and even overtake larger ones. Smaller trees are also much cheaper.

MAIL-ORDER PLANTS

Many trees and shrubs are available from mail-order companies. The young plants are mailed in special packages that minimize damage during transit.

ROOTBALLED PLANTS

A rootballed *Taxus* (yew). The ball of soil around the roots of the plant is held together by a net and strong elastic bands. It protects the roots and prevents desiccation.

BARE-ROOT PLANTS

During the dormant season, bare-root plants are often sold with a wrap to protect their roots. If it is too frosty or wet to plant them, leave in the wrappings until conditions improve.

Specialist nurseries carry a wide range of trees and shrubs. Many have a mail-order service, which can be invaluable if the nursery is not easy for you to reach.

What size tree?

Trees are generally sold as two sizes: standards and half-standards, although you may find variations from some suppliers. Standards have a clear trunk to 1.8m (6ft) or so and are ideal for large trees that will form a specimen in a lawn or at the back of a border. Half-standards have a clear single stem, to at least 1.2m (4ft), and are useful planted in a mixed border or to provide a focal point nearer the edge. You can also buy trees as single-stemmed young plants (known as whips) or with new side branches (known as feathered maidens), which you can train yourself into a half-standard or standard by removing the lower branches as the tree grows.

Choosing shrubs

A garden or area of a garden can accommodate more shrubs than trees, so you can choose plants that offer spectacular displays for a relatively short period. However, it is important to create collections of shrubs that flower at different times to extend the period of interest. If you are planting a large area, plant shrubs in groups of threes or fives to achieve a more natural-looking overall display. Also include a proportion of evergreens to provide structure and colour to the borders in winter – as a rule, aim for about two-thirds evergreen to one-third deciduous plants.

What to look for

When buying trees and shrubs, whether container grown, rootballed or bare root, the signs to look out for are the same. Choose a plant with a well-balanced shape and healthy looking foliage with no signs of pest or disease damage. Grafted plants should have a strong, well-healed union. Look for plants that are well established in their pots but avoid those that have roots coming through the bottom of the pot or where roots are circling inside the pot because these have been left too long in their container. Also avoid plants with unnaturally yellowing leaves or weeds in the container because they have been neglected. Faded labels are also a sign the plant has been hanging around too long.

Look for healthy plants of bushy habit (centre) without any signs of leaf yellowing (right), stunted, straggly growth (left), or premature leaf fall, which may be caused by irregular watering.

Planting trees and shrubs

Trees and shrubs need to get off to the best possible start if they are to establish quickly. The secrets of success are preparing the ground well, preventing competition from other plants and keeping the new specimen well watered.

When to plant

Generally, the larger the specimen, the more work it will be to plant successfully. Container-grown deciduous plants can be planted at any time of the year, but they will establish more quickly and be easier to look after if they are planted in spring or autumn when the soil is moist and warm, which encourages rapid root growth and so establishment. Bare-root specimens, however, have to be planted during the dormant season, which is between autumn and spring. Evergreens, particularly conifers, are best planted in late spring so that they have time to establish before the onset of winter.

How to plant

If planting in a lawn, remove a 1m (3ft) wide circle of turf. Dig a hole large enough to accommodate the full spread of the roots (for bare-root plants) or twice as wide as the rootball for all other types. The hole should be the same depth as the rootball. Fork over the soil in the bottom of the hole. Place all excavated soil on a sheet near to the planting hole. Traditionally, the soil would be augmented with well-rotted manure and a handful of bonemeal, but recent research has shown that it is more beneficial to mulch after planting to prevent competition from weeds and to help retain soil moisture around the roots.

Water the rootball thoroughly before planting and allow it to drain. If staking, drive in a stake at this

Trees often look best planted in isolation on the lawn. Here, the pale pebbles at the tree's base draw the eye to the feature, and enhance the decorative red leaves.

1 Before you start, check that the plant has been watered. If not, give it a thorough soaking, preferably at least an hour before planting. This ensures that the rootball is moist and has the ability to absorb water after it has been planted.

2 If the soil in the bed has not been recently prepared, fork it over, removing any stones, weeds and other debris. Add a slow-release fertilizer and fork it into the soil well. If you use bonemeal, apply the fertilizer wearing rubber or vinyl gloves.

point. Position the tree or shrub at the same depth as it was in the pot or the nursery bed – there is usually a tell-tale dark soil mark on the stem about 5cm (2in) above the highest root. With container-grown specimens, tease out the roots from around the rootball before planting to encourage them to spread into the surrounding soil. Check the planting depth by laying a cane across the planting hole, then add or remove soil as necessary.

Backfill the first few centimetres (inch) of the hole with the excavated soil, and give bare-root trees or shrubs a gentle shake to settle the soil. Firm the first layer around the roots with your heel before adding a second layer and repeating the process until the hole is filled. This will prevent any air pockets. Also check that the specimen is upright from time to time as you work. With trees that you are staking, fit the tie. Water well, then cover the soil around the new tree or shrub with an 8cm (3in) deep layer of well-rotted, loose organic mulch. In exposed gardens, protect the tree or shrub after planting by erecting a windbreak and add rabbit guards if these are a pest in your garden.

How to stake a tree

If you are planting a tree over 1.5m (5ft) tall, hammer in a stake on the windward side of the tree to leave just 60cm (2ft) above ground level. Normally this can be done before positioning the tree.

If planting a large specimen you may need to put in the stake after planting, angling it to avoid the rootball. When planting bareroot specimens, spread the roots around the stake.

1 Place a strong stake of rot-resistant wood or one treated with preservative in the hole, knocking it in so that it cannot move.

2 Place the tree in the hole, pushing the rootball up against the stake, so that the stem and stake are 8–10cm (3–4in) apart.

3 Firm down the soil around the plant with the heel of your boot.

4 Although it is possible to use string, proper rose or tree ties provide the best support. Fix the lower one 15cm (6in) above the soil.

5 Fix the second tie near the top of the stake, slightly below the head of the plant.

6 Water the ground around the plant thoroughly and mulch with chipped bark or a similar material.

3 Dig a hole twice as wide as the rootball. Place the plant, still in its pot, in the hole and check that the hole is deep enough by placing a stick or cane across the hole: the top of the pot should align with the top of the soil. Adjust the depth of the hole accordingly.

4 Remove the plant from its pot, being careful not to disturb the rootball. If it is in a plastic bag, cut the bag away rather than trying to pull it off. Place the shrub in the hole and pull the earth back around it. Firm the soil down around the plant and water well.

5 Finally, mulch round the shrub, covering the soil with 5–8cm (2–3in) of chipped bark or similar material. This will not only help to preserve the moisture in the soil but will also help to prevent weed seeds from germinating.

Moving trees and shrubs

It is of course best to plant a tree or shrub in its final position, but even in the best planned garden this isn't always practical. Moving established plants, even small ones, is hard work and needs careful forethought. However, with a few helpers and good preparation, many plants can be moved successfully.

When to move trees and shrubs

The best time for transplanting most established trees or shrubs is during the dormant season (late autumn to early spring). However, the soil should not be waterlogged or frozen as this will damage the soil structure and make it more difficult for the plant to re-establish itself. Spring planting gives a full season's growth before the winter; an autumn move allows the plant to develop a good root system before spring. Evergreens, including conifers, are best moved in mid-spring when the soil is moist and warm enough to encourage rapid root growth.

What size rootball?

The rootball diameter and depth should depend on the size of the plant you are trying to move. The diameter should be about the same as the spread of the branches of shrubs and about one-third the height of a tree. The depth of the rootball depends on the type of soil in your garden. The lighter the soil the more penetrating the roots and so the deeper the rootball will have to be. For example, a 30cm (12in) deep rootball on clay soil may need to be twice that depth on a light, sandy soil. Bear in mind that rootballs with soil attached can literally weigh a ton if you are moving a small tree or large shrub. Make sure you have sufficient help before you start.

HOW TO MOVE A SMALL SHRUB

1 Before moving a shrub, make sure that the planting site has been prepared and the hole excavated. Water the plant well the day before moving it.

2 Dig a trench around the plant, leaving a large rootball (the size depends on the size of the plant). Carefully sever any roots that you encounter to release the rootball.

3 Dig under the shrub, cutting through any vertical taproots that hold it in place.

4 Rock the plant to one side and insert sacking or strong plastic sheeting as far under the plant as you can. Push several folds of material under the rootball.

5 Rock the shrub in the opposite direction and pull the sacking or plastic sheeting through, so that it is completely under the plant.

6 Pull the sacking round the rootball and tie it firmly at the neck of the plant. The shrub is now ready to move. If it is a fairly small plant, one person may be able to lift it out of the hole and transfer it to its new site.

7 If the plant plus the soil is heavy, it is best moved by two people. Tie a length of wood or metal to the sacking. With one person on each end, lift the shrub out of the hole.

8 Lower the transplanted shrub into the prepared planting hole. Unwrap and remove the sheeting from the rootball. Make sure that the plant is in the right position, refill the hole, and water well.

Root pruning

The chances of successfully moving very large shrubs and trees can be improved by pruning the roots in advance of the move, a technique known as root pruning. It should be done up to a year before the move.

To root prune, simply dig the vertical trench at the correct distance from the tree or shrub and sever any roots you find, then refill the trench with soil. The plant will produce more fibrous roots in the soil nearer to the trunk, and these will form part of the rootball, increasing the plant's chances of survival after the move.

Making moves

Before you start, decide on the new position of the plant and prepare the planting hole, which should be about twice as wide and as deep as the rootball. Fork over the bottom of the hole, incorporating a bucketful of grit on heavy soils to improve drainage.

Use a spade to cut a slit-trench around the tree or shrub being moved to mark out the size of the rootball and to sever any roots near to the surface. Then cut a second slit-trench about 30cm (12in) further out and dig out the soil in between to form a trench around the specimen. Make this trench as deep as the rootball.

Undercut the rootball from the trench by inserting the spade at an angle of about 45 degrees all the way round. Small rootballs should then be completely undercut and can be wrapped. Larger rootballs may need further excavation to expose any vertical roots under the middle of the rootball.

After the rootball has been freed, carefully rock it back and slip a sheet of folded heavy-duty polythene or hessian (burlap) under one side then rock it over the other way and then pull the folded polythene through. Tie the corners of the sheeting over the top of the rootball around the main stem to form a neat package, so that the soil is held firmly. Use rope or strong string to reinforce the rootball on all sides.

Move the tree or shrub by pulling on the polythene sheeting, not the trunk. Use a short plank (board) or pair of planks as a ramp out of the hole and then drag it to its new position or get a gang of helpers to lift it. It may be easiest to fix a pole to help carry the tree or shrub.

Replant immediately and water and mulch well. Stake if necessary. Spray the foliage of evergreens after planting and every few days for the first month to help prevent scorching. It is also worth putting up a windbreak around conifers. Keep all transplants well watered throughout the first growing season.

A shrub may need to be moved because it is too vigorous and is crowding out other plants, or because the re-design of its bed makes a move desirable. Prune the shrub after planting if required to create a balanced shape. Water the shrub well throughout the first growing season.

Even very small conifers such as this *Chamaecyparis lawsoniana* 'Bleu Nantais' are hard work to move. Always check the final height and spread of a plant before choosing where to plant it.

Aftercare of trees and shrubs

Once they are established, most trees and shrubs will look after themselves. However, it can take more than a growing season to reach this point of independence. There are also some ornamental types that produce much better displays if they are given a little extra pampering.

Watering techniques

The main reason new trees and shrubs fail in their first season is because they cannot take up sufficient water. Since they have not had time to root into the soil, new specimens should be treated like container-grown plants elsewhere in the garden. Water them thoroughly once a week in dry weather or if your soil is well drained, rather than giving them a light sprinkling every day. Aim to give new shrubs at least a full watering can of water and new trees twice this amount each time you water.

It is essential that the water soaks the soil around the plant and doesn't run off elsewhere. There are a number of techniques you can employ to make sure this happens. Insert a plastic pipe at an angle into the soil

This evergreen *Pieris japonica* had sufficient water in its first year after planting, and now produces an everchanging display of foliage with very little maintenance required.

so that the bottom is at the root zone and the top just proud of the soil surface. Fill the pipe with gravel so that other rubbish cannot accumulate in it and pour water into the pipe each time you water. Alternatively, ridge up the soil about 30cm (12in) away from the main stem to create a

moat each time the plant is watered. The water will then have time to soak into the soil exactly where it is needed. A more sophisticated method is to use circles of seep hose or leaky pipe with a snap-lock connector around individual plants and clip these to a hosepipe (garden hose) each time you water. The water will be released slowly without running off. If you are planting a whole garden, consider installing an automatic watering system.

Mulching

There are many benefits to mulching the newly planted tree or shrub with organic matter. It smothers the ground, preventing weed seeds from germinating and getting established. It also prevents water evaporation from the soil, helping to conserve soil moisture. As it is incorporated into the ground by soil-living creatures, such as earthworms, it helps improve the soil structure and

HOW TO LOOK AFTER TREES AND SHRUBS AFTER PLANTING

A newly planted tree or shrub needs to be watered well in order to become established.

Mulch with straw or garden compost to conserve the moisture in the soil.

releases valuable plant nutrients as it decomposes. A mulch also helps to insulate the soil from excessive heat in summer and cold in winter.

A wide range of materials can be used for mulching. Apply a 5–8cm (2–3in) deep layer around new plants and top up to this layer each spring thereafter. Around established shrubs and trees you can use grass clippings as a free organic mulch. Although some nitrogen is removed from the soil by micro-organisms as the clippings are broken down, only the very surface layer is affected.

Weed control

Limiting weed growth is important in the first few years but is less so as the canopy fills out. Keep all weeds under control during the early years. Use a hoe shallowly around each plant to avoid damaging the roots and hand weed near shallow-rooted plants, such as azaleas, as well as trees and shrubs, such as lilac, that are prone to suckering (throwing up shoots from below ground level) if they suffer root damage. If a weed gets established, use a chemical spot weedkiller to deal with it.

WEEDING AROUND TREES AND SHRUBS

Using a hoe to remove weeds from around young trees or shrubs is the surest way of catching them all. It is best carried out in hot weather so that any weeds hoed up die quickly.

As its name suggests, *Hippophaë rhamnoides* (sea buckthorn) is tolerant of strong, salt-laden winds and can be planted as a windbreak to protect frailer plants. Its long, silvery green leaves, yellow flowers and orange berries are all decorative in their own right.

Windbreaks

A severe winter storm can cause considerable damage to trees and shrubs, sometimes breaking whole branches. If your garden is exposed you should consider erecting some sort of windbreak. In the short term this can be a special plastic windbreaker, but in the longer term it is probably better to create a more permanent solution by planting a living windbreak. A number of trees and shrubs can be used for this, and it should be fairly easy to find one that fits seamlessly into your garden design.

Leyland cypress grow very fast, and, for this reason, they are often used as windbreaks, but are best avoided for more suitable alternatives. They are thirsty, hungry plants that take a lot of nutrients from the soil for some distance around the roots. They also continue to grow rapidly past their required height.

It is best to get the windbreaks established before the shrubs or ornamental trees are planted, but if time is of the essence, plant them at the same time, perhaps temporarily shielding both from the winds with windbreak netting.

Good windbreak plants

Acer pseudoplatanus (sycamore)
Berberis darwinii
Buxus sempervirens (box)
Cotoneaster simonsii
Fraxinus excelsior (ash)
Griselinia littoralis
Hippophaë rhamnoides
    (sea buckthorn)
Ilex (holly)
Ligustrum ovalifolium (privet)
Lonicera nitida (box-leaf honeysuckle)
Pyracantha (firethorn)
Rosmarinus officinalis (rosemary)
Sorbus aucuparia (rowan)
Taxus baccata (yew)

Conifers

After years in the wilderness, slow-growing dwarf conifers are now coming back into fashion. They are easy to grow, require practically no maintenance and offer year-round interest.

Grouping conifers

Conifers can be grown as single specimens or in groups, in a mixed border with other shrubs, perennials and bulbs or in a special conifer area, where a variety of forms can be combined to good effect. Although an evergreen conifer display is very low maintenance and looks good all year, it can seem static, because it remains exactly the same from one season to the next.

Choosing a position

Most conifers prefer a position in full sun, but many will tolerate partial shade or being in deeper shade for just part of the day. They will not grow well in dense shade or waterlogged soil, however. If your soil is heavy, you could try draining it, improving the structure, by adding plenty of well-rotted organic matter and grit before planting, or creating a special conifer raised bed. Many slow-growing dwarf conifers also do well in containers.

Conifers develop a range of habits, including upright, conical and spreading. Planted together in the garden they can make a striking group.

HOW TO PLANT A CONIFER

1 Place the conifer in the prepared hole and check the planting depth. The soil mark should be at the same level as the surrounding soil.

2 When the plant is in position, untie the wrapper and slide it out of the hole. Avoid disturbing the ball of soil around the roots.

3 Replace the soil around the plant and firm down to eliminate large pockets of air. Apply fertilizer, if necessary, and water well.

Planting

The best time to plant conifers is mid-spring, when the soil is moist and starting to warm up. This allows the plants to establish before the onset of winter. However, container-grown conifers can also be planted at other times of year (particularly early autumn), provided they are kept well watered in summer and protected from cold winds in winter. If the weather or soil conditions are not suitable for planting when the conifers arrive, plant them roughly in a trench in a sheltered spot (known as heeling in) until conditions improve. Do not take container-grown plants out of their pots until you are ready to plant them properly.

Plant conifers in the same way as other trees and shrubs but after planting protect the plants from cold and drying winds by erecting plastic windbreak netting held up on well-anchored posts as a windbreak. Once the conifer is well established this protection can be removed. Tall trees may also need staking to prevent damage from storms.

Do not feed conifers unless they are showing signs of starvation (unnatural yellowing foliage). If they are given too much food, conifers

4 It is worth mulching the ground after planting. It will conserve moisture, and some mulches, such as chipped bark, look attractive.

HOW TO REMOVE A COMPETING LEADER

1 Where two or more leaders have formed a fork in the conifer tree, leave the strongest unpruned. Cut away the other stem or stems at the point of origin.

will grow more quickly, producing lush, often uncharacteristic, growth that does not look attractive and is prone to damage caused by drying and cold winds.

Pruning

Conifers do not need extensive pruning and most are best left to assume their natural shape, with the occasional pruning of an overly long shoot. Occasionally, however, you may need to undertake more substantial pruning if the conifer starts to get too big for its position.

Plants can be clipped annually with shears to keep them small and neat. Do not prune back to leafless brown stems because these will not re-sprout. Cut back whole stems to restrict the size of ground-hugging conifers, making the cut under a newer, shorter shoot that will hide it. Conifers that have become too overgrown should be removed.

Another problem that should be pruned out as soon as it occurs is reversion: all-green growth on variegated forms. Use secateurs (pruners) to remove these vigorous shoots, otherwise they may dominate the more decorative foliage.

2 If the remaining leader is not growing strongly upright, tie a cane to the conifer's main stem. Tie the new leader to the cane to encourage vertical growth.

Most conifers produce resinous sap that bleeds freely from the stems if they are cut while the tree is in active growth. Pruning is therefore best carried out from autumn to mid-winter while the tree is dormant. Use sharp, clean pruning tools as blunt blades will snag the wood and may provide an entry point for disease. Wear gloves and goggles and, if you are using power machinery, the protective clothing recommended.

Aftercare

Once established, conifers will largely look after themselves. Mites and aphids can be problems on pines and spruces respectively, causing the needles to drop and producing unsightly bare stems. Aphids are easy to control with insecticidal sprays, but mites are more persistent (you may wish to get in a professional to treat an affected specimen). Mites are particularly active during warm, dry years when conifers are under stress. You can help prevent outbreaks by watering conifers during a drought and spraying the foliage occasionally to increase air humidity. Do this in the evening to avoid scorching the foliage on a sunny day.

Hedges

A living screen makes an excellent marker for a garden boundary and an attractive garden divider. Hedges will be around for a long time, so careful preparation before planting and regular maintenance are essential to keep them looking good.

Choosing a hedge

Many shrubs and some trees make excellent hedging plants, and the species will be largely a matter of personal preference. However, there are a few key points to bear in mind when you are making your selection.

First, decide whether you want a deciduous or evergreen hedge. An evergreen hedge will provide cover throughout the year but a deciduous one is often hardier and so is better in cold or very exposed positions. A few deciduous plants, such as hornbeam and beech, offer the best of both worlds because they keep their dead leaves on the plant until spring. You will also have to decide whether you want to grow it informally (unclipped) or formally (clipped).

Perhaps the most important consideration is the desired height of the hedge, and you must match the vigour and ultimate height of the hedging plant to this. If you choose a fast-growing variety for a small hedge, for example, the results will be quick, but you will need to trim it many times each growing season and the overall appearance of the hedge may deteriorate with time. Remember that the taller the desired height of the hedge, the more work it will be to maintain – anything over 1.5m (5ft) will be difficult to clip from ground level.

How much time and effort you are prepared to devote to your hedge is also something to consider. Although the thought of having a hedge that needs clipping just once a season can be appealing, the growth that it puts on means the trimming task is a lot of work. You may prefer to spread the work by choosing a hedge that responds to pruning several times each growing season. Alternatively, if you want a low-maintenance option choose a compact, slow-growing variety or consider having a no-prune informal hedge instead.

Planting a hedge

Hedges are planted in the same way as other trees and shrubs. Instead of making a planting hole for each plant, however, you simply prepare the planting trench for the whole hedge in one go. Bear in mind that this will be hard work, especially on heavy soils.

In the autumn, when weather and soil conditions allow, dig over a strip 60–90cm (2–3ft) wide, double digging down its entire

HOW TO PLANT A HEDGE

1 Prepare the ground thoroughly. Excavate a trench at least 60cm (2ft) wide and fork in plenty of manure or garden compost.

2 Add fertilizer at the rate recommended by the manufacturer. Use a controlled-release fertilizer if planting in the autumn.

3 Use a garden line, stretched along the centre of the trench, as a positioning guide. If the area is windy or you need a particularly dense hedge, plant a double row.

4 Use a piece of wood cut to the appropriate length as a guide for even spacing. Make sure the roots of bare-root plants are well spread out. If planting container-grown plants, tease out some of the roots before planting.

5 Firm the plants in and water well. Water the hedge regularly in dry weather for the first season. Mulch to keep down weeds until the hedge is filling out, after which it should suppress weeds naturally.

length. For shorter, less vigorous hedges you can get away with single digging. Remove any weeds and other debris as you proceed and incorporate plenty of well-rotted manure or garden compost into the soil and a handful of bonemeal for every 1m (3ft) of hedge. Allow the soil to settle for a fortnight before planting or delay planting until spring.

Aftercare

The general care after planting a hedge is exactly the same as for any other tree or shrub. However, as a general rule, vigorous deciduous hedging plants, such as privet, should be cut back to 15cm (6in) and evergreens and flowering shrubs cut back by about one-third after planting to encourage thick growth from the base of each plant. Pruning is not required after planting for slower growing deciduous plants, such as beech, and all types of conifers until they have reached the desired height of the hedge.

Annual pruning of an established hedge will vary according to the variety. As a general rule, prune flowering hedges, such as quince or firethorn, after the flowering is over and use secateurs (pruners) rather than shears or hedge trimmers for hedges of large-leaved plants such as cherry laurel.

SHAPING A CONIFER HEDGE

Conifer hedges are best shaped with an inward slope, called a batter, to prevent damage by heavy snowfalls and allow light to reach lower parts of the hedge.

HOW TO PRUNE A HEDGE

1 Take the hard work out of clearing up trimmings by laying down a cloth or plastic sheet under the area you are clipping and move it along as you go.

2 When you use shears, try to keep the blades flat against the plane of the hedge as this will give an even cut. If you jab the shears forward with a stabbing motion, the result is likely to be uneven.

3 When trimming the top of a formal hedge, use canes and string as a guide to help you get it completely flat.

4 Keep the blades flat when you cut the top of a hedge. If it is a tall hedge, you will need to use steps rather than trying to reach up at an angle. Stand back from the hedge periodically to check that the trim is even.

5 Power trimmers are much faster than hand shears and, in consequence, things can go wrong more quickly. Concentrate on what you are doing and have a rest if your arms feel tired. Wear adequate protective gear and take the appropriate precautions if you are using an electrically operated tool.

6 Some conifers are relatively slow growing and produce only a few stray stems, which can be cut off with secateurs (pruners) to neaten them. Secateurs should also be used for large-leaved shrubs, such as *Prunus laurocerasus*. This avoids the leaves being cut in half by mechanical or hand shears, which always looks a bit of a mess and can encourage die-back.

Routine care

Some trees and shrubs need regular maintenance to produce their best displays. Pruning is the main task, but there are a few other important techniques worth carrying out.

Feeding

Trees and shrubs are often fed with bonemeal at planting time but, once established, feeding should not be necessary except in a few special circumstances. If your soil is very poor or free-draining give an annual application of a general fertilizer around each plant in spring. Some free-flowering shrubs, such as roses and lilacs, will produce a better display if given a high-potash fertilizer such as tomato fertilizer or rose feed, in spring and early summer.

Foliar feed can also be applied as an emergency measure when soil nutrients are in short supply or unavailable because of drought, for example. The feed is very dilute and can be easily applied, even to quite large plants and large areas, using a hose-end feeder fitted to the end of a garden hose. The nutrients are readily absorbed through the leaves.

Get better, long-lasting displays from flowering shrubs by applying a high-potash feed in spring.

Deadheading

The removal of fading, dying or dead flowerheads after flowering (known as deadheading) not only improves displays directly by tidying up the plant, but also prolongs and improves flowering over time by encouraging the plant to put its energy into growth and flower production rather than producing seeds. With nearly all trees and most shrubs deadheading is not practicable, but it is particularly worth the effort for repeat-flowering shrubs, such as large-flowered (hybrid tea) and cluster-flowered (floribunda) roses, as well as free-flowering plants such as lilacs. Pinch off the old blooms between finger and thumb or

HOW TO DEADHEAD RHODODENDRONS

1 Deadheading stops the plant putting energy into seed production that could be used for new flowers or foliage. New growth emerges below the flower truss.

2 Pinch out the dead flowerheads, using your finger and thumb to minimize potential damage to the emerging new leaves.

3 After the flowerhead is removed, the point at which soft and tender new leaves will emerge can clearly be seen.

HOW TO DEADHEAD HEATHERS

Trim heathers with shears after flowering. Cut just below faded flowers but avoid cutting into the old wood because it will not resprout.

use a pair of garden snips or secateurs (pruners) for tougher stems. Shrubs that produce a lot of small flowers, such as heathers, are usually easier to deadhead using a pair of shears.

A few shrubs, such as magnolias and rhododendrons, produce next year's blooms just behind those produced this year, so you need to be careful not to break these off too. Hydrangeas are the exception to the deadheading rule because the old blooms should be left on the plant to protect next year's buds in winter. Only in early spring should the faded flowerheads be removed.

Winter protection

If you have any shrubs that are of borderline hardiness for your area, it is worth protecting them over the winter. Even normally hardy shrubs may need protection during a severe

or unseasonably cold spell. Cold and wind or a combination of the two are the main problems. Evergreens in particular can be scorched by cold winds in winter, especially if the soil is frozen, because the plant is unable to replace the water it loses through its leaves. The easiest way to protect individual plants is to erect a windbreak supported on wooden stakes. Groups of small shrubs can be protected by covering them with netting firmly anchored on all sides and held off the plants on canes topped with upturned pots. A more long-term solution is to choose hardy trees or shrubs as windbreaks.

Some shrubs, such as hardy fuchsias and eucalyptus, will die down to ground level in cold winters and sprout again in the spring. In severe spells of cold weather, however, the roots can be killed, so they are worth protecting with an insulating layer of leaves or straw. Make an enclosure over the root area using plastic mesh and fill it with dry leaves in autumn, or cover the roots with a 15cm (6in) layer of bark chippings. This can be removed in spring and used as a border mulch.

HEAVY SNOW FALLS

Some evergreens, particularly conifers, are susceptible to damage caused by the weight of accumulated snow. The plant can be either pulled out of shape or have limbs broken. Prevent damage by tying up susceptible plants before winter or routinely knock heavy falls of snow from exposed plants before damage is caused.

A few shrubs, such as bay, cordylines and myrtle, are worth wrapping up in winter. Make an insulating duvet out of two layers of fine-mesh netting stuffed with insulating material. Wrap the plants in late autumn or early winter and uncover them in early spring.

HOW TO PROVIDE WINTER PROTECTION

1 To protect a tender shrub using a shield, insert three stout stakes firmly into the ground around the plant, then wrap a plastic sheet or several layers of horticultural fleece around the outside of the stakes. Tie securely and peg down the bottom to secure.

2 If you don't want to erect a shield, perhaps on aesthetic grounds, cover the plant with a large plastic bag or horticultural fleece sleeve, pegged to the ground, when very severe weather is forecast. Remove it afterwards.

Shrubs worth deadheading

Azalea	Paeonia
Camellia	Pieris
Choisya	Rhododendron
Erica	Rosa
Hypericum	Syringa
Kalmia	

Pruning basics

Most trees and shrubs will need an occasional prune to maintain health, control their size and improve the display of flowers or foliage. It is a straightforward process provided you use the correct pruning technique and get the timing right.

Pruning tools

Despite having acquired a reputation for being difficult, all pruning follows a few basic rules, which are easy to understand and to put into practice. The first rule is to have good quality tools with sharp, clean blades. Sharp well-maintained blades will make clean cuts without damaging the surrounding tissues left on the plant. By keeping the blades clean you will also minimize the chance of spreading disease when you prune. If you are removing diseased material it is a good idea to use a garden disinfectant to wipe the blades between cuts.

It is also important to use the right pruning tools for the thickness of the stem. For cutting stems up to 1cm (½in) thick use a pair of secateurs (pruners), for stems 1–3cm (½-1¼in) thick a pair of long-handled loppers would be best. For stems more than 3cm (1¼in) thick you will need a pruning saw.

Pruning cuts should also be made in the right way. As a rule, cut just above an outward-facing, healthy looking bud (or pair of buds) so that new growth does not increase the congestion in the centre of the plant. Make the cut angled away from the bud so that it sheds water. With shrubs such as potentilla and spiraea, which have a lot of thin, wiry stems, pruning in this way is not practicable. You will get just as good a result if you use shears to cut back the plant. Indeed, recent research has shown that even thick-stemmed bush roses can be "rough pruned" without a noticeable decline in their health or flowering potential.

Simple pruning

Most shrubs and trees do not require regular pruning, but some will produce bigger and better displays of flowers

GOOD AND BAD PRUNING CUTS

1 A good pruning cut is made about 3mm (⅛in) above a strong bud. It should be a slanting cut, with the higher end above the bud. The bud should generally be facing outward from the plant rather than inward; the latter will throw its shoot into the plant, crossing and rubbing against others, which should be avoided. This is an easy technique and you can practise it on any stem.

2 If the stem has buds or leaves opposite each other, make the cut horizontal, about 3mm (⅛in) above the buds.

3 Always use a sharp pair of secateurs (pruners). Blunt ones will produce a ragged or bruised cut, which is likely to provide easy access to disease spores.

4 Do not cut too far above a bud. The piece of stem above the bud is likely to die back and the stem may well die back even further, causing the loss of the whole stem.

5 Do not cut too close to the bud, otherwise the bud might be damaged by the secateurs (pruners) or disease might enter. Too close a cut is likely to cause the stem to die back to the next bud.

6 It is bad practice to slope the pruning cut towards the bud because this makes the stem above the bud too long, which is likely to cause die-back. It also funnels rain on to the bud, and moisture can collect in the join which may cause rot or other problems.

HOW TO PRUNE

1 Cut any diseased or damaged wood back to sound wood, just above a strong bud. It may be necessary to cut right back to the main stem. The wood is quite easy to spot. It may not be dead, but still in the process of turning brown or black. Damaged wood will not grow and may harbour diseases.

2 Crossing stems should be removed while they are still young, otherwise friction may damage them and let in disease spores. They also make the bush look congested if not removed, and make it harder to prune. Use secateurs (pruners) to cut the stem at its base where it joins the main branch.

3 Tips of stems often die back, especially those that have carried clusters of flowers. Another cause of die-back is when the young growth at the tip of shoots is killed by frost. If the die-back is not cut out, it can eventually kill off the whole shoot. Cut the shoot back into good wood, just above a strong bud.

if they are pruned in the right way and at the right time. If left to their own devices, however, even those types that don't normally need pruning will become congested with unproductive wood. For this reason the most basic form of pruning can be applied to all woody plants and is often known as the three Ds: the removal of dead, diseased and damaged stems. This can be done at any time of the year.

If you want to go a step further the pruning method you use and the time you prune will depend on what you are trying to achieve. For example, if you are pruning to

improve flowering you will need to know whether the shrub you are about to prune blooms on wood produced during the previous season or on new wood produced during the current season. However, if you do not know anything about the shrub

you could use the fail-safe one-in-three method. Prune one-third of the shrub back to the ground every year, choosing the oldest stems, so no stem is more than three years old. The one-in-three technique is also a good way of rejuvenating old shrubs.

No-prune shrubs

Aucuba japonica
Berberis thunbergii
Choisya ternata
Cordyline australis
Cotoneaster microphyllus
Euonymus fortunei
Fatsia japonica
Genista lydia
Magnolia stellata
Prunus laurocerasus
Skimmia japonica

This *Olearia* x *haastii* puts forward a glorious display of white flowers in summer. After flowering, prune back the oldest one-third of the shoots following the one-in-three method.

Pruning popular shrubs

Most of the popular shrubs can be grouped according to their pruning requirements. Prune little and often, ideally once a year, rather than waiting many years until the plant is overgrown and unmanageable.

Better flowering

Shrubs such as *Buddleja davidii*, large-leaved hebes, *Hydrangea paniculata*, lavatera and *Potentilla fruticosa*, which flower on the current year's growth and bloom from midsummer, need pruning in early spring, just before new growth starts. Prune out as much of last year's growth as you want – the harder you prune the more new growth will be produced.

Early-flowering shrubs, such as escallonia, forsythia, *Kerria japonica* and philadephus, which bloom before midsummer, generally produce their blooms on wood produced during the previous season. In this case, prune as soon as flowering has finished by cutting back one in three of the old shoots to a new shoot

Salix integra 'Hakuno-nishiki' should be pruned annually in early spring to ensure its colourful foliage gives the best display.

lower down or a plump outward-facing bud. The new growth put on during the summer months will flower the following year.

Better foliage and stems

Many shrubs, such as *Cornus* (dogwood), *Rubus cockburnianus*, *Salix alba*, *Sambucus nigra* and *Spiraea japonica* 'Goldflame', are principally grown for their foliage displays or brightly coloured stems. These shrubs should be pruned in early spring by removing all the previous year's growth to near ground level or to a low framework of woody stems. This pruning will encourage larger, more brightly coloured foliage in spring and summer and more colourful stems in winter.

Evergreen foliage

Most shrubs grown for their evergreen foliage are pruned only when they need restricting or when diseased or damaged wood is found. Some shrubs, however, such as *Elaeagnus pungens*, *Griselinia littoralis*, *Lonicera nitida*, *Photinia x fraseri*, *Prunus laurocerasus*, *Prunus lusitanica* and *Viburnum tinus*, may need pruning to keep them in shape. Cut back overly

HOW TO PRUNE BACK HARD FOR COLOURED FOLIAGE AND STEMS

1 Plants such as this *Rubus cockburnianus* are cut back to the ground annually in spring to prevent growth becoming congested. The colour on young stems is more pronounced so the plant is more attractive if all the canes have been produced in the current year.

2 Cut the old canes to just above the ground using secateurs (pruners). The height you cut to is not critical as new shoots will grow from the base. Although pruning does not come much simpler than this, it is not without its hazards. Protect your hands from thorny stems by wearing thick gloves.

3 You may find it easier to use long-handled pruners (loppers) to prune thick canes. Do not worry about trying to cut back to a bud as new growth will come from the base.

4 Little will be visible, but if you prune in spring new shoots will appear in a few weeks. By the end of the growing season the new shoots will be as long as those removed in the pruning, forming a bushy and compact plant.

HOW TO PRUNE GREY-LEAVED SHRUBS

1 Grey-leaved foliage plants like this brachyglottis look their best with lots of new growth on compact plants. Prune annually from a young age to keep them looking good.

2 Small plants such as cotton lavender, *Santolina chamaecyparissus,* can be pruned hard in early spring provided they are not too old and woody. If new growth is visible near the base of the plant, cut the stems back to within about 5–10cm (2–4in) of the ground.

3 Cut back to just above a young shoot or a developing bud. Do not cut into wood that is very old and thick. Confine the severe pruning to shoots that grew last summer. The plant will look bare when you have finished, but will soon regrow.

long stems and thin out congested stems in late spring. Small-leaved evergreens can be clipped with hand (hedge) shears, but for large-leaved kinds use secateurs (pruners). Formally shaped shrubs may need to be pruned more often if they begin to look untidy. Avoid cutting back to older wood if you can.

Grey-leaved shrubs

Prune shrubs with grey leaves, such as lavender, *Santolina chamaecyparissus,* *Artemisia abrotanum, Helichrysum italicum*

subsp. *serotinum* and *Senecio,* to keep plants compact and the foliage dense. Trim lightly in spring once plants are well established and repeat each spring by cutting back new growth to just above a pair of leaves, about 5–10cm (2–4in) from the old wood. Do not cut back into old wood because this is unlikely to re-sprout.

Pruning large shrubs

When pruning old thick stems on shrubs and limbs from trees it is best to use a pruning saw. The main

problem with cutting large branches is that their weight tends to rip the branch free before the pruning cut has been completed, producing a ragged finish and tearing the branch and bark from well below the cut. This can provide an entry point for disease. To prevent this, make the first cut beneath the branch and upwards until about half-way through. Then cut downwards, about 2.5cm (1in) further out than the first cut. The branch will break off and the cut can then be straightened.

HOW TO PRUNE THICK STEMS

1 Choose a point about 5cm (2in) or more from the position of the final cut and make a saw cut from beneath the branch. Continue sawing until you are about halfway through or until the weight of the branch begins to bind on the saw.

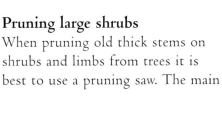

2 Next, make a downward cut from the top of the branch about 2.5cm (1in) or so on the outside of the first cut. When the saw has cut to level with the first cut, the weight of the branch is likely to make the branch split or tear along to the first cut.

3 Sawing from above, cut through the branch at the desired point. Now you have removed most of the weight of the branch, it should be possible to cut cleanly through the branch and thus finish the pruning.

Pruning bush and standard roses

For years rose pruning has been presented as a complicated affair of well-defined rules and precise, well-timed cuts. Then, a few years ago, new research showed it might all be a waste of time. So how should you prune your roses?

Why do roses need to be pruned?

Rose pruning is important for two main reasons. The first is that, left unpruned, the plant will get big and straggly, with an ugly bare base; the second is that the stems will bear flowers for only a few years before becoming exhausted. Pruning tackles both problems in one go, keeping the plant small and the shoots young and vigorous.

Pruning roses correctly

The same basic rules apply when rose pruning as for any other shrub, so use sharp, clean blades and a pair of thornproof gloves.

Bush roses The traditional method of pruning bush roses is probably still the most reliable. Cut back all the stems of large-flowered (hybrid tea) roses by about half their length. Cut back old stems of cluster-flowered (floribunda) roses to the base. The remaining younger stems of cluster-flowered roses should be pruned back to about 45cm (18in).

All cuts should be made just above a healthy, outward-facing bud using a cut that slopes slightly away from the bud so that the lower edge of the cut is still above the top of the bud. You should also remove all dead, damaged or weak wood and thin out the centre of the plant. Pruning should be carried out annually in early spring.

It is now known that, although the results won't be quite as good, all bush roses can be pruned roughly, cutting all stems back to 15–20cm

LARGE-FLOWERED BUSH

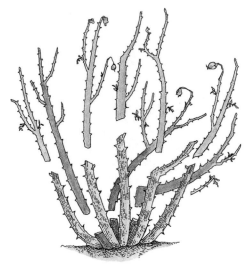

Cut out any badly positioned, diseased or dead wood (shown here coloured orange-brown) close to the base. This will leave fewer stems about which pruning decisions have to be made, and the extra space makes the job easier. Shorten the remaining stems by about half, cutting to an outward-facing bud.

STANDARDS

Prune an ordinary standard rose (left) by shortening the summer's growth by about half. Prune a weeping standard (right) by cutting back each long shoot to a point where there is a new one to replace it. If no suitable replacement shoots can be found, do not prune the main stems; instead, shorten the sideshoots on the flowered stems to two buds.

(6–8in) once every few years without worrying about cutting to just above a bud. You can even use a hedge trimmer if you have a lot of roses and time is short.

CLUSTER-FLOWERED BUSH

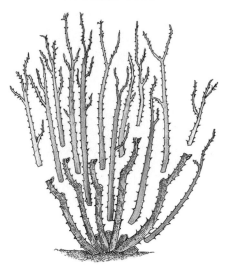

First cut out any badly placed or very old shoots that are dying or diseased (shown here coloured orange-brown), then shorten the remaining main shoots to about 45cm (18in), or about one third of their length. Cut back to an outward-facing bud where possible.

SHRUB

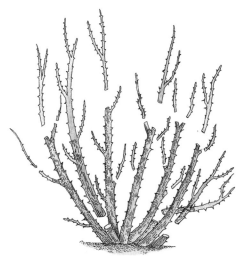

Pruning should always be modified to suit the growth characteristics of the plant but, as a guide, shorten the main stems by between a quarter and a half, and any sideshoots that remain by about two-thirds. Cut out any badly positioned growth and remove weak, diseased or dying stems completely.

Standard roses Prune lightly as cutting back severely will encourage over-vigorous shoots that may spoil the shape. Shorten the main stems in the head and any sideshoots.

Prune standards in late winter or early spring, but prune weeping standards after flowering, in summer.
Shrub roses Prune lightly, either annually or once every other year. Remove between a quarter and a half of the new growth and cut out any dead, diseased or congested growth.
Miniature roses These require little or no pruning other than to keep growth thick and compact. Use shears to trim back vertical new growth in spring. Again cut out any dead, diseased or weak growth.

This floribunda rose has been well pruned and now displays plenty of new, vigorous growth and an abundance of flowers.

HOW TO PRUNE ROSES

1 Moderate pruning is the most appropriate for established large-flowered roses. Cut back all the main stems by about half, or to within 20–25cm (8–10in) of the ground. Cut to an outward-facing bud to keep the centre of the bush open, with no congestion.

2 You can treat cluster-flowered roses in the same way, but if you prune some shoots severely and others lightly, flowering may be spread over a longer period. Prune the oldest shoots back close to the base, but those that grew last year by about one third only.

3 Whichever type of rose you are pruning, cut back any dead or diseased shoots to healthy wood. Also remove any very thin, spindly shoots, cutting either to their point of origin or to two or three buds from the base of the shoot.

Problem solving

Although trees and shrubs are usually trouble free, there are some problems that can occur from time to time, especially if the plant is not growing well or if there is a prolonged spell of dry weather.

Pests and diseases

Generally speaking, a good garden plant that is vigorous and growing well will simply shrug off most pests and diseases. If the plant is suffering from stress, such as water shortage in a drought, it might succumb. However, if the source of the stress is removed (by watering in this example) most established trees and shrubs will recover by themselves. This is fortunate, because using chemical controls on large plants is expensive and often quite impracticable. Many pests will attack the foliage of trees and shrubs, eating holes or defoliating whole twigs. This will almost always be localized and have little impact on the tree as a whole, however. Similarly, diseases tend to disfigure the plant if weather conditions allow, but the effect is usually temporary, and most plants will soon recover. There are a few more serious

BOTRYTIS

Botrytis is a fluffy grey-white/brown fungal mass formed on seedlings or on growth damaged by other causes such as frost. Use a fungicide on seedlings. Remove the affected parts of a mature plant, cutting back into live wood, then spray with fungicide.

exceptions, such as fireblight, honey fungus, canker and silver leaf. If you think your plant has one of these diseases, check the symptoms in a good plant pest and disease encyclopedia before taking action.

Plant fails to establish

Failure to establish can be the result of a number of problems, but the most common is that the soil conditions are inappropriate for the plant in question. Check the pH of your soil and test for the presence of nutrients such as nitrogen, potassium and phosphorus. Look up

LEAF-CUTTING BEE

Neatly notched leaves indicate the presence of leaf-cutting bees. Damage is largely cosmetic and will not affect the health of established plants. Bees are beneficial pollinators and the small amount of damage caused does not justify the use of chemicals.

the conditions the plant prefers in a good plant encyclopedia. If the soil conditions were correct for the plant, the problem might have occurred if the shrub was planted incorrectly. Another reason for plants failing to establish is a shortage of water after planting. It is important to always water well until established.

Foliage problems

Variegated plants often spontaneously produce an all-green shoot that is more vigorous than its more ornamental counterparts. This is known as reversion. It is important

Suckers

Some trees and shrubs are prone to producing shoots from the roots below ground (known as suckers). If the plant is grown on a rootstock, as with many roses, the sucker shoot will bear flowers of the rootstock variety rather than of the ornamental plant. The rootstock is usually much more vigorous, and could eventually take over the ornamental plant, and so the sucker should be removed. Do not prune off the shoot at ground level because this will encourage even more suckers. Instead use the following technique.

1 Remove suckers at their point of origin – you will have to excavate the soil to expose the bottom of the sucker.

2 If possible, pull the sucker off; otherwise, try to cut it off flush with the main stem using a sharp knife.

CUTTING OUT REVERSION IN SHRUBS

Green-leaved shoots have appeared in this *Spiraea japonica* 'Goldflame'. If left, they may take over the whole plant. The remedy is simple. Remove the offending shoots back to that part of the stem or shoot where the reversion begins.

to cut out all reverted shoots as soon as you can because if they are left they will outgrow the ornamental shoots, eventually dominating the whole plant. Variegated plants that are planted in deep shade also lose their variegation. In this case, you will need to move the plant to a more suitable position.

Discoloured leaves can also be a problem on all plants. Yellow leaves, for example, can be caused by a range of problems. Lack of water and starvation are common causes, but lack of iron can be the cause when lime-hating plants are grown on chalky soil. You can either give the plant a fillip with a dressing of chelated iron or you will have to move it to a container filled with ericaceous compost (acid soil mix.)

Leaves with scorched edges are usually a sign of drought, but they can result from hot winds in summer and, on evergreens, cold winds in winter. Severe late frosts can burn the edges of new growth in spring too. Established plants will recover and disfigured stems can be pruned out. If the problem recurs year after year, you will either have to provide shelter or move the plant to a more sheltered position. During hot,

Azaleas are a form of rhododendron. In a good year, if protected from unseasonally late frosts, they produce masses of flowers, making a spectacular spring display.

sunny weather in summer shrubs that like lightly shaded conditions can also suffer from scorched leaves. Plants with golden foliage are particularly vulnerable.

Flower problems

Many flowering shrubs don't flower well for a few years while they are getting established, so be patient. If your plant's flowering has declined it might need feeding with a high-potash fertilizer. If the shrub has been pruned recently you may have used the wrong method or pruned at the wrong time of the year.

Early flowering shrubs can lose their blooms to late frosts, while those that flower later in the year can drop buds in response to drought.

A few large-flowered shrubs, notably roses, are also susceptible in prolonged periods of wet weather to a physiological problem (known as balling) that causes the blooms to rot on the plant.

DEADHEADING CAMELLIAS

Some cultivars of *Camellia japonica* do not shed their flowers as they fade, and will need deadheading regularly.

Climbers

Climbing plants have much to offer the modern gardener. They are fairly easy to grow and usually take up little growing space. Many climbers produce spectacular displays of flowers, and others provide an attractive backdrop to other plants for most of the year before taking on glorious tints in autumn.

Climbers have many uses and are an important element in most gardens. They are often trained up supports to cover walls and fences or tied into free-standing structures. Many are suitable for scrambling through mature trees and shrubs or for use as weed-suppressing ground cover.

There is a wide range of climbers, varying in both vigour and preferred position, so it is important to choose carefully. Match the climber to the size of the support as well as the prevailing conditions in your garden. There are climbers to suit almost any situation, including most soils in sun or shade. When you are buying climbing plants follow the same rules as described for shrubs.

Walls offer perfect support and protection for climbers such as this *Clematis montana* 'Elizabeth', which produces a mass of flowers in early spring.

Planting climbers

Most climbers should be planted in the same way and at the same time as trees and shrubs, although the technique varies slightly depending on the type of support they are being trained against.

Preparing the soil

The soil next to vertical surfaces, such as walls and fences, is usually drier than the soil in the rest of the garden because the ground is in the rain shadow of the wall or fence. Walls also draw water from the soil, further reducing the moisture content. It is essential, therefore, to improve the water-holding capacity of the soil before planting and to set the climber a little way away from the wall so that the roots have a chance to spread out. This is also the best method when planting next to free-standing supports. Before you plant a new climber it is a good idea to put up the support. Prepare the soil by digging it over thoroughly and removing any debris, which can include builders' rubble if the border has not been properly dug before. Incorporate plenty of organic matter as you go.

Planting

Once the soil has settled, dig a hole 30–45cm (12–18in) away from the wall or fence, large enough to accommodate the full spread of the roots (for bare-root plants) and about twice as wide as the rootball for container-grown types. The planting hole should be the same depth as the rootball.

As you dig, place all excavated soil on to a sheet next to the planting hole. Fork over the soil in the bottom of the hole. Add well-rotted manure or organic matter, such as garden compost to the soil as well as a handful of bonemeal and gently fork it in (use latex gloves for protection when handling bonemeal). Remove container-grown specimens

Match the vigour of the climber to the climbing space available. This *Rosa* x *alba* 'Alba Semiplena' grows to 2m (6ft) high.

from their pots and tease the roots out from around the rootball before planting to encourage them to spread into the surrounding soil.

With the exception of clematis, position the climber at the same depth as it was in the pot or the nursery bed – look for a soil mark on the stem – angling it back at 45 degrees towards the bottom of the support. Check the planting depth by laying a cane across the hole, then add or remove soil as necessary.

Backfill the first few centimetres (inches) of the hole with the excavated soil and give bare-root climbers a gentle shake to settle the soil. Firm the first layer around the roots with your hands before adding a second layer and repeating the process until the hole is filled. Water in well and cover the soil around the new specimen with an 8cm (3in) deep layer of well-rotted, organic mulch but take care not to pile it up against the stems.

HOW TO CHOOSE A CLIMBER

1 Many climbers are sold in containers. Look for strong-growing plants with plenty of shoots arising from the base of the plant.

2 Small plants with fewer stems are sometimes available. They are usually cheap but will probably need good aftercare if they are to establish themselves properly.

3 Check the root system by sliding the plant from its container. Reject the plant if the roots are congested or tightly coiled around the pot. The root system of this plant is in good condition.

HOW TO PLANT CLIMBERS

1 Dig over the proposed site, loosening the soil and removing any weeds. If the ground has not recently been prepared, work some well-rotted organic material into the soil to improve soil texture and fertility.

2 Add a general or specialist shrub fertilizer to the soil at the dosage recommended on the packet. Work into the soil around the planting area with a fork. A slow-release organic fertilizer is best.

3 Water the plant in the pot. Dig a hole that is much wider than the rootball. The hole should be next to a free-standing support or at least 30cm (12in) from a wall or fence, and angled back towards the support.

4 Stand the plant in its hole and place a cane across the hole to check that it is at the same level. Take the plant from the pot or cut the bag away. Holding the plant steady, fill in the soil. Firm as you go with your hands.

5 Train the stems of the climber up individual canes to their main support. Tie the stems in with string or plastic ties. Even twining plants or plants with tendrils will need this initial help. Spread them out, so that they ultimately cover the whole of their support.

6 Water the climber thoroughly. Put a layer of mulch around the plant, to help preserve the moisture and prevent weed growth. Do not pile mulch up against the stems of the climber, however.

Planting near established plants

The soil next to established trees and shrubs is often dry and full of roots and it may be difficult for a climber to become established.

The best position for a new plant is at the edge of the tree or shrub canopy, where water will run off when it rains – the "drip zone". When digging the planting hole try as far as possible to do this without disturbing the surrounding soil or any major roots. Cut off any minor roots that become exposed in the planting hole. Improve the soil with well-rotted garden compost and bonemeal, and then line the sides of the planting hole with pieces of old timber. This will give the climber a chance to establish without suffering from too much competition from surrounding plants. The timber will eventually rot away without you having to remove it.

Planting clematis

It is good practice to plant clematis about 8cm (3in) deeper than other types of climber so that the bottom of the stems are below ground level. Then, if the clematis suffers from wilt, which kills all top growth, it will be able to produce new shoots the following year from unaffected buds at the base of the stems underground.

Providing wall support

When choosing a support for a climbing plant it is important to take into consideration the method by which it climbs. Some climbers such as ivy can be grown on a bare brick wall, but most will need a trellis to support them as they grow.

Types of climbers

Climbers hold on to their supports in a number of ways. Some are self-clinging and can cover a vertical surface without the need for any support at all. Ivies and climbing hydrangeas, for example, produce modified roots on their stems that attach themselves to rough surfaces, while other climbers, such as Virginia creeper, produce tiny suckers that will stick to any surface, including glass. Many self-clinging climbers need a support or another plant to climb up but will hold on by themselves. Clematis, for example, have twining leaf stalks, and passion flowers and sweet peas produce tendrils. A few plants, such as akebia, honeysuckle and wisteria, have twining stems that coil snake-like

SELF-CLINGING CLIMBERS

Hydrangea anomala subsp. petiolaris clings to wall surfaces by putting out modified roots.

around their supports. There are also climbers, including climbing and rambler roses, that are not self-clinging and need to be tied in to their supports.

Supports for vertical surfaces

There are several types of support to choose from, but it is important to provide one that matches the size and vigour of the climber it is to

TWINING CLIMBERS

Clematis have twining leaf stalks that grow round a supporting structure.

support. Against a wall or fence you have the choice of fixing trellis panels, expanding trellis or plastic mesh to the surface or attaching a series of sturdy parallel wires.

Trellis panels Wooden or plastic panels are very strong and look attractive. They are also easy and quick to erect, but they are fairly costly. Trellis panels are available only in a small range of specific

HOW TO TRAIN A CLIMBER OR WALL SHRUB ON WIRES

1 Without supporting wires or a trellis, a wall shrub will grow out in all directions.

2 Drill pilot holes into the wall and insert vine eyes to support the wires. If you use vine eyes with a screw fixing, insert a plastic or wooden plug in the wall first. Vine eyes are available in several lengths, the long ones being necessary for vigorous climbers, such as wisteria, that need wires further from the wall.

3 The simplest vine eyes are wedge shaped. Hammer them directly into the masonry and then feed the wire through a hole. Although wedge-shaped eyes are suitable for brick and stone walls, the screw type are better for wooden fences and posts.

HOW TO FIX A TRELLIS TO A WALL

1 The trellis should be sturdy and in good condition. Ensure it has been treated with wood preservative. Take the trellis panel to the wall and mark its position. The bottom of the trellis should be about 30cm (12in) from the ground. Drill holes for fixing the spacers and insert plastic or wooden plugs.

2 Drill the equivalent holes in the wooden batten and secure it to the wall, checking with a spirit (carpenter's) level that it is horizontal. Use a piece of wood that holds the trellis at least 2.5cm (1in) from the wall. Fix another batten at the base, and one halfway up for trellis more than 1.2m (4ft) high.

3 Drill and screw the trellis to the battens, first fixing the top and then working downwards. Check that the trellis is straight using a spirit level. The finished trellis should be secure, so that the weight of the climber and any wind that blows on it will not pull it away from its fixings.

sizes, so are suitable for only some climbers and walls.

Expanding trellis This is sold in a compact form, is easier to transport than panels, but is not as strong. It comes in specific sizes, but expansion can be adjusted to fit an area.

Plastic mesh This is cheap but less robust than trellis panels. It is also less pleasing to the eye until it is covered with growth.

Wires and netting Fixing vine eyes into a wall to support galvanized wire is time-consuming, but once up, wires are a good support for climbers. Even when not covered with plants they are barely visible, and are very versatile, covering any shape or size of surface. If you are growing annual climbers, such as morning glory and sweet peas, less robust netting or even string can make a suitable support.

Access for maintenance

To make maintenance of the wall easier in the future, consider attaching the bottom of the trellis panel to the bottom spacer batten with galvanized hinges so that when the screws fixing the panel to the other battens are removed the panel can be swung away from the wall or fence, providing easy access for repointing or painting.

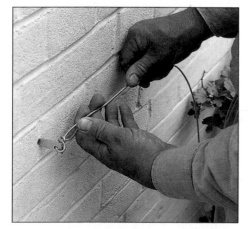

4 Thread galvanized wire through the hole in the vine eye and wrap it around itself to form a firm fixing. Thread the other end through the intermediate eyes (set at no more than 2m/6ft intervals and preferably closer) and fasten the wire around the end eye, keeping it as taut as possible.

5 Spread out the main stems and attach them to the wires, using either plastic ties or string. Tie at several points, if necessary, so that the stems lie flat against the wall and do not flap about in the wind.

6 When all of the stems are tied in to the wires they should form a regular fan shape. Tying the stems in like this, rather than allowing the climber to grow up the wall naturally, covers the wall better and encourages the plant to produce flowering buds all along the top edge of the stems.

Providing free-standing support

It is not always convenient to grow a climber against a wall, and a free-standing support gives flexibility in planning which climbers to grow and where to place them. Climbers can be used to shield an unsightly part of the garden from view as well as adding variety to already attractive areas.

Growing into established plants

If you wish to grow a climber through a tree or a shrub, you must make sure that you have compatible candidates. Neither plant should compete unduly for moisture or nutrients or both will suffer. The established plant must also be strong enough to bear the weight of a full-grown climber, which can be

considerable. Hedges and apple trees are good candidates for large climbers. The tree should be neither too young nor too old: a young tree may be smothered by the vigorous climber, while the additional burden may be too much for an older, weaker tree during winter storms.

Position the climber on the side of the prevailing wind so that it will blow the stems into the support as it grows. After planting the climber, hammer in a short stake next to it and attach one end of a piece of rope to the stake. Tie the other end of the rope up into the canopy of the supporting plant. Untie the climber from its supporting cane that was supplied when you bought it and unravel the stems. The climber can

then be tied into the rope and the longer stems up into the canopy of the tree or shrub. Do not, as is sometimes recommended, secure the bottom of the rope by looping it under the rootball because the climber is likely to be pulled out of the ground by the first strong gust of wind that catches the branch holding the other end of the rope.

Arches and pergolas

Garden structures, such as arches and pergolas, are available in a wide range of styles. The style you choose should fit in with the rest of the garden design and be strong and large enough to support the chosen climbers. There are many ready-made kits on sale in a variety of materials.

PLANTING A CLIMBER NEXT TO AN ESTABLISHED SHRUB

1 Choose a healthy shrub, such as this *Salix helvetica*, and preferably one that flowers at a different time from the climber.

2 Dig a hole at the edge of the supporting shrub so that the climber will receive rain. Improve the soil if necessary.

3 Using a cane, train the climber, such as this *Clematis alpina*, into the shrub. Spread out the shoots so it grows evenly through the shrub.

4 Water the new plant thoroughly and mulch if necessary. Continue to water, especially in dry weather, until the climber is established.

The white flowers of the scented rambling rose 'Seagull' look spectacular against the dark green of the conifer it is climbing through.

Single posts, tripods and hoops

Many climbers are suitable for training up single posts, often called pillars, although it is probably best to avoid very vigorous climbers. If space permits, a series of pillars can be erected along a path, linked garland-fashion by chunky rope along which climbers can grow. Climbers also look effective trained up tripods or, alternatively, you can make your own supports from canes.

Training a climber over a hoop allows you to direct the growth so that it covers the available space with an abundance of flowers. Bending the new growth into curving arches encourages flowering buds to be formed along the whole stem rather than just at the tip. A hoop will also keep the climber in proportion to the border in which it is growing, and is a useful method of growing vigorous plants in a limited space.

Whichever free-standing support you choose, it is essential that it is anchored securely into the ground.

The rich purple flowers of *Clematis* 'Jackmanii' can be seen clearly as it climbs up a tripod, bringing interest to an otherwise neglected corner of the garden. Once it is fully grown, the clematis will cover the support completely, so that the tripod cannot be seen.

HOW TO ERECT A PILLAR FOR A CLIMBER

1 Dig a hole at least 60cm (2ft) deep. Put in the post and check that it is upright. Backfill with earth, ramming it firmly down as you work. In exposed gardens a more solid pillar can be created by filling the hole with concrete.

2 Plants can be tied directly to the post but a more natural support can be created by securing wire netting to the post. Self-clinging climbers such as clematis will then be able to climb by themselves with little attention from you other than tying in wayward stems.

3 Plant the climber a little way from the pole. Lead the stems to the wire netting and tie them in. Self-clingers will take over, but plants such as roses will need to be tied in as they grow. Twining plants, such as hops, can be grown up the pole without wire.

Aftercare of climbers

Most climbers are easy to look after and, apart from pruning, require the minimum of care. Do keep an eye out for potential problems, however, as early action is most effective. A little general maintenance will keep your plants in tip-top condition.

Watering and mulching

Most climbers are planted in dry soil at the base of walls and fences, which is why they are more likely to suffer from drought during prolonged dry spells. Always keep climbers well watered until they are established. Thereafter, soak the soil thoroughly once a fortnight during a period of drought or if the climber is showing signs of stress.

Each spring top up the loose organic mulch so that it is about 8 cm (3 in) thick but is not piled against the stems of the climber. The mulch will not only help to retain moisture in the soil but will also prevent any competition from weeds.

Feeding

With new plants, apply a general-purpose fertilizer on the surface of the soil in spring. Thereafter, if your soil is very poor or free-draining apply an annual dressing of a general fertilizer around each plant in spring. Some free-flowering climbers, such as roses, will produce even better displays if given a high-potash fertilizer, such as rose feed, in spring and early summer. Foliar feed can also be applied using a hose-end feeder fitted to the end of a garden hose. The nutrients are readily absorbed through the leaves.

Keeping plants tidy

Tie in new growth while it is still flexible enough to be bent into position against the support. Prune out any dead, diseased or dying growth as well as any unwanted, crossing stems. Also remove any all-green shoots produced on variegated climbers (known as reversion) to

Using grass clippings

For a free organic mulch use grass clippings (not treated with weedkiller) in an unobtrusive area, such as at the back of a border or the bottom of the garden, to mulch established climbers each spring. Top it up throughout the mowing season. This is not only a cheap and effective mulch but is also a convenient way of getting rid of lawn clippings.

prevent these more vigorous green shoots from overwhelming the rest of the climber. Check old ties to make sure they are secure and are not constricting the stems.

The removal of fading flowers (known as deadheading) on climbers is desirable although not always practicable if the climber is large or not very accessible. Deadheading not only makes the climber look neater, but also encourages better and longer-lasting flowering displays by stopping the climber wasting energy in producing unwanted fruits and seeds. Where the fruits or seedheads are of ornamental value, simply deadhead parts of the climber that are hidden from view so that you get the best of both worlds.

Winter protection

Although walls and fences give some protection in winter, climbers that are of only borderline hardiness may need extra protection during cold years or in colder areas. Draping a sheet of hessian (burlap) over the climber is the traditional method, but a double layer of horticultural fleece will also do the trick. For real protection, create an insulating duvet by stuffing straw or other insulating material under the sheeting. Remove all winter protection when milder weather returns in spring.

HOW TO TIE IN NEW SHOOTS

HOW TO DEADHEAD CLIMBERS

Once you have pruned out the old stems of ramblers and climbers, tie in vigorous new shoots to replace them.

As the flowers die, remove the flowerheads. This not only makes the climber tidier but also promotes further flowering. With tall climbers, however, this may not always be practicable.

CLEMATIS WILT

Some forms of clematis, mainly large flowered hybrids and *montana*, are susceptible to wilt. This disease is caused by the fungus *Ascochyta clematidina*. The top-growth dies back and, left unchecked, the disease may affect the whole plant. If your clematis shows signs of wilt prune it hard. If it has been planted deeply enough it will usually recover. Drenching with fungicide at monthly intervals in the growing season may help, but if wilt is a persistent problem, replace your clematis with one less susceptible to the disease.

HOW TO PROTECT AGAINST FROST

For light protection against unseasonal frosts a temporary cover such as shade netting or hessian (burlap) can be used to protect new shoots and early flowers. If the climber is grown against a wall, hang the cover from the gutter or from some similar support. Fasten the netting securely so that it remains attached, even in windy weather.

This *Solanum* has been well cared for and is in good condition. The plant has been securely tied to its support, and trained so that it is not growing over the windows or into the guttering. Regular mulching and feeding with a high-potash fertilizer will help improve flowering.

Pruning clematis and wisteria

Most climbers can be kept in good shape and flowering well by simply removing unwanted growth and pruning out any dead, dying or diseased stems. A few popular types, however, including clematis, wisteria and roses, require special pruning for best results.

Pruning clematis

Clematis has gained a reputation for being difficult to prune, mainly because not all clematis are pruned in the same way. However, as long as you know when your clematis flowers and can tell whether it produces blooms on old stems or new growth produced during the current year, you won't go far wrong.

Clematis can be divided into three groups: those that produce all their flowers on old wood (known as pruning group 1); those that produce blooms on both old wood and new growth produced during the current season (known as pruning group 2); and those clematis that flower only on new growth (known as pruning group 3).

Clematis 'Pagoda' is a group 3 clematis, so the flowers are borne on new stems. Hard pruning in winter will lead to a good display of flowers the following summer.

CLEMATIS PRUNING GROUPS

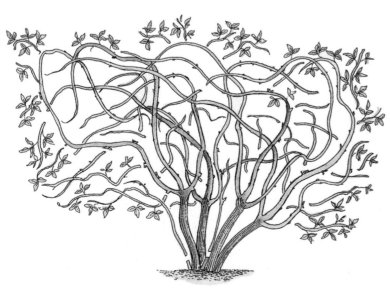

Group 1 These clematis need pruning only when they outgrow their space. Cut out sufficient branches to reduce congestion and take those that encroach beyond their space back to their point of origin.

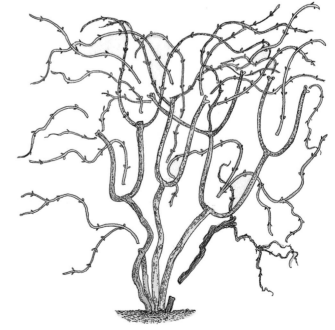

Group 2 After cutting out all the dead, damaged or weak growth, remove any wood that is making the clematis congested, cutting back to a pair of buds.

HOW TO PRUNE WISTERIA

1 In late summer shorten the long shoots produced this year. Unless required for further spread, cut back to about four or six leaves.

2 In midwinter shorten the summer's growth further, cutting back to just two or three buds, so the shoots are 8–10cm (3–4in) long.

WISTERIA TWO-STAGE PRUNING

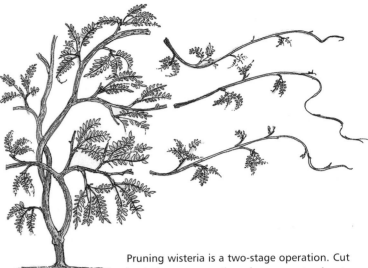

Pruning wisteria is a two-stage operation. Cut back the new growth each summer to about four leaves and reduce this even further with a winter pruning.

Group 1 The spring-flowering clematis belong to this group. Some are vigorous, such as *C. montana*, while others are more restrained. Cut back vigorous species as necessary to keep them in check, but others in this group need little pruning other than the removal of dead, damaged or diseased stems. Prune back unwanted stems to their point of origin or to a pair of plump buds.

Group 2 This group includes late spring and early summer varieties that flower mainly on old wood early in the season and later produce a smaller flush on this year's growth.

They need little pruning other than the removal of dead, damaged or diseased stems. Congested growth can be thinned out by pruning back stems to their point of origin or a pair of plump buds. Alternatively, cut half the stems back to a pair of buds before growth starts to increase the number of blooms produced later in the year.

Group 3 The clematis in this group flower in late summer. Cut back all stems during the winter or early spring to the lowest pair of buds.

Pruning wisteria

Wisteria has an undeserved reputation for being difficult to prune, but in this case it is because it is pruned in two stages, in late summer and then in winter. The pruning itself is straightforward: simply cut back all the whippy new growth to four or six leaves in late summer and then, when the leaves have fallen and it is easier to see what you are doing, cut the same stumps to just two or three buds from the main stem.

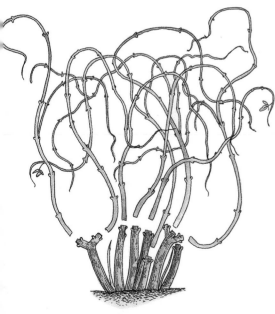

Group 3 These clematis should have all the growth cut back in winter or early spring to the first pair of sound buds above the ground.

Clematis pruning groups

Group 1	Group 3
C. alpina	'Abundance'
C. armandii	'Bill MacKenzie'
C. cirrhosa	'Comtesse de
C. macropetala	Bouchaud'
C. montana	'Duchess of
	Albany'
Group 2	'Etiole Violette'
'Barbara	*C. flammula*
Jackman'	'Gravetye
'Daniel Deronda'	Beauty'
'Ernest	'Hagley Hybrid'
Markham'	'Jackmanii'
'Lasurstern'	'Perle d'Azur'
'Marie Boisselot'	*C. rehderiana*
'Nelly Moser'	*C. tangutica*
'The President'	'Ville de Lyon'
'Vyvyan Pennell'	'Victoria'

Pruning climbing roses and honeysuckle

Climbers that are grown for their flowers, such as roses and honeysuckles, require only light pruning from time to time to achieve a profusely flowering plant.

Climbing roses

When trained up walls or along fences climbing roses may not need pruning annually, other than to remove dead or dying growth, but regular pruning will keep the plant vigorous and flowering well, with the blooms low down, where they can be appreciated. Roses trained over free-standing supports need annual pruning to keep them within bounds.

Climbing roses can be divided into two main groups: those that produce blooms in one flush on short sideshoots from an established framework of stems, and those that are repeat-flowering, bearing blooms in a series of flushes throughout summer. Once-flowering climbers should be pruned after flowering by removing up to one-third of the stems, starting with the oldest. Cut back near to the base or to a new sideshoot produced low down. If there isn't much new growth, cut back older branches to about 30cm (12in) to encourage more next year. Trim sideshoots on other stems to two or three leaves.

Repeat-flowering climbers or those that produce attractive hips should be pruned in winter to remove the weakest and oldest stems. Trim any sideshoots on the remaining stems to within two or three buds.

Rambler roses

These roses have a single flush of blooms in summer, which are produced on growth that was formed the previous year. They produce long shoots from the base. For each vigorous new young shoot prune out an unproductive old one back to ground level after flowering. Do not prune out an old shoot unless there is a new one to replace it, but remove completely any very old, dead or diseased wood.

On a well-established, once-flowering climber, cut out one or two of the oldest stems to a point just above a new shoot near the base.

PRUNING A RAMBLER ROSE

Ramblers are straightforward to prune. Cut out old canes that have flowered, taking them back to a point where there is a new replacement shoot.

HOW TO PRUNE A ONCE-FLOWERING CLIMBING ROSE

1 These climbing roses have a stable framework of woody shoots and are always pruned in summer after flowering, so they can seem intimidating to prune. Fortunately, these roses usually flower even with minimal pruning, provided you keep the plant free of any very old stems and any dead and diseased wood.

2 Cut out one or two of the oldest stems each year to encourage new growth. Cut old stems off just above young replacement shoots near the base. If there are no low-growing shoots, choose one that starts 30–60cm (1–2ft) up the stem, and cut back to just above this level.

3 If there are strong young replacement shoots, prune back a proportion of stems that have flowered to just above the newer growth. Tie them in if necessary. If possible, always prune to an outward-facing bud or shoot.

4 Go along the remaining stems and shorten the sideshoots, pruning back to leave two or three buds. Do not remove more than a third of the stems, otherwise flowering will suffer next year.

HOW TO PRUNE A RAMBLER ROSE

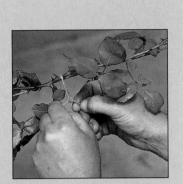

1 Prune the rambler rose after flowering – late summer is a good time. Older, congested plants can be more off-putting than younger ones, but all rambler roses are fairly straightforward to prune if you work on them methodically.

2 Once you have a well-established rambler, try to balance the shoots that you remove with those available to replace them. First, cut out any dead or damaged shoots or those that are very weak and spindly. Do not remove very vigorous, young shoots.

3 Cut out old stems that have flowered, but only where there are new shoots to replace them. This will vary from plant to plant and year to year. Shorten the sideshoots on old stems that have been retained (those that have flowered) to leave two or three leaves.

4 Tie in the flexible new shoots to the support. Wherever possible, tie loosely to horizontal wires or a trellis. After pruning, rambler roses will produce new stems from the base, rather than growing taller on existing stems, which gives them a lower, more spreading habit.

Honeysuckle

These climbers can be divided into two groups: those that flower on the current year's growth and those that bear blooms on stems produced last year. Those that flower on new wood do not need regular pruning unless they outgrow their allotted space. In this case, cut back all stems in winter to allow for the new growth the following season. If the climber gets overcrowded remove about one-third of the oldest stems, cutting back to near ground level. Honeysuckles that flower on the previous year's growth should have old growth that has flowered cut back to a newer shoot produced lower down on the stem.

HOW TO PRUNE HONEYSUCKLE

1 Prune honeysuckle only if it has become sparse at the base and the flowers are too high, or if the tangled mass of stems is too thick. This sometimes happens if the plant is grown on a trellis of limited height: when the stems reach the top, they cascade downwards and begin to grow upwards, using the already tangled stems for support.

2 If you prune back hard you will lose flowers for a season or two. Avoid this by shearing off only dead or badly placed shoots, especially those beneath healthy growth. You could use secateurs (pruners), but the job will be very tedious among the mass of tangled stems.

3 If it is done carefully, the plant will not look very different yet much of the redundant growth will have been removed. As you will almost certainly have severed stems that remain entangled, you may notice dead stems, which will need to be pulled out; sever the stems in several places if this helps to disentangle them.

Tackling overgrown climbers

Overgrown and unproductive climbers can be given a new lease of life by hard pruning. The method you use will depend on the type of climbers you are tackling.

Renovation pruning

If your climbers have got out of control or produce all their flowers out of sight at the top of the plants, you may need to take decisive action. The best time to carry out drastic pruning of climbers is during the dormant season, between autumn and spring. When there are no leaves it is easier to see what you are doing and make the cuts in the right place. Choose a mild day to make the task as pleasant as possible and arm yourself with a good pair of secateurs (pruners) and long-handled loppers. For stems over 3 cm (1½in) thick you will also need a special pruning saw.

HOW TO PRUNE A SELF-CLINGING CLIMBER

1 Vigorous self-clinging climbers can reach great heights if planted against a tall wall. They may need pruning to keep shoots clear of windows and doors, or areas where they can cause damage such as blocking gutters or loosening roof tiles.

2 The actual pruning, best done in early spring, is very simple but you may need ladders to reach the offending stems. If necessary pull the shoots clear of the wall (this may require some force) so that you can use the secateurs (pruners) freely.

3 On this wall, a hard edge after the plant has been cut back is acceptable, but around windows you may prefer to cut the shoots by different amounts to avoid a clipped or straight-line appearance.

Evergreen plants such as this ivy 'Green Ripple' can be particularly difficult to prune as it is hard to see the stems under the leaves. When pruning is necessary, carry out the task methodically, working your way along the wall.

Overgrown clematis

Clematis are often left unpruned for years so that the climber ends up as a mass of bare, non-flowering stems at the base with the few blooms produced way up on top. All clematis respond well to pruning back hard: cut back stems to within 1m (3ft) of the ground. Those that flower on new wood can be cut back even harder, to 30cm (12in). If your clematis flowers on old wood, you will not get any blooms for a year or two, but thereafter the climber will flower with renewed vigour.

Climbing and rambler roses

If they are neglected climbing roses slowly get bigger and bigger, forming large gnarled bare stems at the base with the flowers produced on growth higher up on the plant. Tackle an overgrown monster by removing one stem in three back to a newer shoot lower down or cut right back to the base if there is not one. Repeat over a three-year period to reinvigorate the plant completely.

Rambler roses by contrast throw up new shoots from the base, and these form impenetrable thickets of thorny growth if left to their own devices. In this case, thin out the tangle of stems by removing all but the newest shoots.

Honeysuckles

These often form a top-heavy mass of spindly shoots, and when they are grown on free-standing supports and fences they tend to catch the wind and rock the support. The best way to tackle an overgrown honeysuckle is to trim back all the thin growth on the top to reveal the main stems. These can then be pruned with secateurs (pruners). Reduce their number by removing awkwardly placed stems and the oldest ones

HOW TO RENOVATE A NEGLECTED CLIMBER

1 This neglected climbing rose has lost vigour and is flowering very poorly, and so needs renovative pruning.

2 Use loppers to cut back old growth that is too thick for secateurs (pruners).

3 Thick stems may need a pruning saw. Support the branch to prevent it tearing off bark from the main stem.

4 Use a sharp knife to pare off the rough edges of any large pruning wounds.

first. If all else fails, honeysuckles respond well to hard pruning, so if yours gets out of hand try cutting it back in winter to within 30cm (12in) of the base. It should regrow, although it may be a couple of years before it is flowering well again.

RENOVATING HONEYSUCKLE

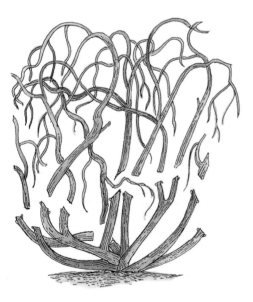

If you prune honeysuckle hard you will lose flowers for a season or two, but in the long term you will have fresh growth that you can retrain. This drastic treatment means that the support will look bare for a while, but new shoots should grow fairly rapidly in the first summer. Tie the new shoots in or train them to the support to give even and relatively untangled growth.

Hard pruning can sometimes restore all of the former glory of a rose, such as this 'Frühlingsgold', which is now showing a healthy crop of primrose-yellow flowers.

Flowers

Bulbs, annuals and perennials are the principal players in any garden scheme. Combined with the right backdrop of trees, shrubs and climbers, they steal the show with superb displays of colour.

Flowers provide the eye-catching highlights of each season. In spring, early bulbs produce a succession of colour until early summer, when exotic bulbs make their brief but triumphant entrance. Glorious annuals then make their mark, along with early-flowering perennials – shooting stars that transform the shape, colour and feel of the border.

As the summer marches on, the banks of summer bedding are dwarfed by the long-flowering, daisy-faced perennials, which, in turn, link up with the late summer and autumn perennial fireworks. Even after the early frosts a few flowers soldier on, supplemented by colourful autumn-flowering bulbs. Evergreen perennials combine with winter bedding and the subtle charm of dainty winter bulbs to complete the cycle.

Irises and primulas produce a stunning combination of fresh, bright colours to liven up an informal border in spring.

Buying bulbs

The plants grown from bulbs are superb for adding much-needed colour to spring borders, but there are other types, flowering at other times of the year, that are equally rewarding. It is important to choose bulbs suited to the conditions your garden has to offer.

Selecting bulbs

Bulbs can be bought from garden centres, from gardening websites on the Internet or by mail order from specialists. Most are sold as dry bulbs during the dormant season, either loose or in prepacks. A few select varieties are available as container-grown plants in spring.

Dry bulbs can deteriorate quickly in the warmth of a garden centre and so are best bought as soon as they arrive – check with your local branch to find out in advance when they are due to take delivery. In general, bulbs sold loose are more variable in quality than those sold in prepacks, but you have the opportunity to select the best and leave poorer

Bulbs is an umbrella term, referring to tubers and corms as well as true bulbs. A bulb's internal structure and external shape give vital clues to identifying them. True bulbs (such as the galtonia, shown top) have onion-like leaves within them, while corms (such as the gladiolus, bottom) have solid flesh and, usually, a regular outline like a bulb. Tubers (such as the anemone, centre) also have solid flesh within, but their outline and shape is often more lumpy and irregular.

quality bulbs behind – another good reason for buying bulbs early. Loose bulbs are usually cheaper than pre-packed ones. Check them over carefully and make sure they are not damaged and have not got mixed up with bulbs from adjacent bins. Even when you are buying pre-packed bulbs, it is worth checking over the packs to find the best bulbs. If you cannot see or feel the bulbs through the packaging, you may be better off buying from a different source, where you can inspect the bulbs or opt for loose bulbs.

What to look for

Bulbs should be firm to the touch, with the outer skin (called the tunic) as complete as possible. The skins should not be loose, cracked or showing signs of mould. Avoid bulbs that are soft, which indicates rot, or hard and mummified. Also reject bulbs that are covered in soil or shooting at the growing point or producing roots from the base. Before you make your final selection, press the base of each bulb to make sure it is firm – if it is soft it could indicate basal rot.

When buying daffodils, pick bulbs with only one or two "noses" (growing points), avoiding those with multiple noses because they are less likely to flower well in the first season.

A massed display of *Tulipa praestans* 'Fusilier' is very effective as each stem has up to six flowers.

Bulbs from the wild

Selling garden bulbs is big business, and each year unscrupulous dealers trade in bulbs that are taken from the wild – either stolen from native woodland or uprooted from countries around the world. Do not buy bulbs in bulk unless you are sure of the source.

Choosing the right bulb

Naturalizing in woodland	Normal borders
Allium	Allium
Anemone (some)	Anemone (some)
Chionodoxa	Chionodoxa
Crocus	Colchicum
Cyclamen	Convallaria
Eranthis	Crocus
Erythronium	Cyclamen
Fritillaria (some)	Eranthis
Galanthus	Erythronium
Leucojum	Fritillaria
Muscari	Galanthus
Narcissus	Hyacinthus
Scilla	Iris
Tulipa	Leucojum
	Muscari
	Narcissus
Dry borders	Ornithogalum
Amaryllis	Oxalis
Iris (bulbous)	Puschkinia
Cyclamen	Scilla
Gladiolus	Trillium
Nerine	Tulipa
Tigridia	

Muscari armeniacum (grape hyacinth) thrives in most places and multiplies freely. It is ideal for planting in bold drifts amongst shrubs or in woodland.

Which type?

Make sure you have a good idea of what you are looking for before you buy your bulbs and do not buy on impulse. Different species of bulbs like different conditions, and it is important to choose a suitable type for the position you have in mind. Also consider the colour, size and flowering time of the bulbs so that they fit in with your existing planting schemes. If you are combining several species of bulb, either choose types that flower at the same time for a dramatic splash of colour or combine forms that flower at slightly different times to provide a succession of colour throughout the season.

In the green

Some bulbs, notably snowdrops (*Galanthus*) and snowflakes (*Leucojum*), do not transplant very well as dormant bulbs and often do not survive drying out. Instead, buy them shortly after flowering has finished when they are still in leaf (known as "in the green"). Ask at your local garden centre if they supply these bulbs in the green and make sure you buy them as soon as they are available. Otherwise, you will have to go to a specialist supplier.

BULBS FROM SEED

A drift of bluebells makes a soft haze under the canopy of the trees. The display looks better massed, with many plants, so these bluebells have been allowed to self-seed freely. This is an economic way of raising a large number of plants.

Growing bulbs

Bulbs are among the easiest plants to grow and so are an ideal starting point for newcomers to gardening. They need little more than planting and watering to get going and require very little maintenance thereafter.

Planting

As a rule, bulbs should be planted as soon as they are bought. Autumn- and spring-flowering types produce new roots in autumn and should be planted in late summer or early autumn. The main exceptions are tulips, which are best planted in late autumn. Plant bulbs in well-prepared, weed-free soil. If it is poor incorporate a sprinkling of slow-release fertilizer, such as bonemeal.

The depth of planting and spacing depends on the size of bulb. As a rule, all bulbs should be planted in a hole that is three times as deep as the bulb. For example a 5cm (2in) deep daffodil bulb will need a 15cm (6in) deep hole so that the bulb is covered by 10cm (4in) of soil. Similarly, a 1cm (½in) deep crocus corm will need to be planted 3cm (1½in) deep. Small bulbs should be about 2.5–5cm (1–2in) apart and larger bulbs 8–10cm (3–4in) apart.

Creating a natural effect

To get an instant effect you will need to plant bulbs quite thickly – say 70–140 per square metre (7–14 per square foot), depending on the size of bulb. Some bulbs, such as daffodils, spread mainly by offshoots from the bulb so that they form larger and larger clumps. Others, such as crocuses and chionodoxa, will seed themselves, so that after four or five years the original display will be transformed with the new plants.

If you want to create a natural-looking planting scheme it is important to plant in irregular clumps.

HOW TO PLANT BULBS

1 Fork over the ground before planting and, if the plants are to be left undisturbed for some years, try to incorporate plenty of organic material, such as rotted garden compost or manure. Many bulbs like well-drained soil but nevertheless benefit from plenty of organic material, which will hold moisture and nutrients.

2 Avoid adding quick-acting fertilizers in the autumn. Controlled-release fertilizers that provide nutrients according to the soil temperature can be used, but they are best employed in spring. Instead, rake a slow-acting fertilizer, such as bonemeal, which contains mainly phosphate, into the surface, or apply it to the planting holes.

3 Where there is space and the plants will benefit from planting in an informal group or cluster, dig out a hole about three times the depth of the bulbs and wide enough to take the well-spaced bulbs.

4 Space the bulbs so that they look like a natural clump, using the spacing recommended on the packet as a guide. Wide spacing will allow for growth and multiplication, but if you intend to lift the bulbs after flowering, closer spacing will create a bold display.

5 Draw the soil back over the bulbs, being careful not to dislodge them in the process. Firm the soil with the back of the rake rather than treading it down, which may damage the bulbs and compact the soil.

6 So that you do not disturb the bulbs when you are weeding, mark their position with canes. Don't forget to include a label.

If you are planting several varieties together, do not mix them up, but keep them in roughly separate clumps for the best effect. The easiest way to get a natural distribution of bulbs is to toss them gently on to the ground and plant them where they land. Individual bulbs can be planted using a cylindrical bulb planter. Push the planter vertically into the ground and remove a core of soil that is deep enough for the bulb being planted. After positioning the bulb replace the core and firm down. Clumps of bulbs are best planted by digging a trench or hole with a spade and planting in this.

Planting bulbs the correct way up

Most bulbs have an obvious top and bottom and present no problem. Others, especially tubers, can lack an obvious growing point. If in doubt, plant them on their side – the shoot will grow upwards and the roots down.

Some bulbs that do have an obvious top are planted on their side because the base tends to rot in wet soil, though these are rare exceptions. *Fritillaria imperialis* is sometimes planted in this way. It is always worth planting vulnerable bulbs on a bed of grit or sand to encourage good drainage around the base and prevent them from rotting.

Bulb planner

Type of bulb	planting time	depth	spacing	flowering time
Allium	early autumn	5–8cm (2–3in)	15–30cm (6–12in)	late spring to early summer
Anemone	early autumn	5cm (2in)	10cm (4in)	late winter to mid-spring
Arum	midsummer	15cm (6in)	10cm (4in)	mid- to late spring
Begonia	spring	2.5cm (1in)	23–30cm (9–12in)	summer
Chionodoxa	early autumn	2.5–5cm (1–2in)	8cm (3in)	late winter to mid-spring
Colchicum	late spring	8cm (3in)	10–15cm (4–6in)	autumn
Crocus, spring	late summer	5–8cm (2–3in)	10cm (4in)	spring
Crocus, autumn	midsummer	5–8cm (2–3in)	10cm (4in)	autumn
Cyclamen	late summer	2.5cm (1in)	15cm (6in)	autumn to spring
Eranthis	late summer	2.5–5cm (1–2in)	10cm (4in)	late winter to mid-spring
Erythronium	late summer	5–8cm (2–3in)	10cm (4in)	mid- to late spring
Fritillaria	early autumn	5–8cm (2–3in)	15–45cm (6–18in)	spring
Galanthus	late summer	8–10cm (3–4in)	10cm (4in)	late winter to mid-spring
Gladiolus	mid-spring	8–10cm (3–4in)	10–15cm (4–6in)	midsummer
Hyacinthus	early autumn	10cm (4in)	20cm (8in)	spring
Iris reticulata	autumn	8–10cm (3–4in)	10cm (4in)	midwinter to early spring
Leucojum	late summer	8–10cm (3–4in)	10–20cm (4–8in)	mid- to late spring
Lilium	mid-autumn	10–15cm (4–6in)	15–45cm (6–18in)	late spring to late summer
Muscari	late summer	5–8cm (2–3in)	10cm (4in)	spring
Narcissus	late summer	5–12cm (2–5in)	10–20cm (4–8in)	spring
Nerine	spring	2.5cm (1in)	15cm (6in)	late summer to early autumn
Ornithogalum	mid-autumn	5–8cm (2–3in)	10–15cm (4–6in)	spring
Puschkinia	early autumn	5–8cm (2–3in)	8cm (3in)	spring
Scilla	late summer	5–8cm (2–3in)	5–10cm (2–4in)	spring
Sternbergia	midsummer	8cm (3in)	12cm (5in)	autumn
Tigridia	late spring	5–8cm (2–3in)	15cm (6in)	late summer
Tulipa	late autumn	8–15cm (3–6in)	10–20cm (4–8in)	spring

Aftercare of bulbs

Bulbs need very little routine aftercare, although deadheading, weeding and keeping the bulbs well fed and watered will help to make sure that they give good displays for years to come.

Deadheading

Most bulb displays benefit from regular deadheading to remove dead and dying flowers. Not only does this keep the display tidy, but it also stops the bulbs using up vital energy in producing unwanted seed. This is draining on their food reserves and can adversely affect their flowering performance the following season. Some bulbs, including alliums and bluebells, should be deadheaded to prevent them from self-seeding prolifically and becoming invasive.

Do not remove the foliage from bulbs until at least six weeks after flowering. This will allow the bulb to build up plenty of reserves for the following year's flowering display. Ideally, leave bulb foliage until it has turned brown.

Narcissus 'Tête-à-Tête' is a welcome sight in spring. Once flowering has finished, the leaves should not be cut back for at least six weeks to allow the bulbs a chance to build up reserves of nutrients ready for flowering the next year.

After removing the foliage from daffodil bulbs, use a hoe to break up the soil and fill any holes that would provide easy access for narcissus bulb flies.

Weed control

Growing bulbs and dormant, shallowly planted small bulbs are best weeded by hand. It is safe to weed around deeply planted bulbs with a hoe while they are dormant as long as you keep the blade near the surface.

Individual deep-rooted perennial weeds can be controlled with a wipe-on weedkiller containing glyphosate, which is applied directly to the leaves of the weed. If the border is heavily infested with perennial weeds, you would be better off lifting the bulbs when they are dormant and thoroughly digging over the border to remove all traces of the perennial weed roots before replanting.

Once you have achieved weed-free soil, many bulbs, including daffodils, tulips and lilies, benefit from a thick mulch of loose organic matter, such

HOW TO LIFT DAHLIA TUBERS

1 Dahlias are not hardy and should be lifted and overwintered in a frost-free place. Lift the tubers once frost has blackened the foliage. First, cut off the stems to about 15cm (6in) above the ground and remove stakes.

2 Use a garden fork to lift the clump of tubers, inserting it far enough away to avoid the risk of spearing the tubers. If possible, do this when the soil is fairly dry.

3 Carefully remove as much soil as possible before taking the tubers into a shed or greenhouse to dry off. This will be easier if the soil is not too wet.

as well-rotted manure or garden compost. This not only prevents further weeds from germinating, but it also helps retain soil moisture. The mulch will improve the nutritional value and structure of the soil as it is broken down by soil-borne creatures.

Feeding

Unless you are growing bulbs for a single season and then discarding them, all bulbs, apart from those naturalized in grass, will benefit from feeding. If you feed bulbs growing in a lawn you will encourage the grass to grow more vigorously, which may obscure the flowering display. On poor soils give bulbs a top-dressing of sulphate of potash two or three times during the growing season, otherwise a single application of a balanced, slow-release fertilizer, such as growmore is usually sufficient. Do not use high-nitrogen fertilizers because they encourage leafy growth at the expense of the flowering display.

Lilies reward care and attention with a sumptuous display. Deadhead the flowers to keep the bed looking its best and weed regularly to prevent unwanted plants from gaining toe-hold.

Winter care

Some bulbs, such as tuberous begonias, are frost tender and will perish if left outside in winter. Others, such as dahlias or gladioli, are well protected below the ground and will probably survive a mild winter provided the soil does not become too wet. Except where winters are mild and frosts do not penetrate more than a few centimetres (inches) into the soil, it is best to lift vulnerable bulbs and overwinter them in a cool, frost-proof place.

HOW TO STORE TUBERS

1 Stand the tubers upside down so that moisture drains easily from the hollow stems. Using a mesh support is a convenient way to allow them to dry off. Keep them in a dry, frost-free place.

2 After a few days the tubers should be dry enough to store. Remove surplus soil, trim off loose bits of old roots and shorten the stem to leave a short stump. Label each plant.

3 Pack the tubers in a well-insulated box with peat, vermiculite, wood shavings or crumpled newspaper placed between them. Store in a frost-free location. Check from time to time, and discard any that feel soft, which could be a sign of rot.

Buying annuals

The usual definition of an annual is a plant that grows and dies or is discarded in a year. Annuals can be raised from seed or bought as plants in a range of stages of development. The way you decide to buy them will depend on how many you need, the amount of time you have and how much you are prepared to spend.

Annuals in the garden

Widely available and cheap to buy, annuals offer a quick, easy and, above all, cheap way of adding instant colour to your garden. Annuals come in a wide range of colours from very bright to soft and subtle shades. They can be used almost anywhere in the garden from beds and borders to patio containers, hanging baskets and window boxes – they can even be used to decorate the vegetable plot.

Raising plants from seed

This is a cheap and easy way to raise a lot of plants. Hardy annuals can be sown directly in autumn but half-hardy annuals should not be planted outside until the threat of frost has passed. You may need propagating facilities and somewhere to grow the plants on. A few types of annual have to be sown in early spring to be in flower by early summer, but most can be sown in mid-spring. Seeds generally germinate at a temperature of 15–18°C (59–65°F), but some may need temperatures as high as 21°C (70°F) to germinate reliably. Quick-maturing annuals, such as alyssum and French marigold, can be sown as late as late spring and still produce a good display.

Choosing annuals

Traditionally, the best way to get annuals was to raise the plants yourself from seed. Although

HOW TO CHOOSE ANNUALS

1 Young plants are sometimes grown in small cells, known as plugs. These are cheaper than those in larger packs, but can become potbound. Plants left too long in the cells can be starved if the tangled mass of roots cannot find enough food. The plants should be potted on and allowed to grow for a while before being planted out.

2 When they are grown individually in larger cells, young plants have plenty of room to develop good root systems. Plants can stay in these larger packs longer and with less danger of becoming overcrowded.

3 Some of the best plants come in individual pots, but they are more expensive to buy because more work was required to raise them. The plants have more compost (soil mix) in which to grow and can be left in the pots longer than when in packs or plugs.

4 When choosing plants always check the root system. It should be evenly spread and not overcrowded (right). If the roots have wound themselves around the inside of the pot and are obviously overcrowded (left), you should reject the plant.

bedding plants were available in garden centres, the choice was very limited and the quality variable. In recent years, however, there has been a revolution in bedding plants, with many types being offered as seedlings, individual tiny plants and flowering plants in cellular packs or individual containers. The range being offered increases every year, and many are the most recent and

best varieties available. This is an ideal way of buying bedding without having to go to the trouble or risk of raising your own from seed, and if you want a range of different species it can be cost effective too. Some bedding plants, notably pelargoniums, are expensive to buy as seed, and it is quite tricky to raise plants early in the season, so buying a few ready-grown plants can make

Sowing times for annuals

Type	sowing time	minimum sowing temperature
Ageratum	mid-spring*	18°C (65°F)
Alyssum	late spring	15°C (59°F)
Antirrhinum	early spring*	10°C (50°F)
Begonia	early spring*	21°C (70°F)
Dianthus	mid-spring	18°C (65°F)
Gazania	early spring	15°C (59°F)
Impatiens	mid-spring*	21°C (70°F)
Lobelia	early spring*	15°C (59°F)
Nemesia	mid-spring	18°C (65°F)
Nicotiana	mid-spring*	18°C (65°F)
Pelargonium	early spring	21°C (70°F)
Petunia	mid-spring*	18°C (65°F)
Salvia	early spring	18°C (65°F)
Tagetes (African)	mid-spring	15°C (59°F)
Tagetes (French)	late spring	15°C (59°F)
Verbena	mid-spring	21°C (70°F)
Viola x wittrockiana	mid-spring	15°C (59°F)
Zinnia	late spring	18°C (65°F)

Key: * = sow on surface of compost (soil mix) because seeds need light to germinate.

Popular bedding plants, such as these marigolds, can be bought as seed, seedlings, plugs and flowering plants.

good economic sense. Buying ready-grown bedding plants is, however, an expensive way of buying a lot of the same type of bedding for something like a massed bedding scheme.

Tender summer bedding often appears in the garden centres before the last frost has occurred, so make sure that you have somewhere cool but frost-free to keep your plants until they can be safely planted out. Otherwise, wait before buying and let the garden centre take the risk.

Which way to buy annuals?

Whether you decide to grow annuals from seed or buy them as plants will probably depend on the amount of money and time you have, how big an area you intend to cover and the time of year you start.

Seed Good for unusual varieties and is a cheap way of growing lots of the same variety of plant.

Seedlings Overcomes the need to buy propagation equipment and is a cheap way of growing a few dozen of the same variety.

Plugs A cheap way to grow a few plants of the same variety. Easier than seedlings or raising from seed.

Cellular packs Plants are growing in their own cell, so good for plants such as *Impatiens* that resent root disturbance when planting.

Small pots Individual plants that are slightly larger and more expensive than those sold in plugs or cellular packs, but good for planting a single container or hanging basket.

Individual pots Mature plants, often in flower. They are expensive, but ideal for creating instant displays.

What to look for

Plants should be compact and, unless naturally coloured, should have healthy green leaves. Avoid any plants with unnaturally yellowing foliage – a sign of starvation – or a blue tinge to the outer leaves, which is a tell-tale sign that the plant has been allowed to get too cold. Don't buy seedlings (or plants) that are tall and straggly because they have been packed together too tightly for too long, and check the compost (soil mix) to make sure that it is moist but not waterlogged. Avoid plants that have any signs of pest and disease attack, such as aphids in the growing tips and under the leaves. Always make sure that plants you buy have been hardened off properly by the garden centre: ask if you are not sure.

The annuals should not be in flower unless they are sold in summer, in cellular packs or individual pots. Pinch off flowers and buds when you plant so that the new specimen establishes quickly.

Sowing annuals

Hardy, half-hardy and tender annuals are a cheap and easy way of adding colour to your garden. They are perfect for filling gaps and for making a cheerful display in a new garden before you have had a chance to draw up longer-term plans or before perennials and shrubs have filled their allotted space.

Types of annual

Hardy annuals can be sown directly into the soil in autumn and they will survive the winter unprotected ready to produce flowers in the late spring or early summer. Half-hardy annuals cannot tolerate frost, so they should either be grown in a greenhouse, hardened off and planted in late spring, or sown directly into the soil once there is no danger of frost.

Tender annuals must be raised in a greenhouse in order for them to flower early in the year.

Sowing direct

Some people are put off growing annuals because they have sown them *in situ* outside and the seeds have failed to come up or the results have been sparse and patchy. The secret to success is good soil preparation and careful sowing.

The soil does not need to be very fertile, because many annuals can tolerate fairly impoverished conditions. A week or two before sowing, cultivate the soil and remove any weeds, stones and other debris. Rake the soil level and remove any lumps. Cover with clear plastic to warm the soil and encourage weed

seeds to germinate. Hoe lightly just before sowing to kill off the new flush of weed seedlings.

The easiest way to sow directly is to scatter the seed in rows. For a more natural effect, combining several varieties, mark out the seed-bed into irregular blocks. A series of arcs drawn with sand is usually recommended, but any shape will do.

Press a cane into the soil to create drills at the correct spacing (see the seed packet for details), varying the direction of the drills in each block. Sow the seed thinly, at the recommended spacing, and lightly cover with soil or compost (soil mix). Weed as necessary, and when the seedlings are large enough to handle, remove the weakest to leave the plants at the correct spacing.

SOWING HARDY ANNUALS

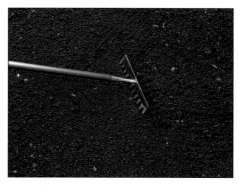

1 It pays to prepare the ground thoroughly by clearing it of weeds and raking the surface to a fine, crumbly tilth.

2 If you are growing just for cutting, sow in rows in a spare piece of ground, but if you want to make a bright border of hardy annuals, "draw" your design on the ground with sand or grit.

3 Use the corner of a hoe or rake to draw shallow drills, but change the direction of the drills from one block to the next to avoid a regimented appearance. Check the packet for spacing between rows.

4 Scatter the seeds as evenly as possible in each marked out area. If the weather is dry, run water into the bottom of each drill first and allow it to soak in.

5 Write and insert a label, then cover the seeds by raking the soil back over the drills. Try not to disturb the seeds unnecessarily.

6 Water the area thoroughly, particularly if the soil is dry and rain is not forecast. Continue to water in dry weather until the seedlings have emerged.

If time is short or if you have a large area to cover, you can broadcast sow. In this case measure out sufficient seed for each sector and place it in the palm of your hand. Then carefully scatter it over the area as evenly as possible by tapping your hand gently. Use a soil rake to mix the seed into the surface soil. Weed and thin out overcrowded plants as before.

Weeding around annuals that were broadcast sown can be a nightmare because it is so difficult to tell the weed seedlings from the flowers. Sowing in rows does overcome this problem to some extent, especially if you use sterilized potting compost to cover the drills after sowing. The lines of flower seedlings stand out clearly, making identifying weeds less of a problem.

Using a greenhouse

Heavy soils, wet weather and prolonged cold spells can take their toll, even with hardy annuals. You can still win the day if you have a greenhouse or cold frame, by raising hardy annuals from seed in trays (flats) – just as you would tender annuals and vegetables.

Sowing in trays is far less wasteful of seed than sowing directly outside, and the results are more predictable. Sowing in trays also means that you can place the plants exactly where they are needed, producing better displays. If space under glass is at a premium, you can still have the best of both worlds by sowing most of the seeds directly into the bed and, say, 10 per cent in trays to use for filling gaps and in places where direct sowing is impracticable.

It is important that any annual raised in the greenhouse is hardened off thoroughly before planting outside in its final position.

HOW TO SOW OR PLANT A MIXED BORDER

1 Remove any old plants and weeds from the area. Dig over the soil, taking care that you do not disturb the roots of nearby plants, and add well-rotted organic material if the soil has not been rejuvenated recently.

2 Work well-rotted compost into the soil and break the soil down to a fine tilth. If the soil is impoverished, add a base dressing of slow-release general fertilizer and rake into the surface before sowing or planting.

3 If sowing, carefully level the soil with a rake before scattering the seed evenly over the ground. Rake in and water using a watering can fitted with a fine rose. When the seedlings appear, thin them to the desired distance apart.

4 Bedding plants can be used instead of seeds. Arrange the plants in their positions before you start to plant as changes are easy to make at this stage. Try to visualize the final height and spread, and do not be tempted to plant them too close together.

The intricate flowers of *Nigella damascena* (love-in-a-mist) make it a popular choice for the border. This is a hardy annual, so sow seeds directly in the autumn.

Growing annuals

Vigorous but delicate young bedding plants need to be planted carefully at exactly the right time, otherwise they will receive a check in growth and may never recover.

Planting

Prepare the ground by digging over the soil and removing weeds and other debris. Incorporate well-rotted organic matter, such as manure or garden compost, if the soil is poor. Make sure all the plants have been hardened off well beforehand and keep tender bedding in a frost-free place until it is safe to plant outside.

The stems of young bedding plants are delicate and easily damaged, so it's advisable to handle them by their rootball or leaves rather than holding them by the stems. For this reason the best way to remove the plant from its container is by turning it upside down in the pot with the plant between two fingers and tapping the pot or pushing on its base to dislodge the

HOW TO PLANT EDGING

1 Prepare the soil, removing any weeds and adding some well-rotted compost if the soil is impoverished. Break the soil down to a fairly fine consistency. Set up a garden line at an even distance from the actual edge of the border. Alternatively, for a curved border, use a standard measure, such as a length of stick, between the edge and each plant.

rootball. Plant at the same depth as the plant was in the pot and firm the soil lightly around the rootball. Water well after planting.

2 Plant the edging plants along the line at the correct spacing (depending on the variety), checking the distance between each one with a measuring stick. Firm in each plant and water. For an informal planting, you can use a mixture of plants in uneven rows so that the edging merges into the other plants in the border.

Late frosts

Protect new bedding from damaging late frosts by covering plants with a double layer of horticultural fleece or sheets of newspaper when late frosts are forecast. If unprotected tender plants are touched by frost, minimize the damage by covering them in the morning, before the temperature rises, to slow down the thaw. It is the rapid thaw that causes most damage to plant tissues.

Hardening off bedding plants

About two weeks before you want to set out your bedding plants, they will need to be weaned off the cosy temperatures inside the greenhouse to the harsher environment outdoors. This is known as hardening off. It simply means that you get plants slowly accustomed to conditions outside over a period of time. Normally, this is done with a cold frame. Start off by opening the top slightly on mild days and closing it at night, then increase this ventilation each day until the top is removed altogether. If you don't have a cold frame you can use shelves near vents in the roof of a greenhouse to harden plants off or construct a makeshift cold frame out of a large cardboard box cloche or layers of horticultural fleece in a sheltered part of the garden.

Puddling in

If your soil is dry or you are planting during a warm spell in summer, use a special technique called puddling in. Water the plants well in their pots as usual. Prepare the planting hole and fill it right up with water. When the water has had a chance to soak away, position the plant and replace the soil around the roots. Water thoroughly after planting and keep well watered until established.

An informal edging of *Chrysanthemum tenuiloba* 'Golden Fleck' sprawls out over a path.

Bedding planner

Bedding type	planting distance
Ageratum	20cm (8in)
Alyssum	15cm (6in)
Antirrhinum	23cm (9in)
Begonia	15cm (6in)
Dianthus	20cm (8in)
Gazania	20cm (8in)
Impatiens	20cm (8in)
Lobelia	15cm (6in)
Nemesia	20cm (8in)
Nicotiana	30cm (12in)
Pelargonium	30cm (12in)
Petunia	25cm (10in)
Salvia	20cm (8in)
Tagetes (African)	20cm (8in)
Tagetes (French)	20cm (8in)
Verbena	25cm (10in)
Viola x wittrockiana	20cm (8in)
Zinnia	25cm (10in)

HOW TO PLANT ANNUAL CELLULAR PLANTS

1 Several hours before planting out, or the evening before, water the tray of plants and leave them to stand so excess water drains away. The plants are less likely to be stressed by the move if they are growing well.

2 Remove a plant from the pack by pressing on the bottom. In strips, where the plants are not segregated, remove the lot from the pack and carefully remove one, trying not to tear off too many of its neighbour's roots.

3 Using a small trowel, dig a planting hole that is wider and slightly deeper than the plant's rootball.

4 Adjust the depth of the planting hole so that the top of the rootball is level with the surrounding soil.

5 Fill in the hole around the plant with soil and gently firm down with your hands.

6 Water the plant with a watering can fitted with a fine rose. Keep well watered thereafter until the plant is well established.

Aftercare of annuals

Once they are established and growing well most annuals will look after themselves, but to get better and longer-lasting displays you need to pamper them a little.

Watering and feeding

Keep an eye on annuals because they will be among the first plants to indicate if they are running short of water or nutrients. Even before planting out they may show signs of starvation: poor growth and yellowing lower leaves. While still in their containers water them with a balanced liquid feed.

Once established in the ground, most bedding won't need regular feeding, but to get the best flowering displays apply a high-potash feed every month while they are actively growing. It is important not to let annual bedding suffer from drought. If they are allowed to wilt some, such as lobelia, are reluctant to recover, while others, including verbena, will be more susceptible to diseases such as powdery mildew.

For sheer architectural grandeur there is little to beat the giant spires of *Verbascum* (mullein), which tower 2.1m (7ft) or more above the border.

PINCHING OUT

If left to their own devices, many annuals will grow up as a single stem. In a bedding scheme this would result in a forest of tall spindly spikes rather than a desirable carpet of foliage and flowers. To avoid this effect, pinch out the growing tip of each main spike. The stem will produce sideshoots and the plant will become completely bushy and much more attractive. Cut through the stem with a sharp knife just above a leaf joint.

FEEDING

An application of high-potash fertilizer during the growing season will help promote better flowering. If using granular feed, take care not to get any on the leaves. Apply the fertilizer at the manufacturer's recommended dosage, as given on the package.

SUPPORTING

In exposed gardens taller annuals may need supporting. Use sticks pushed into the ground around the clump. Bend the sticks over and weave or tie their tops together to create a network through which the stems will grow. Alternatively, use special plant supports.

General care

Some annuals, such as antirrhinums, tend to produce a single main stem that will get taller through the summer. You can encourage bushier growth by pinching out the growing tip after planting. If necessary, repeat the process a couple of weeks later by pinching out the tips of the sideshoots that are produced.

Taller annuals may also benefit from staking, especially in exposed gardens or borders. Traditionally, twiggy sticks have been used, pushed into the ground around young plants with the tops woven together to form a firm support. Alternatively, use any of the plant supports that you would for perennials.

Pests and diseases

Slugs and snails have a particular liking for some bedding plants. Put down beer traps or patrol the garden after dark with a torch (flashlight) when these pests are most active and collect and dispose of any you see. Protect new plants with slug-proof barriers, such as cut-down large

TIDYING UP

Some edging plants spread out over the grass, possibly killing it or creating bald patches, as this *Limnanthes douglasii* (poached-egg plant) has done. If the plant has finished flowering, it can be removed completely. Otherwise, just cut back the part that is encroaching on the grass. If cascading over a path, there may be no problem, although it could still cause people to stumble.

plastic drinks bottles, or surround plants with a layer of grit or broken eggshells, which slugs and snails find uncomfortable to cross. If all else fails, scatter slug pellets sparingly around susceptible plants.

Mammals and birds can also be a problem in some areas: use suitable barriers and netting to protect plants if these are pests in your garden.

Deadheading bedding plants

A few plants need to be deadheaded regularly to keep flowering well. If left, the plants will produce seeds at the expense of new flowers, and some, such as sweet peas (*Lathyrus odoratus*), will stop flowering altogether. Large-flowered bedding plants, such as pelargoniums, are also worth deadheading as a matter of routine. Many types of bedding have too many tiny flowers to make deadheading worthwhile, but a few, such as pansies, will flower better if you cut back leggy stems with scissors. Ageratum, calendula, dianthus, erigerons, marigolds, mesembryanthemums, mimulus, osteospermum, phlox and poppies are also worth deadheading.

If you have masses of soft-stemmed bedding, such as begonias and impatiens, you could try speeding up the process by deadheading with a nylon-line trimmer, but this is a tricky procedure to get right without damaging or destroying the plants. After deadheading clear up the discarded material and compost.

WEEDING

Where plants are close together, the best way to remove weeds is either to pull them out by hand or to dig them out using a hand fork. Perennial weeds must be dug out whole and not simply chopped off or they will soon resprout. Where there is more room, hoes can be used in a border, but take care to avoid the delicate plants. In hot weather hoed-up weeds can be left to shrivel, but it looks neater if they are removed to the compost heap.

MULCHING

It is a good idea to apply or renew a mulch after weeding. As well as helping to prevent weeds from reappearing, this will also preserve moisture. Composted bark, chipped bark or gravel will set the plants off well. You could also consider using garden compost or leaf mould as a mulch. Other mulches such as black polythene, grass clippings and straw work well but look unattractive.

DEADHEADING

Regular deadheading helps to ensure a continuing supply of new flowers. If any of the flowers are allowed to run to seed, vital energy that would otherwise be channelled into producing new blooms is used up. Removing dead flowers and any developing seedheads helps to conserve this energy.

Buying perennials

Spring is the best time to buy perennial plants. Garden centres, specialist nurseries and gardening websites offer the greatest range of varieties at this time of year, and the plants will also be coming into growth and be ready to plant.

Choosing perennials

Perennials are a large and varied group and there are types to suit every garden situation, regardless of soil type or whether the garden is in sun or shade. Most perennials are herbaceous, which means they die back to ground level during the winter months and then produce new growth each spring from dormant underground roots.

A few perennials are evergreen, however, keeping their leaves throughout the winter. Some even flower in the winter, so it may be worth considering planting a winter garden to enjoy in the colder months of the year. Some shade-tolerant perennials can be grown beneath a deciduous tree or shrub, so that they are in full view when at their best, but hidden from sight the rest of the year.

The wide choice of perennials can be bewildering for the beginner so it is a good idea to consider exactly what you want from each plant from the start. That way you can drastically reduce the number of options available to make the selection a more manageable task.

Another tip is to start by visiting your local garden centre, which will stock only a limited range of plants, all of which should be suitable for growing in your area.

Evergreen perennials

Ajuga	Helleborus
Artemisia	Heuchera
Bergenia	Kniphofia
Carex	Lamium
Epimedium	Pulmonaria
Euphorbia	Sempervivum
Festuca	Stachys

Winter-flowering perennials

Anemone nemorosa (wood anemone)
Eranthis hyemalis (winter aconite)
Euphorbia rigida
Helleborus niger (Christmas rose);
  H. orientalis (Lenten rose);
  H. purpurascens
Iris unguicularis (Algerian iris)
Primula vulgaris (primrose)
Pulmonaria rubra (lungwort)
Viola odorata (sweet violet)

Spring in the cottage garden heralds the appearance of ever-popular perennials such as primulas and columbines.

Buying pot plants

It is a good idea to choose perennials sold in 9cm (3½in) pots because they will establish more quickly than larger plants and cost you a lot less. The exception to this rule is if you want a large number of the same variety, for ground cover, for example. In this case, a bigger plant that is well established in its pot is worth buying because it can be divided into many smaller sections before planting.

It is also worth buying a few perennials, such as peonies and Japanese anemones, in large pots because they tend to sulk if they get potbound in tiny containers. Perennials in larger pots are also worth opting for if you are buying later in the season, because plants in smaller containers will have suffered more from irregular watering.

What to look for

Choosing the healthiest plants you can will ensure your garden display looks its best. The points to consider change throughout the year.

Early spring If you buy plants early in the season, before new growth

Planting perennials in the right combination can make for a truly spectacular summer display. Here, *Tanacetum parthenium* has been planted with *Galega* x *hartlandii* 'Alba' to create a bright white border, softened with the yellow centres of the tanacetum flowers and green foliage.

starts, make sure the perennials have recently been delivered from the nursery and are not left-over stock from the previous season. Weeds, faded labels and scruffy pots are all tell-tale signs of older plants.

Late spring Once new growth starts, choose plants that have fresh, healthy-looking, new shoots and foliage with no signs of pests or diseases. Make sure the plants are well established in their pots and avoid those with loose compost (soil mix) because they probably have been only recently potted up and are not ready to be planted out. Avoid plants with lots of bright green leaves because they will have been forced into growth and need hardening off before planting.

Summer and autumn Later in the season, choose plants with strong, even growth that look as if they have been well cared for. Avoid those plants with weeds, straggly foliage and lots of roots growing out of the base of the pot. The foliage of most perennials naturally turns yellow in autumn, so don't let this put you off at this time of year.

BUYING POT PLANTS

Most perennials are now bought in pots. You should find a reasonable range in your local garden centre suitable for growing in your area. Before you buy, always check that the plant is healthy and free from pests or disease, and make sure that the surface of the soil is free of liverwort.

HARDENING OFF

Make sure that perennials have been hardened off properly before you plant. If not, place them in a cold frame for a week or two. Close the top in the evening and on cold days, otherwise ventilate freely. Be aware of the weather, and if frost threatens, cover the frame with insulation material.

Growing perennials

Perennials should be considered permanent residents of the garden and so soil improvement should be carried out before planting. If you are planting a new bed, dig the area thoroughly and remove all weeds and other debris, including the roots of perennial weeds. Improve the soil by incorporating plenty of well-rotted organic matter, such as farmyard manure or garden compost. Also add a base dressing of a slow-release fertilizer, such as bonemeal.

Planting

Nearly all perennials are now sold as container-grown specimens, which means that they can be planted out at any time of the year as long as the ground is not frozen or waterlogged. However, they will establish a lot more quickly if they are planted either in spring or autumn. Summer planting can be hard work, because new additions will need regular watering during dry spells.

Before removing the plants from their pots place them on the bed and adjust the arrangement until you are satisfied with the result. Larger specimens can be used individually, but smaller perennials and ground cover plants are best grouped in odd numbers of threes or fives if you want to achieve a natural-looking scheme. Also bear in mind that herbaceous perennials die back in winter, so you might want to include a proportion of evergreen plants or evergreen trees and shrubs to provide structure and interest throughout the coldest months.

Water the perennials thoroughly while they are still in their containers and leave to drain. When you have decided on the positions of the plants, dig planting holes. Starting with the central perennials, plant them at the same depth as they are

HOW TO PLANT PERENNIALS

1 Always prepare the soil first. Dig it deeply, remove weeds, and incorporate a fertilizer and well-rotted garden compost if the soil is impoverished. Most perennials are sold in pots, so space them out according to your plan. Change positions if the associations don't look right.

2 Water thoroughly about half an hour before knocking the plant from its pot, then dig a planting hole with a trowel. If the roots are wound tightly around the rootball, carefully tease out a few of them first. Work methodically from the back of the border or from one end.

3 Carefully firm the soil around the roots to remove any large pockets of air.

4 Always water thoroughly after planting and keep plants well watered in dry weather for the first few months.

in their pots. Firm the soil around them, not too heavily, and water well. Finally, apply a mulch, 5–8cm (2–3in) deep, of loose organic material, taking care not to pile it up against the plant stems.

Raising perennials from seed

Many perennials are also easy to grow from seed. This is much cheaper than buying container-grown

plants and many perennials grown this way will flower in their first year, while nearly all will be in bloom by their second summer. It is particularly well worth raising plants from seed if you want a lot of one variety such as ground cover plants, or are planting a new garden from scratch.

Seed can be sown in several ways: outside in a well-prepared seedbed; in a cold frame between early spring

Good perennials to raise from seed

Achillea	Helenium
Aquilegia	Lobelia
Coreopsis	Lupinus
Gaillardia	Polemonium
Geum	Viola

and midsummer; or in pots of fresh compost (soil mix) as you would sow bedding plants and vegetables. When the seedlings are large enough to handle, prick them out into 8cm (3in) pots. As soon as the young plants are well established they can be planted out into their final flowering positions.

Lupins make a good border plant, and their attractive flowers also have a distinctive, peppery scent. If you want a massed planting of lupins it may be worth raising them from seed.

HOW TO SOW SEED IN OPEN GROUND

1 Prepare the soil in the bed thoroughly, carefully removing all weeds and the roots of perennial weeds and breaking the soil down into a fine tilth with a rake.

2 Draw out a shallow drill with a corner of a hoe. It should be about 1cm (½in) deep. Keep the drill straight by using a garden line as a guide.

3 If the soil is dry, water the drill with a watering can and wait until the water has soaked in before sowing.

4 It is essential to mark the ends of the row, to help you identify the seedling flowers when weeding and hoeing later on.

5 Sow the seed thinly along the drill. Larger seed can be "station sown" at intervals.

6 Gently rake the soil back into the drill, covering over the seed. In dry weather water regularly and do not allow the soil to dry out.

Aftercare of perennials

Maintaining beds and borders is part of the enjoyment of gardening, and gives you a chance to examine the perennials thoroughly, to check on their general health and well-being and to admire their beauty at close quarters.

Feeding

Once they are established, perennials don't require regular feeding unless they are growing on poor soil or are becoming congested. Apply an annual feed of balanced fertilizer in the spring. Scatter 70g per square metre (2oz per square yard) around the plants, taking care not to get any fertilizer on their foliage. Over-crowded perennials are best lifted and divided in either spring or autumn to reinvigorate them.

Staking

It is worth staking taller-growing perennials or types with large blooms that are prone to flopping in windy conditions or heavy rain. Perennials grown in exposed gardens or plants that are crammed together may also benefit from some form of support.

Perennials that produce just one or two tall stems are best staked individually with a bamboo cane and string. Clump-forming perennials are easier to support with special interlocking structures, which are available from most garden retail outlets. If you are on a tight budget you can make your own support from short pieces of old bamboo cane linked together with string. Alternatively, use twiggy sticks pruned from beech or another well-branched deciduous woody plant during the dormant season.

Pests and diseases

If you choose good varieties, most plants do not suffer from pests and diseases unless they are under stress – during a drought, for example. A few types, however, including hostas and delphiniums, are prone to slug damage when they are first planted and each year as the new shoots emerge. Try to prevent damage by reducing pest numbers, and use barriers of sharp grit and roughly crushed eggshells that these pests don't like to cross. If your plants are

Diversity in the garden

The greater variety of plants you grow, the less chance there is that any individual pest or disease will reach epidemic proportions. Choosing many types of plant will limit the number that are susceptible to attack, and will also provide a variety of homes for the pests' predators.

still suffering from damage, scatter slug pellets around susceptible plants early in the season before any new shoots emerge or get some slug-destroying nematodes from a biological control supplier.

Deadheading

Many repeat-flowering perennials can be persuaded to produce bigger and longer-lasting displays by regular deadheading. For most perennials, simply nip the fading flowers off just above the first leaf down the stem to encourage a second flush of blooms. For perennials such as delphiniums and hollyhocks, which throw up flower spikes, cut back to the first sideshoot lower down on

HOW TO STAKE PERENNIALS

Proprietary hoops with adjustable legs can be placed over a clump-forming perennial. The new shoots grow through the grid, gaining support from the frame and eventually hiding it.

Tall flowering stems can be staked individually by tying them to a cane that is shorter than the eventual height of the plant and hidden from sight behind the stem.

Wire netting can be used vertically, creating cylinders, held firmly in place with posts. The plant grows up through the centre, with the leaves coming through and covering the sides.

Perennials that are worth deadheading

Aconitum	Erigeron
Alcea	Gaillardia
Anchusa	Geranium
Centaurea	Leucanthemum
Chrysanthemum	Lupinus
Delphinium	Penstemon
Digitalis	Scabiosa

CLEARING AWAY SUMMER BEDDING

Old bedding plants are ideal for the compost heap. Being non-woody, they rot down easily, making excellent compost.

TOP-DRESSING PERENNIALS

In autumn apply a mulch of garden compost around the crowns of your perennials. This will help to conserve moisture.

the stem when the last bloom on the original flower spike starts to fade. These sideshoots will develop to flower during late summer. Some early-flowering perennials, notably hardy geraniums, look untidy by midsummer and so are worth cutting back to ground level with shears. If watered and given a feed, they will produce an attractive mound of new leaves and perhaps even a further flush of flowers later in the season.

Cutting back

At the end of the season, most perennials start to look tatty as the foliage begins to die back. In early autumn cut back the foliage to near ground level with shears or secateurs (pruners) for thicker stems and consign them to the compost heap. Shred or chop up woody stems before adding to the compost heap to speed the decomposition process.

The crowns of borderline hardy species should be covered with an insulating layer of leaves held in place with fine netting or a 15cm (6in) thick layer of bark chippings.

The insulating layer should be removed in spring after the worst of the cold weather is past and before new growth starts.

A few perennials, including agapanthus, chrysanthemums, red-hot pokers, schizostylis and sedums, are worth leaving intact over the winter months because they have attractive seedheads. These can be particularly eye-catching on a sunny morning after a hoarfrost.

Hostas are sometimes subject to viruses, usually apparent as a yellowing in blotches on the leaf surface. Dig up and burn any affected plant to prevent the spread of the virus.

Patios and containers

Tubs, baskets and other containers can be filled with annuals and short-lived perennials to brighten up your patio. Planted with perennials, climbers, shrubs and even trees they provide a long-term structure in an otherwise empty part of the garden.

Anything that can hold soil and has drainage holes can be used for planting. Pots are the most popular option, but hanging baskets, troughs, window boxes, wall-mangers and urns can look equally attractive, and provide a splash of colour at eye-level.

Containers are made in a range of materials. Terracotta has a natural tone and fits with almost any garden design or planting scheme. Plastic pots are cheap and lightweight but may not be sufficiently stable for tall plants. Wood and stone have a natural appeal and are suitable for almost any setting, but metal or fibreglass containers may be better options for contemporary designs.

This garden makes the most of a small space with the clever use of containers. They make the patio an inviting area to step into.

Planting window boxes and baskets

Window boxes, troughs and hanging baskets filled with annual bedding plants are an ideal way of adding colour and interest to all parts of the garden in summer. They can also be used to brighten up the dull, dark days of winter by planting them with evergreens and winter-flowering perennials.

Choosing a hanging basket

When you are choosing a basket, opt for the biggest you can find – ideally 40cm (16in) – because this holds twice as much compost (soil mix) as the most popular size – 30cm

(12in). It will also weigh twice as much, so make sure you buy suitable brackets and have a system of watering that doesn't involve lifting the hanging basket down each time.

There are basically two types of hanging basket: open-mesh wire baskets and solid-sided plastic baskets. The open-mesh style, which includes wrought iron types, is the most common but in many ways the most difficult to master. The wire mesh is plastic coated to prevent corrosion, and the large holes make planting the sides easy. However, they will dry out more quickly than solid-sided baskets,

HOW TO PLANT A HANGING BASKET WITH ANNUALS

1 Stand the basket on a large pot or bucket to make it easier to work. Carefully place the liner in position so that it fills the basket.

2 Half fill the liner with compost (soil mix), then mix in some water-retaining granules to help prevent the basket drying out. Add some slow-release fertilizer; this will overcome the need to feed throughout the summer.

3 Cut holes 4cm (1½in) across in the side of the liner. Shake some earth off the rootball of one of the plants and wrap it in a strip of plastic. Poke it through the hole, remove the plastic and spread out the roots. Add more compost containing water-retaining granules and slow-release fertilizer.

4 Plant up the rest of the basket, packing the plants much more tightly together than you would in the open ground. Smooth out the surface of the compost, removing any excess or adding a little more as necessary. Water, then keep the basket indoors until all danger of frost has passed.

although this can be overcome by using a waterproof liner. Solid-sided plastic baskets cannot be planted at the sides, so the display is less appealing, but they need watering less often, especially if there is a built-in water reservoir.

Types of liners

Open-mesh baskets need to be lined before they can be planted to stop the compost (soil mix) falling out. Traditionally, a 5cm (2in) thick layer of sphagnum moss was used, but this is expensive, and many gardeners have turned to alternatives on environmental grounds. This has led to the appearance of manufactured liners in a variety of materials, including recycled wool and cotton, coconut fibre and foam.

Window boxes

The type of window box you choose should fit comfortably with the style of your house. There is a wide range of materials and styles to choose from: stone and terracotta look attractive as they age but they are fairly heavy. Plastic, wood and galvanized tin window boxes are all lighter options.

HOW TO PLANT A WINDOW BOX WITH ANNUALS

1 Assemble all the items you will need. If the window box is light, assemble it on the ground. If it is heavy, make it up in position, especially if it is to be fixed high up.

2 Place irregularly shaped stones over the drainage holes to prevent the compost (soil mix) falling through.

3 Partially fill the window box with compost containing water-retaining granules. These granules will help retain moisture so that the planted window box will not require watering so frequently.

4 Plant the flowers to the same depths as they were in their pots or trays. For instant impact, postion plants closer together that you would in open ground.

5 Regular feeding is important: the nutrients in the compost will quickly get used up. Add a liquid feed to the water every week or push special slow-release fertilizer tablets into the compost at planting time.

6 Water thoroughly. The plants will soon spread out to fill the window box. If the box has been planted away from its final position, it can be left for a while until the plants are all in full flower before being put on display.

Trouble-free plants for hanging baskets

Flowers	**Foliage**
Begonia	*Cineraria*
Bidens	*Glechoma*
Brachycome	*Hedera*
Felicia	*Helichrysum*
French marigold	*petiolare*
Gazania	*Lysimachia*
Heliotrope	*Plectranthus*
Impatiens	
Osteospermum	**Trailers**
Pelargonium	*Anagallis*
Petunia	*Convolvulus*
Portulaca	*sabiatus*
Scaevola	*Diascia*
Verbena	*Fuchsia*
Viola	*Lotus*
	Nasturtium
	Pelargonium
	Sanvitalia
	Sutera

Pale orange pansies make this an eye-catching summer hanging basket.

Planting tubs

The beauty of tubs and other large containers is that with the minimum of effort they will transform a patio, bringing the bright colours of the garden closer to the home. They can be filled with annuals or bulbs for a seasonal display, or planted with small ornamental trees or shrubs.

Which compost?

It is important to choose a good-quality compost (soil mix) if you want reliable results in your container. There are three main types: traditional loam-based composts and peat-based mediums or those based on a peat-substitute.

Loam-based composts These are made to a special formula and contain a mixture of soil, peat and sand. They are heavy and variable in quality, but maintain their structure and nutrients well over a long period of time. Loam-based composts are ideal for long-term schemes and permanent plants in containers.

Peat-based composts Lighter and easier to use than loam-based composts, these composts are a good choice for planting bedding.

Peat-substitute composts These new composts are based on composted bark, coir or other organic waste material. Use in the same way as peat-based composts.

Planting containers

Although the traditional technique of adding broken pots to the bottom of the tub is not necessary, if you are planting top-heavy trees or shrubs, a heavy layer of stones will improve stability. If you are planting shallow-rooted bedding plants in a deep container you can save compost and reduce the weight of the container by filling the bottom third with polystyrene (styrofoam) chips. In small containers, which are more prone to drying out, consider using a special hanging basket compost, which contains a wetting agent to help the water soak in. Some plants, such as camellias and azaleas require acid conditions and so are best planted using a specially formulated ericaceous compost (acid soil mix).

HOW TO PLANT IN A CONTAINER

1 Filled tubs and pots can be heavy to move, so plant them where they are to be displayed. Cover the drainage holes with a layer of broken pots, gravel or chipped bark.

2 Use a loam-based compost (soil mix) for permanent plants such as trees and shrubs. A peat-based or peat-substitute compost is a better bet for annuals.

3 Choose a tall or bold plant for the centre, such as *Cordyline australis* or a fuchsia, or one with large flowers such as the osteospermum that has been used here.

4 Fill in with bushier plants and trailing types around the edge. Choose bright flowers if the centrepiece is a foliage plant, but place the emphasis on foliage effect if the focal point is a flowering plant.

5 Water thoroughly. If much of the surface of the compost is visible, you can add a decorative mulch such as chipped bark, which will help conserve moisture; with a dense planting, there is no need.

HOW TO PLANT A PERMANENT CONTAINER FOR WINTER AND SPRING INTEREST

1 When creating a winter interest display, choose attractive evergreen plants with contrasting habit and form. Here, a dwarf conifer and small-leaved variegated ivies have been used with spring flowering bulbs to provide a colour boost in the spring.

2 Position the bulbs on the surface first so that they are evenly spaced around the container. Small bulbs that multiply freely, such as *Muscari armeniacum*, scillas, chionodoxas and *Anemone blanda*, can usually be depended upon to improve year by year.

3 When you are happy with the position of the bulbs, plant them with a trowel, being careful to disturb the roots of the conifer and ivies as little as possible. Water the container thoroughly and mulch if necessary.

Planting large specimens

A useful technique that will save a lot of effort when planting a semi-mature specimen in a large pot is to partly fill the container with compost. Remove the pot from the specimen plant and position the pot where you want the plant to go, making sure it is at the right level. Then pack compost around the empty pot and use it as a mould for the plant's rootball. Remove the empty pot, and simply slip the plant into position. Lightly firm the soil to remove air pockets. Top up the container with compost if necessary and water thoroughly. After watering cover the surface with large pebbles for an attractive ornamental effect. The extra weight will also help keep the specimen in position.

Flowers for containers

Ageratum (floss flower)
Antirrhinum (snapdragon)
Begonia
Bidens
Brachyscome
Cerinthe
Chrysanthemum
Dianthus (carnations, pinks)
Echium
Felicia
Laurentia (syn. *Isotoma*)
Lobelia
Myosotis (forget-me-not)
Nicotiana (tobacco plant)
Schizanthus (butterfly flower; poor man's orchid)
Senecio
Tagetes (marigold)
Tropaeolum (nasturtium)
Viola x *wittrockiana* (pansy)

Lathyrus odoratus (sweet pea), one of the best-loved of all fragrant annuals, can be used as trailing plants, instead of growing them to climb up an obelisk or frame.

Planting perennials in containers

Some hardy perennials make ideal container plants. Although they do not flower for as long or as prolifically as bedding plants, they are generally easier to look after and can cope with a wider range of different conditions.

Perennials for containers

When you choose perennials for containers, select plants that have decorative foliage so that they look attractive throughout the growing season. Evergreen plants will also offer winter interest. Several perennials, including hostas and agapanthus, make excellent specimen plants. If the flowers are their main feature, as in the case of agapanthus, they can be given a prominent position while in bloom and then tucked out of the way at other times of the year. Where foliage is the main attraction, as in the case of hostas, the plant can be given a prominent position for most of the summer. Some smaller perennials, such as lamium and *Festuca glauca* (blue fescue), can be combined with

other plants to create a permanent container display or used as a long-term filler between bulbs and seasonal bedding. This will save you time and money in the long run because you won't have to buy so many bedding plants to fill your pots.

Many perennials are also more tolerant of shady conditions than annual bedding plants and so are

useful for brightening the gloom in these areas. Ideal candidates include hostas, hardy ferns and variegated ivy. Other perennials, such as diascias and sempervivums, are drought-tolerant and can go for long periods between waterings, so are ideal for hot sunny spots, or for window boxes or baskets that aren't easily accessible for watering.

Corners in the shade

This permanent window box contains three different sorts of fern, and is ideal for a dark, damp, shady spot. These conditions are disliked by many plants, but ferns will thrive here. Provided the plants are not allowed to dry out, they will grow happily for many years.

HOW TO PLANT AN URN

1 Assemble the items you will need: a terracotta pot, your choice of plant (in this case, a cordyline), some stones to cover the drainage holes, compost (soil mix), slow-release fertilizer (either loose or in pellets) and water-retaining granules.

2 Cover the bottom of the container with small stones or some pieces of broken tile or pottery, to prevent the compost washing out of the drainage holes.

3 Partly fill the pot with a good-quality potting compost – loam-based compost is best for permanent displays. If you wish, mix some slow-release fertilizer and water-retaining granules into the compost before you fill the pot.

LEFT
The foliage and flowers of the perennials *Stachys byzantina* and *Nepeta* x *faassenii* blend perfectly in a container.

Unusual containers

Containers also give you the opportunity to grow plants that would otherwise struggle in your soil conditions as well as invasive perennials that would swamp your borders or even your whole garden. The giant ornamental rhubarb, for example, *Gunnera manicata*, can reach 2 x 2m (6 x 6ft) in a moist spot, but in a large container, such as a half-barrel, it can be kept to a more manageable size.

Alpines grow well in containers, too, thriving on the good drainage and airy conditions. The container also brings their dainty form and intricate markings closer to the eye where they are more easily appreciated. When they are grown in a trough, they can be combined with other dwarf plants and rocks to create an attractive miniature landscape or alpine bed.

4 Scoop a hole in the compost and insert the plant, positioning it so that the top of the rootball is level with the surface of the compost.

5 Place any extra plants that you wish to include around the edge of the main plant. Add more compost to fill any gaps and firm down. Insert a fertilizer pellet at this stage if fertilizer granules were not added to the compost mixture.

6 Water thoroughly. The plants will soon grow and fill out the container.

Patio trees and shrubs

Tough, drought-tolerant trees and shrubs make superb container plants, and they can be used to create a focal point or to provide shelter and shade on the patio.

Planting for a patio

Trees and shrubs add structure to permanent containers just as they do to other planting schemes around the garden. Although almost any species can be grown in a pot, it's a good idea to choose trees and shrubs that are not too vigorous to avoid having to carry out regular pruning and repotting. Trees and shrubs can be used as effective focal points around the garden, and when they are grown in a container you can alter the way a garden is viewed by moving the plants around. They also provide shelter and privacy on the patio during the summer months as well as adding colour and interest throughout the rest of the year.

By planting trees and shrubs in containers you can grow types that would not thrive in your garden soil. For example, if your soil is alkaline

A small tree in a container can be moved around the garden at will. A change in position will draw attention to both the tree and its surroundings.

you will not be able to grow acid-loving plants such as heathers, rhododendrons, camellias and azaleas in the border, but you could grow them in containers filled with ericaceous compost (acid soil mix). You can also grow exotic plants that

are not hardy in your area provided you have somewhere frost free, such as a conservatory or greenhouse, to keep them safe over winter.

Which container?

Choose any large, wide-bottomed container with drainage holes that will be stable once it is planted up. Wooden tubs, half-barrels and even empty water tanks can be used. Ideally, the container should be on outdoor castors to make moving it around easier. However, if this is not possible, position the container carefully before planting because it will be difficult to adjust its position afterwards. For a small collection of plants a tub of at least 45cm (18in) diameter will be required, filled with a loam-based compost (soil mix).

Choosing trees and shrubs

If you are looking for a focal point, choose neat plants with dense foliage, such as box or bay, but if you want to add a little colour too, choose a variegated shrub, such as *Aucuba japonica*. Seasonal displays from

HOW TO PLANT A TREE OR SHRUB IN A TUB

1 Choose a large tub or pot with an inside diameter of at least 45cm (18in), unless you are planting very small shrubs. Make sure it is heavy (clay or stone, for instance, not plastic) and place pieces of broken clay pots or chipped bark over the drainage hole.

2 Part-fill the tub or pot with a loam-based compost (soil mix). Do not use lightweight alternatives because the weight is required for stability.

3 Knock the plant from its pot, and if the roots are tightly wound round the rootball carefully tease out some of the roots so that they will grow into the surrounding soil more readily.

HOW TO PLANT A CLIMBER IN A HALF-BARREL

1 Fill a half-barrel with a loam-based compost (soil mix). You need a large, deep container and heavy potting mixture, which will secure the canes as well as the plants.

2 Plant the climbers, using the right number of plants. For instance, in a barrel of this size, you will need three to four clematis. Angle the root-ball of the plant so that it points slightly inwards.

3 Tie the canes together with string or use a proprietary plastic cane holder. If the growth reaches the top of the canes, it will tumble down again and make the planting look even denser.

shrubs, such as rhododendrons and camellias, can also be very effective. By growing them in containers you have the added advantage that once the flowers fade, the tub can be moved to a less prominent position for the summer. The type of shrub you choose can also influence the general ambience of the garden – for example, by combining a yucca or cordyline with the lush leafy growth of *Fatsia japonica* (false castor oil plant) to create a steamy, tropical atmosphere around the patio.

Two types of trees make excellent container plants: slow-growing specimens with attractive foliage, which can be left largely to their own devices, and fast-growing trees, which respond to annual heavy pruning to keep them in check. Vigorous trees, such as eucalyptus, *Betula pendula* (silver birch) and *Salix* (willow), are ideal for adding instant maturity to a new garden and can have all their new growth cut back in early spring to create eye-catching multi-stemmed or lollipop shapes. Containers are also an ideal way of growing trees that sucker and would otherwise be a nuisance in the garden. As with other plants, trees vary in their ability to cope with a lack of moisture, so if you find regular watering a problem, choose a drought-tolerant tree such as *Caragana arborescens* (pea tree).

4 Test the plant for size and position. Add or remove soil as necessary, so that the top of the rootball and soil level will be 2.5–5cm (1–2in) below the rim of the pot to allow for watering.

5 Backfill the soil around the roots firmly, because trees and shrubs offer a great deal of wind resistance. Water thoroughly after planting, thereafter water as necessary including during the winter months.

Shrubs for containers

Arundinaria	*Hydrangea*
Aucuba	*Juniperus*
Berberis	*Picea* (dwarf
Buxus	forms)
Caragana	*Rhododendron*
Chamaecyparis	*Rosmarinus*
Choisya	*Skimmia*
Cordyline	*Viburnum*
Euonymus	*Yucca*
Fatsia	

Permanent container aftercare

Growing plants in permanent containers requires a fair amount of maintenance. They require regular feeding and watering: perhaps more watering than other containers because the plants are bigger. Many will also need annual repotting, pruning or tidying up to keep in good shape. But don't be put off as there are all sorts of advantages to growing plants in this way.

Perennials

These plants fall into three broad groups when it comes to their aftercare: short-lived perennials that need replacing every few years; long-term perennials that need dividing every other year to maintain a neat habit and good flowering; and a few long-term perennials, such as agapanthus, that flower better if

they are a little pot-bound. Instead of dividing these perennials, simply replace the top few centimetres (inch) of compost (soil mix) with fresh each spring and push a few slow-release fertilizer pellets into the compost.

All perennials will need tidying up at the end of the season. Remove all yellowing stems and leaves. Pests, such as slugs and snails, which can be a menace in the border are often less of a problem in pots. However, powdery mildew, which can ruin aquilegias and pulmonarias among others, is more serious because container-grown plants are more likely to suffer from stress caused by uneven watering. If the attack occurs early in the season spray with a systemic fungicide, but later attacks are best ignored.

Lily-of-the-valley (*Convallaria majalis*) grows very well in containers and will thrive in the shade, where its delicately scented white flowers stand out from the greenery.

HOW TO PROTECT FROM COLD

1 If you are using plastic bubble wrap or horticultural fleece, wrap it around the plant in its container, allowing a generous overlap, and cut it to the correct size using sharp scissors. For particularly vulnerable plants, cut enough for a double layer.

2 Place four or five tall canes in the container and wrap the protective sheeting around the plant. If you are using a sleeve, it can be simply slipped over the canes.

3 If you are using plastic bubble wrap, leave the top open for ventilation and a gap at the bottom to permit watering if necessary. If you are using horticultural fleece, tie the top closed to help to conserve warmth.

Trees and shrubs

Most trees and shrubs require little regular maintenance, apart from an annual tidy up with secateurs (pruners) to remove any unwanted growth or to tidy the overall shape of the plant. Some clipped specimens, such as bay, will require trimming more often through the growing season to keep their neat form. Flowering shrubs, such as rhododendrons and camellias, are worth deadheading once the flowers start to fade to tidy the display.

Every couple of years in spring, permanent specimen plants will need repotting. Where practicable move them to a larger pot or repot into the same container. To do this you will first need to remove the plant from its pot – this is easier said than done with a large specimen, but pulling the pot on to its side will help. Use your fingers to remove any loose compost from around the rootball and trim any roots that are winding around the base of the pot. After cleaning the container, place a

PROVIDING SUPPORT

Check the potential size of any climber you plant and place canes in the container to support it. With regular feeding and watering, a small climber will send up strong stems that can be trained into a permanent structure around cane supports. It may be necessary to tie in the climber as it grows.

little fresh compost in the base and position the specimen so that it is at the same level as before. Trickle fresh compost down the sides of the rootball, carefully pushing it down with a short stick to get rid of any air pockets. Top up with compost and add slow-release fertilizer pellets before watering thoroughly.

GENERAL CARE FOR PLANTED CONTAINERS

1 Most composts (soil mixes) contain fertilizer, but it will run out after about six weeks. Either feed plants with a liquid fertilizer every time you water or add a slow-release fertilizer to the compost each spring that will last for the whole growing season.

2 Leave the top of the compost as it is, or cover it with a decorative mulch, such as large pebbles or gravel. These not only give the container an attractive finish but also help keep the compost cool and prevent water from evaporating.

3 Water the container thoroughly and continue to do so at regular intervals. During hot weather, this is likely to be at least daily. Occasional watering will also be necessary during dry spells in the winter months.

Planting up a patio

Don't restrict yourself to planting in containers to bring life to your patio because there are many attractive plants that are well-adapted to growing in cracks, crevices and planting pockets in and around the patio.

Creating large planting pockets

Planting pockets large enough for a small shrub or climber can be created by lifting one or two adjacent slabs from part of the patio. Choose an area that is not used very often and away from points of access. Prise up the slab with a garden spade or use a cold chisel and club hammer if it is cemented into position. Use a garden fork to break up the rubble or hardcore base before removing it. Dig down about 30cm (12in), removing any additional hardcore and subsoil, then use a garden fork to loosen the soil in the bottom of the hole. The soil is likely to be fairly poor quality, so incorporate plenty of organic matter, such as well-rotted garden compost, and top up with fresh topsoil from elsewhere in the garden or use a loam-based compost (soil mix).

PLANTING IN PAVING

Chisel out a space in your paving to a depth of at least 5cm (2in). Add loam-based compost (soil mix) and plant your seedling. Trickle more compost around the roots and firm in. Water regularly, using a fine mist sprayer to avoid washing the compost away.

Plant the pocket as you would a bed, putting the larger plants in first and then filling the gaps with the smaller plants. All plants should be drought-tolerant. Take care not to create an obstruction or hazard when using larger plants. After planting, water thoroughly and cover the surface of the compost with a decorative mulch of pebbles to prevent weeds germinating and help retain water. Continue to water until the plants are established.

Planting cracks in paving

Cracks between paving stones and at the edge of the patio, which often get colonized by weeds, can be used to grow a range of ground-hugging, drought-tolerant plants that are tough enough to be walked on occasionally. They will also prevent the weeds from returning.

To prepare the crack, first remove any weeds. Perennial weeds are best killed with a translocated weedkiller that will kill the whole plant, including the roots. Use a screwdriver to dig out the loose material between the paving slabs, reaching down as far as possible. Fill the crack with a loam-based compost (soil mix), poking it into the hole with the screwdriver to eliminate any air pockets. Level the compost and firm gently.

If you are planting seeds directly into the crack, sow them thinly and evenly. Use a garden sieve to dust compost over the seed, then water with a fine mist sprayer or a watering can fitted with a fine rose to prevent the seed and compost from being washed away. Thin seedlings when they are large enough to handle, leaving the strongest.

HOW TO CREATE A LARGE PLANTING POCKET

1 Lift one or two paving slabs, depending on their size. If they have been mortared into position, loosen the slabs with a cold chisel and club hammer, then lever them up with the chisel or a crowbar.

2 If the paving slab has been bedded on concrete, break this up with a cold chisel and club hammer. Fork over the soil, adding well-rotted garden compost or manure and a slow-release fertilizer.

3 Plant the shrub or climber, firming it in well and watering thoroughly. Arrange decorative pebbles or gravel to make the feature more attractive and reduce the chance of soil splashing on to the paving.

PLANTING IN A DRY-STONE WALL

Press moist loam-based compost into the crevice using a small dibber or your fingers. Firm in to avoid air pockets. Insert the plant into the crevice and add more soil. Keep the compost moist until the plants become established by spraying with a fine mist.

If you are using small plants in the crack, press the rootball between your palms to form a wedge shape. Carefully ease the rootball between the paving stones and water well.

Continue to water the crack as needed, until the plants or the seeds are established, especially during prolonged dry spells.

Planting crevices in walls

Garden walls or walls around raised beds can be planted using a similar technique to that described for cracks. The crevice in the wall will have to be made large enough to accommodate the rootball of the plant and deep enough for the plant to become established. Only drought-tolerant plants can be used.

Place a small, flat stone at the base of the crack to prevent the compost from falling out before you position the plant and pack in more compost around its roots. Water carefully until the plant is well established. You can sow seed directly into the crevice by mixing the seed with some compost in your hand, moistening it and pressing it into the crevice.

Good specimens for planting in the patio

Plants for cracks	Plants for crevices	Plants for pockets
Aubrieta deltoidea	*Globularia cordifolia*	*Armeria maritima*
Dianthus deltoides	*Lewisia tweedyi*	*Campanula*
Erinus alpinus	*Saxifraga callosa*	*portenschlagiana*
Scabiosa graminifolia	*Sedum spathulifolium*	*Cerastium tomentosum*
Thymus	*Sempervivum*	*Sedum telephium*
	Thymus	*Veronica prostrata*

Erinus alpinus   *Thymus serpyllum*   *Veronica prostrata*

The formality of regular shaped paving edged in brick has been softened with an exuberant planting of low-growing herbs. The herbs spill out of their planting pockets and from cracks between paving slabs in this charmingly informal patio.

Watering container plants

Keeping plants moist is of critical importance throughout the growing season and watering should be continued, although less frequently, during the winter months. It can be time-consuming, but there are many techniques and products that can be employed to make the job easier.

Hanging baskets

A large basket that holds plenty of compost (soil mix) will retain water better than a smaller basket. Line wire-mesh baskets with polythene before planting. Use a special hanging basket compost that contains a wetting agent to make watering easier. Incorporate water-retaining granules that hold on to water longer and choose drought-tolerant plants that can go for longer periods without water and recover well if they do suffer a shortage.

Patio containers

Choose the largest container you can and line porous containers, such as those made from terracotta, with a sheet of polythene, taking care not to cover the drainage holes. Mix water-retaining granules into the compost before planting, or trickle water-retaining granules into holes made with a bamboo cane into the compost in existing permanent containers. Cover the surface of all containers with a mulch of stone chippings or pebbles to prevent moisture evaporating.

Watering problems

When a container plant goes short of water, the compost can dry out and be difficult to rewet. If the water sits on the surface without soaking in, add a drop of washing-up liquid (dishwashing detergent) to the watering can before watering. This will act as a wetting agent, making it

Hanging baskets are vulnerable to drying winds and should always be kept well watered.

HOW TO USE WATER-RETAINING GRANULES

1 Pour the recommended amount of water into a bowl. Scatter the granules over the surface, stirring occasionally until it has absorbed the water.

2 Add the hydrated granules to compost (soil mix) at the recommended rate. Mix the hydrated granules thoroughly before using the compost mixture for planting.

Watering acid-lovers

Acid-loving plants growing in ericaceous compost (soil mix) will suffer if they are watered with hard water, direct from the tap. If you live in a hard-water area, either collect rainwater (which is slightly acidic) in a water butt or add an old teabag to a full watering can and let it stand for 24 hours before watering.

easier for the water to be absorbed. Alternatively, place a few ice-blocks on the surface of the compost. These will slowly soak into the surface as they melt, and you will then be able to water as normal.

In severe cases of drought, the rootball may shrink away from the sides of the container so any water simply runs between the rootball and the inside of the pot and out of the drainage holes. Prevent this from happening by adding compost to the top of the rootball and pushing it in to fill any gaps. Then water.

During hot periods it is best to water in the early morning or late evening to minimize evaporation.

Water acid-loving plants, such as this variegated pieris, with rainwater collected in a water butt if you live in a hard water area.

1 One of the easiest ways of watering is with a watering can. This allows you to deliver just the right amount of water to each plant. However, it is very time-consuming, so only really suitable for a small number of containers. Always make certain that the soil is well soaked and that you have not just dampened the surface.

3 For large collections of containers, a hose-end trigger spray is a more efficient method of watering. If you have several hanging baskets to water, consider buying a spray lance (wand) instead.

Watering equipment

A wide range of aids to make watering easier are available. Choose one that can cope with the types of containers you have and that fits in with your watering regime. Watering cans and garden hoses fitted with a hose lance (wand) make watering containers a lot easier. You can either direct the hose at individual plants or mount the hose so that a group of plants is watered by the spray.

Self-watering containers, which have a reservoir of water, are widely

2 You can apply water more quickly to established containers using a watering can without a rose fitted, but it is still hard work and quite time-consuming.

4 If you have not used a slow-release fertilizer, you can feed your plants at the same time as watering them by adding a liquid fertilizer to the watering can. Feed containers once a week when plants are growing rapidly or flowering a lot.

available, and are especially useful in hot, sunny poistions. However, if you have a number of containers you can make your life even easier by installing an automatic watering system. This is basically a network of small-bore tubes attached to a water source. It delivers water to each container by way of an adjustable drip nozzle pegged into the compost. The system can be made completely automatic by adding a water timer or watering computer to the outside tap (faucet).

Water and rock gardening

Water features add a new dimension to your garden, providing colour, movement and gentle sound, which can be used to create a relaxing atmosphere. If well planned and given the right setting, water features are easy to look after and a joy to behold.

The most important consideration when creating a water feature is to site it correctly. It needs a sunny, open position well away from overhanging trees and dense shade. Choose a type of pond that complements the style of your garden and position it where it will be most appreciated.

When creating a pond, consider adding other complementary features to your garden at the same time. A bog garden blurs the divide between pond and garden and allows you to grow some wonderful plants, while a rock garden can be as natural or as dramatic as you like.

The purple flowers of *Iris sibirica* make a striking edging to a charming and informal garden pond.

Small water features

No contemporary garden would be complete without introducing water somewhere in the design. With modern equipment, small water features are easy to install.

Choosing a feature

Creating a water feature used to require considerable planning and some serious excavation, but the development of easy-to-install kits and reliable low-voltage submersible pumps means that even a novice can build an attractive, working feature in less than a day. Of course, careful planning is advisable to avoid errors, but once you have decided on a suitable position, the time required to install a water feature is short.

There is a huge range of features to choose from, but they can be grouped according to their function: a watercourse, which creates a stream effect; spouts, where a jet of water spills from a wall mask; gurgle ponds, where a water spout splashes over a feature such as a heap of pebbles; and still-water pools.

Bear in mind that the temperature of a small pond, situated in a suntrap, may fluctuate too much for fish to thrive.

Moving water features

All small features with moving water have the same basic equipment: a submersible pump and a reservoir to hold the water. The reservoir can be bought for the purpose or made from anything that holds water, from an inexpensive central-heating header tank to a hole lined with flexible pond liner. The reservoir needs only to be deep enough to completely cover the pump with water, but larger reservoirs are much easier to maintain because they require topping up less frequently, especially in summer.

HOW TO MAKE A PEBBLE FOUNTAIN

1 Mark out the diameter of the reservoir and dig a hole slightly wider and deeper than its dimensions. Place a shallow layer of sand at the bottom. Ensure the reservoir rim is slightly below the level of the surrounding soil.

2 Backfill the gap between the reservoir and the sides of the hole with soil. Firm in. Create a catchment area by sloping the surrounding soil slightly towards the rim of the reservoir. Place two bricks at the bottom to act as a plinth for the pump. Then position the pump.

3 Ensure the pipe used for the fountain spout will be 5–7cm (2–3in) higher than the sides of the reservoir. Line the catchment area with a plastic sheet and either cut it so the plastic drapes into the reservoir, or cut a hole in the centre for the fountain pipe. Fill with water.

4 Position the plastic sheet over the reservoir, with the fountain pipe protruding through the hole and fit the fountain spout.

5 Place a piece of galvanized mesh (large enough to rest on the rim of the reservoir) on top to support the weight of large wet cobbles. If you are using small stones, place a smaller mesh on top of the larger one to prevent them falling through.

6 Cover the area around the pump with a layer of cobbles. Check the height of the spout is satisfactory. When you are happy with the fountain, finish arranging the cobbles.

The finished gurgle fountain gives interest to what would otherwise have been a neglected corner of the garden.

Plants for miniature ponds

Acorus gramineus 'Variegatus'
Azolla filiculoides
Dwarf water lilies
Eichhornia crassipes
Juncus effusus f. *spiralis*
Marsilea quadrifolia
Trapa natans

What size pump?

The size of pump you require will depend on the amount of water needed to produce the effect you want. A small water feature will require a pump with a flow rate of about 450 litres (about 120 gallons) per hour, while a large fountain will need one that can supply 650 litres (about 170 gallons). If you want to combine features or have a watercourse you will need a much larger pump (see product packaging for details).

The easiest way to create a small water feature with moving water is to sink a reservoir into the ground so that it is about 5cm (2in) below the surrounding soil. Then create a catchment area for the feature by sloping the soil around the hole towards the reservoir, so that when it is lined with heavy-duty polythene or a flexible pond liner, water will drain back into the reservoir. Position the pump in the reservoir and cover with heavy-duty steel mesh and smaller mesh to prevent smaller pebbles from falling through. Arrange cobbles and pebbles on the mesh to hide the reservoir and the catchment area to create a pebble fountain.

You can change the display by adding a millstone or another focal point, or by adding different types of fountain jet on the outlet pipe of the pump to create all manner of display fountains.

Alternatively, use a piece of pipe to connect the outlet pipe to a wall mask or a free-standing waterspout.

Still patio pools

You can create a small attractive pool from a half-barrel or large bucket. Sink it into the ground or stand it on the patio as a raised pool. If the container is not properly sealed, line it with flexible pond liner, stapling the top edge just out of sight below the rim. Trim carefully to neaten the edges and cover the bottom with a layer of gravel. Fill with water and allow to stand for a few days before planting with dwarf pond plants such as dwarf water lilies, corkscrew rush and the variegated form of the Japanese rush.

Larger raised pools are available in kit form from garden retailers or they can be made from fibreglass liners supported with brick walls.

HOW TO PLANT A MINIATURE POND

Choose an attractive watertight container such as a sturdy bucket and fill it with water. Plant with dwarf or miniature varieties of *Nymphaea* (water lily) and *Eichhornia crassipes* (water hyacinth).

Making a pond

After deciding on the best position for a pond in your garden, you need to consider its style and dimensions as well as the construction materials.

Planning a pond

A self-sustaining pond that does not require constant maintenance should be as big as possible. Whatever the shape, it should have at least 5 square metres (over 50 square feet) of surface area, and so that it doesn't heat up too quickly in summer or get too cold in winter it also needs to be at least 60cm (24in) deep over much of that area. A marginal shelf 23cm (9in) wide and about 15cm (6in) below the surface of the water around the edge is needed to accommodate plants that like their roots in water but their shoots and leaves in the air. Before excavating, check that there are no underground obstructions, such as pipes and cables.

Lining a pond

A pond can be made with a rigid, pre-formed liner or with a special flexible liner. Rigid liners are usually made from plastic or fibreglass and

A brick or paved edge creates a fairly formal effect, but the pond has been made more interesting by using the excavated soil to build up a raised bed behind it.

they come in a range of shapes and sizes to suit most styles of garden. Rigid liners tend to be on the small side, with little space for marginal plants, and are more work to install. A flexible liner, made from PVC, butyl rubber or heavy-duty polythene, gives you a lot more control over the design of your

pond. It can be pleated at the corners to fit a rectangular or square-shaped pond, and it is particularly suitable for an informal pond because it can be folded to fit any shape you want. It does, however, require some skill to create a convincing shaped pond, and the liner can be easily damaged, especially on stony soil.

HOW TO INSTALL A FLEXIBLE LINER

1 Mark out the shape of the pond with garden hose or rope for curves and pegs and string for straight edges, then remove any turf and start to excavate the pond. Redistribute the topsoil to other parts of the garden.

2 Dig the whole area to about 23cm (9in) deep, then mark the positions of the marginal shelves. Each should be about 23cm (9in) wide. Dig the deeper areas to 50–60cm (20–24in) deep. Angle all the vertical sides so they slope slightly inwards.

3 Check the level as you work. Correct discrepancies using sieved garden soil. Make sure there are no sharp stones on the base and sides that might damage the liner, then line the hole with builders' sand.

What size flexible liner?

Flexible liners are available in a range of sizes. To calculate the size you will need for your pond, use the following formula:

Length = 2 x maximum depth + maximum length of the pond

Width = 2 x maximum depth + maximum width of the pond

For example, a pond that is 3 x 2m (10 x 6ft) with a maximum depth of 50cm (20in) will require a flexible liner that is 4 x 3m (13⅓ x 9⅓ft).

Edging the pond

The style of edging and the material used should reflect the formality of the pond and the materials used elsewhere in the garden. A formal pond looks best with a neat, straight edge of paving, while an informal one can be paved with irregularly shaped stones or small unit paving, which can follow the gentle curves of the pond. Around the edge of a wildlife pond, a sloping pebble beach would be appropriate so that visiting wildlife can enjoy a bathe and a drink.

HOW TO INSTALL A PRE-FORMED RIGID LINER

1 Transfer the shape to the ground by inserting canes around the edge of the unit. Use a garden hose, rope or sand to mark the outline on the ground.

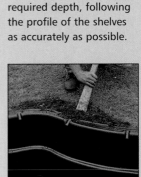

2 Remove the unit and canes and excavate the hole to approximately the required depth, following the profile of the shelves as accurately as possible.

3 Use a spirit (carpenter's) level and straight-edged board, laid across the rim, to check it is level. Measure down to check that it is the required depth.

4 Remove any large stones. Put the pond in the hole, then add or remove soil to ensure a snug and level fit. Check with a spirit level that the pond is level.

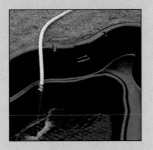

5 Remove the pond and line the hole with damp sand if the soil is stony. With the pond in position and levels checked again, backfill with sand or fine soil, being careful not to push the pond out of level.

6 Fill with fresh water and backfill further if necessary as the water level rises, checking the level frequently to make sure the liner has not moved. Allow to stand for a few days before stocking with plants.

4 On stony soil, you may need to line the hole further with loft insulation or special pond liner underlay. Trim the liner underlay so that it fits neatly into the hole.

5 Ease the liner into position without stretching it unduly. Choose a warm day because this will make it more flexible. Weigh down the edges with stones, then fill the pond slowly. Ease the liner into position so that it follows the contours as the pond fills.

6 Once the pond is full, trim back the excess liner to leave an overlap of at least 15cm (6in) around the edge. Cover the overlapping liner with paving or other edging. To disguise the liner, overlap the water's edge by 2.5cm (1in).

Stocking a pond

It is essential to choose the right blend of aquatic plants to create a natural balance in your pond. Select plants that suit the size of the pond so they don't need regular chopping back to keep them in check.

Types of water plant

Pond plants can be grouped according to the depth of water they require.

Deep-water plants These plants, which include *Nymphaea* (water lily), are essential to the overall health of the pond because the leaves cover the surface and provide shade, which discourages the growth of algae and offers a cool retreat for fish.

Marginal plants The roots of marginal plants are in water but the stems and leaves grow above the surface. Most flower for only a short time between late spring and late summer, so try to combine varieties with different flowering times to prolong the period of interest. In addition, include plants with attractive foliage, such as the variegated irises *I. pseudacorus*

An informal pool, where nature is allowed to have its way, will soon become a haven for wildlife.

'Variegata' or *I. laevigata* 'Variegata', or *Schoenoplectus lacustris* subsp. *tabernaemontani*, which lasts for months.

Submerged aquatic plants Although not as ornamental as other plants, submerged aquatics are important for keeping the pond healthy. They use up excess nutrients that would otherwise encourage blanketweed and other algae. They also oxygenate the water, improving the environment for fish and other pond creatures. Add around ten bunches per square metre (yard) of pond surface area.

Free-floating plants These plants, together with those that live in deep water, provide shade for fish and discourage the growth of algae. Aim to cover about one-third of the surface area with floating foliage.

HOW TO PLANT AQUATICS

1 Fill a basket sold for water plants with special aquatic compost. The hessian (burlap) liner will help prevent the soil from falling through the mesh sides of the basket.

2 Remove the plant from its container and plant it in the basket at its original depth, using a trowel to add or remove aquatic compost as necessary. Firm it in well.

3 Cover the aquatic compost with gravel to help keep it in place when you put the container in the pond and to minimize disturbance by fish. Soak the plant in a bucket of water to remove air bubbles.

Planting

The easiest way to introduce an aquatic plant is to use a special planting basket. If you use one of the traditional mesh-sided baskets, line it with hessian (burlap) before planting so the compost does not wash out. The extra lining will not be necessary if you are using a modern micromesh aquatic basket. Use specially formulated aquatic compost because standard potting compost (soil mix) will allow nutrients to leach out, encouraging excessive algae growth. Good quality topsoil can also be used if you find it difficult to get aquatic compost.

Although you can put more than one plant in a large basket, you are better off planting singly so that individual plants can later be removed and divided or replaced more easily. Top the basket with a 2cm (½in) deep layer of pea gravel to stop fish disturbing the compost and muddying the water. Soak the basket in a bucket of water before positioning it in the pond.

4 Once thoroughly soaked, carefully place the plant on the shelf at the edge of the pool so that the container is covered by 3–5cm (1–2in) of water.

HOW TO PLANT AN OXYGENATOR

Submerged aquatic plants are called oxygenators and are essential for the health of the pond. To plant an oxygenator such as *Lagarosiphon major* (curly water thyme), tie it to a stone, then drop it in the water. The plant will root in the sediment at the bottom of the pool.

STOCKING A WILDLIFE POND

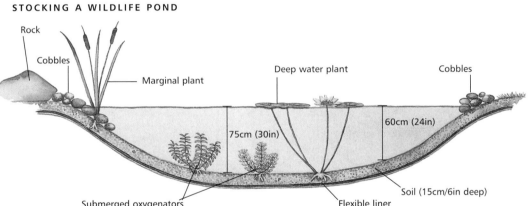

This pool has a sloping edge to allow birds and animals to reach the water easily. Surround it with lush plantings and long grass to provide cover for visiting wildlife.

INTRODUCING FISH

Never place fish directly in the pond. First acclimatize them by floating the plastic bag that you transported them in on the surface of the water for an hour. This will allow the water temperatures to equalize gradually, after which the fish can be allowed to swim out of the bag.

Trouble-free pond plants

Deep-water plants
Nymphaea 'Attraction'
   N. 'Aurora'
   N. 'Ellisiana'
   N. 'Froebelii'
   N. 'Pygmaea Helvola'
Nymphoides peltata (water fringe)
Orontium aquaticum (golden club)

Marginal plants
Acorus calamus 'Variegatus'
Butomus umbellatus (flowering rush)
Caltha palustris 'Flore Pleno'
   (marsh marigold)
Iris laevigata 'Variegata'
Myosotis scorpioides
Pontederia cordata (pickerel weed)
Schoenoplectus lacustris
Typha minima

Submerged and floating plants
Azolla filiculoides (fairy moss)
Eichihornia crassipes (water hyacinth)
Eleocharis acicularis (hair grass)
Fontinalis antipyretica
Hydrocharis morsus-ranae
Ranunculus aquatilis
Stratiotes aloides (water soldier)
Trapa natans
Utricularia vulgaris

Pond care

Once established, a well-planned and constructed pond will largely look after itself. There are, however, a number of seasonal tasks worth carrying out that will help maintain the equilibrium.

Spring

Once the coldest weather is over, you can remove the netting keeping out wind-blown leaves and exchange the pond heater for a pump. The pond will come to life in mid-spring, when marginal plants put on new growth, the first lily pads appear and on a mild day fish can be seen at the surface. This is the time to start feeding the fish and to carry out a pond spring clean. Scoop any dead or rotting leaves from the pond to prevent them from fouling the water.

Mid- to late spring is an ideal time to add new plants to your pond. It is worth adding special fertilizer tablets to the compost of established plants. Make sure they are pushed well into the compost so that nutrients do not leach out into the water and encourage the growth of algae. If the pond tends to go green with algae at this time of year, place a barley straw pad (available from garden retailers) in the pond.

A mature specimen of the water lily *Nymphaea* 'Attraction' in early summer.

Summer

Choose a warm, fine day in late spring or early summer to remove and divide overgrown plants.

Fish will need feeding on a regular basis throughout summer. Try to feed in the morning and clear away any uneaten food left floating on the surface of the water after about 10 minutes using a fine-mesh fishing net. This will prevent it from sinking to the bottom and rotting.

Pond problems often occur in summer. Use a jet of water from a hose to knock off sap-sucking pests from water lily pads. Spreading filaments of blanketweed should be scooped out with a bamboo cane or wire rake. Before placing it on the compost heap, leave the weed on the side of the pond for a couple of hours to allow any pond creatures to make their way back into the pond. Use a fine-mesh net to scoop out floating duckweed, which can quickly spread over the surface of a pond. Top up the water level as necessary and clean the filter of the pump if there appears to be a blockage. In heavy, thundery weather you may

HOW TO DIVIDE A WATER LILY

1 Lift the water lily in spring, put it in a bowl of water and wash it free of compost. Trim back any over-long roots with secateurs (pruners) and remove any damaged leaves.

2 Using a sharp knife, cut the rhizome into pieces, making sure that each section has roots and leaves or leaf buds.

3 Pot the sections up into pots of aquatic compost. Add a layer of gravel to prevent the compost being disturbed. Put the pot in a bowl of water and keep it in a shaded place. New leaves will appear within a few months.

HOW TO OVERWINTER TENDER AQUATICS

1 Net a few plants in good condition. They may already be deteriorating in the cooler weather, so don't save any that appear to be rotting or badly damaged.

2 Put a handful of the plants in a plastic container of pond water. Don't overcrowd them – use extra containers rather than allow them to touch. Some gardeners put a little soil in the bottom to provide nutrients.

3 Keep the plants in a light, frost-free place, such as a greenhouse. You might be able to keep them on a cool windowsill. Top up or change the water occasionally so that it does not become stagnant.

see fish gasping for air at the surface. Increase oxygen levels in the water by turning on the pump or by playing a jet of water from a hose on to the surface.

Autumn

The main tasks of autumn are to clear away the dying foliage of marginal plants and to prevent leaves from nearby deciduous trees from falling into the pond. Cut down marginals so that the tops of their stems are above the water surface when the pond is full. Remove any other organic material. Place tender aquatics in a bucket of pond water

somewhere cool but frost free, such as a greenhouse, until spring. In early autumn use a high-protein fish food to help fish build up sufficient reserves to survive the winter, then when the weather cools stop feeding altogether. Remove the pond pump, store carefully and replace with a pool heater, which will help keep at least part of the water's surface ice free in freezing weather.

Winter

If you completed all the pond-care tasks on time in autumn, little needs to be done other than to keep the pond clear of fallen leaves that are

still blowing about the garden and to make sure that at least part of the pond's surface remains free of ice during prolonged cold weather.

The easiest way to clear an area of ice is to stand a pan of hot water on the surface to melt a hole. Never hit the ice with a hammer to try to break it up because this will send shock waves through the pond that can harm fish. If a substantial ice-sheet has formed on the pond, you could siphon off a couple of inches of water from underneath the ice. The layer of air will help to insulate the water and prevent any more water from freezing.

SUMMER MAINTENANCE

Submerged oxygenators, such as *Lagarosiphon major*, and rampant growers, such as *Myriophyllum aquaticum*, will clog the pond unless you clear them out periodically. Remove the excess with a net or rake.

HOW TO PREPARE A POND FOR WINTER

1 A small pond can be protected from the worst of the leaf fall with a fine-mesh net. Anchor it just above the surface of the pond. Remove the leaves regularly and eventually take the netting off.

2 If you cannot cover your pond with a net, use a fish net or rake to remove leaves regularly – not only from the surface but also from below the surface. Decomposing leaves in the pond will pollute the water.

Bog gardens

Marshy bog gardens associate particularly well with water features, helping to create a natural setting, but they are also worth considering as features in their own right because they allow you to grow a wider range of plants in your garden.

Deciding on a site

Bog gardens are areas of permanently wet soil that are suitable for growing marginal and wetland plants. They look particularly effective alongside water features, where the lush foliage and colourful flowers help to integrate pools into the rest of the garden. A bog garden can be either planted in a permanently water-logged area in your garden or created in a dry spot using a pond liner.

The soil in a bog garden must be kept moist, which may mean regular watering during the summer months. Before planting a bog garden consider installing a seep hose under the soil for automatic watering.

Creating a bog garden

A bog garden is very easy to create. If you are building a pond at the same time you can simply extend the excavation and use a single piece of flexible liner to line both the pond

CREATING A BOGGY MARGIN TO A POND

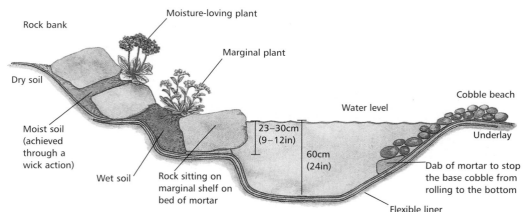

Adding a boggy margin to a pond will make it more attractive and help integrate it into the surrounding garden. It is the perfect spot to experiment with unusual moisture-loving plants.

and the bog area. However, you can also create a bog garden near to an existing water feature or make it a feature in its own right. Simply scoop out an area about 45cm (18in) deep with sloping sides and a flat base to the hole. Don't make it too small, otherwise the soil will be prone to drying out, but try to keep the widest part no more than 2m (6ft) across so that it will be easy to reach and maintain the plants in the centre. Line the hole with sand as you would a pond and then cover with a flexible liner.

If you are building the bog garden at the same time as the pond, make

a ridge of stones along the border between the two and lay some fine-mesh netting on the bog garden side along the inside of the stones. This will stop soil washing through the stones and muddying the pond. To allow excess water to drain away,

Good bog garden plants

Aruncus	*Hosta*
Astilbe	*Iris*
Caltha	*Ligularia*
Cardamine	*Lysichiton*
Filipendula	*Lobelia* (some)
Hardy ferns	*Primula* (some)
Hemerocallis	*Zantedeschia*

HOW TO PLANT A BOG PLANT

1 Adjust the position of the bog plants while they are still in their pots until you are satisfied with the arrangement. Water each container well and allow to drain before planting the centre of the bog garden first.

2 Make a planting hole slightly larger than the container and plant at the same depth. Firm the soil carefully around each plant.

3 Level the soil over the bog garden after planting is complete and cover the surface with a layer of loose organic mulch to help prevent moisture loss. Take care not to pile the mulch against the stems of the plants.

HOW TO PROPAGATE BOG PLANTS BY SEED

1 Fill the base of a seed tray with stones for drainage, then fill with aquatic compost to within 1cm (½in) of the top.

2 Firm down the aquatic compost with a tray of the same size, but do not compact it. Moisten the compost by standing the tray in shallow water for a couple of hours until the surface of the compost darkens with moisture.

3 Scatter the seeds thinly and cover with compost. Spray regularly to keep the compost moist. When they are big enough to handle, pot up the seedlings and grow them on.

make a few well-spaced holes in the bog garden liner and cover with a 5cm (2in) layer of grit. Trim the flexible liner to leave a 15cm (6in) overlap on all sides before filling the bog garden with a mixture of three parts topsoil to one part well-rotted organic matter. Allow the soil to settle for a couple of weeks and then mix in a slow-release fertilizer. Water well before planting up with your chosen bog plants. Start in the centre and work your way outwards. As a finishing touch, cover the liner flap with decorative pebbles or other stones. Alternatively, if it is next to a border, cover it with a thin layer of soil or mulch.

Careful planting of the bog garden will help to make a subtle transition to the wider garden.

Rock gardens

Like ponds or watercourses, rock gardens benefit from an open site. If planned well, they can each enhance the other. In a level garden the soil excavated during pond installation can be used to form the base.

Building a rock garden

When you build a rock garden, aim as far as possible to create as natural-looking outcrop, otherwise it will take on the appearance of a rock-encrusted heap of soil. The most important ingredient is the rocks, which are more likely to "gel" as a rocky outcrop if they are of the same natural stone. Choose a type of rock that has clear strata lines running through it and an attractive texture and colour. Limestone and sandstone are perhaps the best rock types, but it is possible to create an attractive feature from other types of rock.

You will need a range of sizes of rock – anything from 15kg (33lb) to 100kg (well over 200lb) – so make sure you have help to manoeuvre the larger stones. If you live near a quarry, use this as your source, otherwise suppliers can be found in local directories, and a limited selection of rocks is offered at some garden centres.

Rock gardens are perfect for growing a selection of alpine plants.

HOW TO BUILD A ROCK GARDEN

1 The base of the rock garden is a good place to dispose of rubble and subsoil excavated if you have dug out a pond.

2 Use a special soil mixture for the top 15–23cm (6–9in), especially if soil excavated from a pond is used. Mix equal parts of soil, coarse grit and peat (or peat substitute) and spread evenly over the mound.

3 Lay the first rocks at the base, making sure that the strata run in the same direction, and add more soil mixture around them.

Designing a rock garden

The design should suit the situation. On sloping ground you can build a natural-looking outcrop or a series of terraces or a combination of the two for a very large rockery. On a level site a more acute outcrop, with strata lines at a 45 degree angle, can work well, or choose a series of flattish stones to create a pavement effect with horizontal strata lines.

Careful planning is essential. Mark out the site using string and improve drainage if necessary – if you have heavy soil this may mean digging a hole 30cm (12in) deep, half-filling it with rubble and covering it with a layer of sharp sand before topping with good-quality, free-draining topsoil mixture.

Building a rockery on a slope

If practicable start at the bottom of the slope and build in layers. Choose the best-looking stone to start building your rockery and position it in the middle so that the strata lines angle gently back into the ground. About one-third of the stone will be underground, so you will have to scoop out a hole to accommodate it. Then add stones either side so that the strata lines

HOW TO PLANT A ROCK GARDEN

1 Position the plants while still in their pots so that you can see how they look and adjust if necessary. Alpines are a good choice of plant for a rock garden.

2 Use a trowel to take out a hole a little larger than the rootball. You can buy narrow trowels that are particularly useful for planting in the crevices between rocks.

3 Make sure that the plant is at the correct depth, then trickle gritty soil around the roots and firm it well.

4 Finish off by covering the exposed surface with more grit to improve drainage and protect leaves from splashing mud.

fall away at exactly the same angle. Make sure that each stone is set firm before positioning the next by ramming soil around the rock. Repeat the process for each layer of the rockery, then fill any gaps with a

free-draining mixture consisting of equal parts of good quality topsoil, peat (or peat substitute) and coarse grit. Then plant and mulch the surface with stone chippings to match the rocks used in the rockery.

4 Lever the next row of rocks into position. Using rollers and levers is the best way to move heavy rocks around.

5 As each layer is built up, add more of the soil mixture and consolidate it around each of the rocks in turn.

6 Make sure that the sides slope inwards and make the top reasonably flat rather than building it into a pinnacle. Position the plants, then cover the exposed soil with a layer of stone chippings.

Vegetable gardening

Growing your own vegetables is one of the most satisfying aspects of gardening. On a large plot you can even become self-sufficient if you plan carefully and are able to put in the necessary time and effort. Even in a small garden you can grow a wide range of vegetables, which will reduce your grocery bills and provide tasty meals throughout the year.

There are a number of factors to consider before you embark on redesigning your plot to grow vegetables. First, look at the garden itself, its location, aspect, soil type and size. Second, assess the labour force: how good are you at gardening and how much time will you be able to devote to tending your crops? Don't forget holidays, because these tend to fall at the most inconvenient times. Then, consider whether you intend to grow vegetables to eat fresh or to produce sufficient for winter storage. Finally, draw up a list of the vegetables you like to eat.

Wigwams or tepees of long bamboo canes support runner beans.

Planning a kitchen garden

The initial planning is the most important part of growing a range of vegetables for the kitchen. It is essential to plan for a continuous supply and to avoid gluts and shortages.

Choosing a style

Careful planning will help you to achieve a continuity of supply of vegetables for the kitchen table. Timing is critical, and the best way to get this right is to work out when you want particular crops to reach maturity and then to work backwards to decide on the best possible sowing dates.

There are three main systems for growing vegetables: in rows in a designated plot; in permanent vegetable beds; and randomly mixed throughout the garden. The last is perhaps the most aesthetically pleasing in a small suburban garden, but vegetable crops have to compete with neighbouring plants for light, moisture and nutrients, which reduces growth and subsequent yields. For this reason most gardeners prefer the traditional method of growing vegetables in a dedicated area that can be kept clear of other plants and prepared specifically with the needs of the vegetables in mind.

Recently, a system of permanent beds, called no-dig beds, has become fashionable. The vegetables are grown in beds surrounded by permanent paths, which means that they can be grown more closely together, and yields are higher because the soil is not compacted by trampling. This system also requires less effort to prepare the soil – often no digging is needed once the system is set up – and because rows are much shorter, access to all parts of the vegetable area is easier. Furthermore, because the plants are grown close together the opportunities for weeds to become established are minimized. This system can also be

Sowing crops in rows in a designated vegetable plot makes weeding much easier.

used effectively in a small garden, especially if you choose a decorative material for the paths.

Creating no-dig beds

Plan the design of the beds carefully. A series of straight beds may be the most suitable design on an allotment, but in a small garden a system of interlocking beds could be more attractive. However, do not choose too intricate a scheme because this will reduce the amount of growing space and undermine the advantages of growing vegetables in this way.

The beds should be about 1.2m (4ft) wide, so that the centre can be reached from either side, and the paths should be about 30cm (12in) wide. If you want wheelbarrow access you will need to increase the path width accordingly. Use tanalized gravel boards 15cm (6in) wide to make the sides. Support them with stakes 45cm (18in) long and 5cm (2in) square, at the corners and at 1m (3ft) intervals along the sides. Dig the beds over thoroughly, then

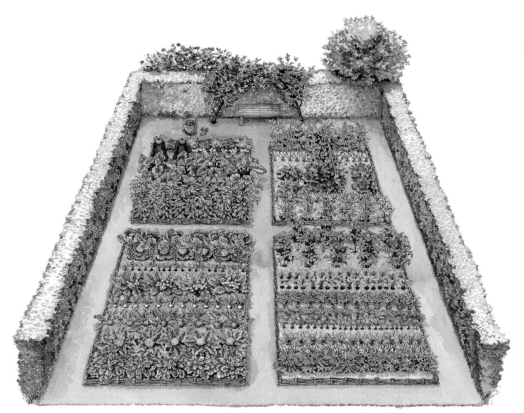

When there is room in the garden, a dedicated plot is the most productive way of growing vegetables. Dividing the vegetable garden into beds makes crop rotation much simpler.

scoop the topsoil from the paths into the beds and top up with a mixture of equal parts of well-rotted organic matter and topsoil. Cover the paths with a weed-suppressing membrane and cover this with chipped bark or another all-weather material.

Crop rotation

If you grow the same family of vegetables on the same ground year after year, soil-borne pests and diseases will build up, reducing yields. The easiest way to avoid this on permanent vegetable plots and beds is to use a crop rotation system over three or four years. This method of gardening also has the advantage of using your time in the garden efficiently. For example, a plot can be heavily manured when it is dug in the autumn, providing ideal conditions for cabbages. The following year the plot can simply be dug over, ready for planting root crops, which do not like the soil to be too rich.

Crops are grouped by their family. Grow each group in a different area, then rotate the crops around the areas with each year. There are four main groups.

Brassicas This family includes broccoli, Brussels sprouts, cabbage, calabrese, cauliflowers, kale, kohl rabi and radishes.

Legumes The vegetables in this group include peas, French (green) beans, runner beans and broad (fava) beans.

Onion family This group includes shallots, garlic, leeks and spring onions (scallions) as well as onions.

Root crops Potatoes, parsnips, swedes (rutabaga), beetroot (beets), carrots and turnips are all defined as root crop vegetables.

If you are using a four-year rotation system, each of these crops can be grown in a different bed, but if you are working on a three-year system, combine the legume and onion crops in one bed. It may also be worth creating a permanent bed

Vegetable beds filled with colourful, strongly growing crops can be as attractive as more conventional ornamental plants.

to grow crops such as asparagus, rhubarb, artichokes and sea kale. Whether you adopt a three- or four-year rotation, make sure that brassicas, in particular, are moved every year.

HOW TO PLAN A THREE-YEAR CROP ROTATION

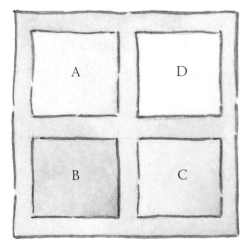

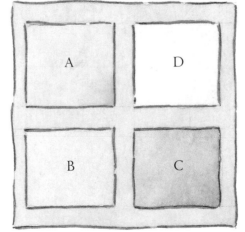

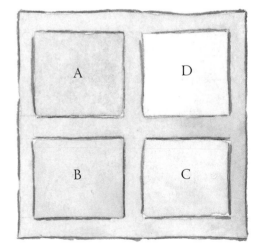

Year 1
There are four beds in the vegetable garden. Crops are grown in a four-year or three-year rotation system.

Bed A   Onions and legumes
Bed B   Root crops
Bed C   Brassicas and lettuces
Bed D   Permanent

Year 2
With the exception of certain vegetables, which need a permanent site, the crops are planted in a different bed each year.

Bed A   Brassicas and lettuces
Bed B   Onions and legumes
Bed C   Root crops
Bed D   Permanent

Year 3
Moving the crops in this way helps to prevent pests and diseases lingering from one year to the next and allows efficient soil management.

Bed A   Root crops
Bed B   Brassicas and lettuces
Bed C   Onions and legumes
Bed D   Permanent

Sowing vegetables

Most vegetables are raised from seed, but the techniques you use will depend on the time and facilities you have available and on the crops you want to grow.

Buying vegetable seed

There is an extensive range of crops available by mail order from seed companies, from gardening websites and from garden centres. If you are buying by post, order seeds during the winter months when you are planning your next year's planting so that you are ready to sow in early spring. There are three main ways of sowing, and the method you use will depend on the crops you grow.

Sowing indoors

Indoor sowing in pots or modular seed trays (flats) is an ideal way of getting vegetables off to an early start. This approach gives the most reliable results, but it is expensive because you need to invest in equipment, such as a propagator, and provide somewhere heated to grow them on. The main advantage is that you can sow exactly when you want to, regardless of the weather and soil

After sowing seeds in blocks or trays, they should be thoroughly watered and then placed in a warm position for germination.

conditions. It is a good system for crops such as tomatoes, which are expensive to buy as seed, and tender crops, such as courgettes (zucchini), which need to be kept under cover until the threat of frost has passed.

Sowing in seedbeds

Some crops, notably brassicas, are best sown in a specially prepared area and then transplanted when they reach a suitable size. The main advantage of this system is that you can use your best piece of ground to raise the crops from seed and give them extra attention during this

Crops planted in a seedbed can be protected from bad weather with cloches. They are transferred to their final position in late spring.

critical growing period. Raising plants in a seedbed also makes it practical to protect the seedlings from the worst of the weather using cloches. This system is of particular value for widely spaced crops that would otherwise occupy a lot of growing area while still young. It is not suitable for crops that resent root disturbance, however.

Sowing direct in rows

Many crops are best sown direct in the rows where they are to grow on to maturity. This is a good system for crops, such as broad (fava) beans

HOW TO SOW SEEDS IN DRILLS

1 Most vegetables grown in rows, such as carrots, are sown in drills. Use a garden line to make sure the drills – and therefore the rows – are straight.

2 Open up a shallow drill with the corner of a hoe or rake. Refer to the seed packet for the recommended depth.

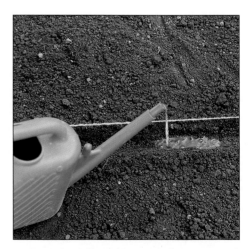

3 Flood the drills with water before sowing if the weather is dry. Do it before sowing rather than after so that the seeds are not washed away or into clumps.

TECHNIQUES FOR SOWING SEED AND PLANTING BULBS

1 Parsnip, carrot, onion and parsley seeds are sometimes germinated then mixed with wallpaper paste, placed in a bag and squeezed over the soil. This is called fluid sowing.

2 Carrots must be sown thinly. Mix the seed with a little silver sand, which makes it easier to sow both thinly and evenly.

3 Large seeds, such as peas, can be sown individually, at the correct spacing in a wide drill. Make sure the trench is the right depth.

4 Shallots are spaced about 15cm (6in) apart. Push the bulbs into the drill so that the tips are just protruding. Pull the soil back around them with a hoe or rake.

and peas, that can be set out at the correct spacing and for crops, such as carrots and radishes, that do not like to be moved once they have germinated. The main drawback is that you waste seed in having to thin plants to the correct spacing, and through variable germination and losses from pests and diseases.

Fluid sowing

In dry soil or during the summer months germination from direct sowing can be erratic. One way to overcome this is to use a technique called fluid sowing. Pre-germinate the seed on sheets of moist kitchen paper. When the roots are just showing, before the leaves open, mix the seeds with a half-strength, fungicide-free wallpaper paste or a special sowing gel. Put the mix into a plastic bag and make a small hole by cutting off one corner. Twist the top of the bag to prevent the paste oozing out, then squeeze out the mixture into the prepared seed drill as if you were icing a cake.

4 Sprinkle the seeds evenly along the drill. Do this carefully now and you will save time later when you have to thin the seedlings.

5 Cover the row of seeds with compost (soil mix) if your soil is stony.

6 Use a rake to return the excavated soil to the drills. Rake in the direction of the row, not across it, otherwise you might spread the seeds and produce an uneven row.

Planting vegetables

A limited number of vegetables are now available to buy, either as seedlings or as plants in pots. They can be good value if you want just a few plants or for those vegetables that are tricky to raise from seed. Plant out these vegetables as soon as you can. You will also need to plant out the crops sown under glass, and those grown in seedbeds.

Buying plants

If you are buying plants from your local garden centre, ask when the next delivery is due and visit as soon as possible afterwards so that the plants are not left in inappropriate conditions. Choose stocky plants with dark green leaves and no signs of discoloration. Yellow leaves are a sign of starvation, and a blue tinge could indicate that the plants have been allowed to get too cold. Also avoid plants with signs of pests and diseases, such as speckled leaves, and check growing tips for pests, such as aphids, which not only weaken plants but also transmit diseases, such as leaf viruses.

PLANTING BOUGHT SEEDLINGS

This courgette (zucchini) has been grown in a fibre pot so that the roots are disturbed as little as possible when it is planted out. Buying seedlings of frost-tender plants is a good option if you are not able to provide the conditions that are needed to germinate the seeds yourself.

Planting vegetables in rows makes it much easier when weeding as you will be able to identify more easily what are weeds and what are wanted plants.

Vegetable planner

Vegetable	germination temperature	sowing depth	planting distance in rows	distance between rows
Bean, broad (fava)	5°C (40°F)	5cm (2in)	15cm (6in)	50cm (20in)
Bean, French (green)	10°C (50°F)	5cm (2in)	8cm (3in)	45cm (18in)
Bean, runner	10°C (50°F)	5cm (2in)	15cm (6in)	60cm (24in)
Beetroot (beet)	7°C (45°F)	2.5cm (1in)	5cm (2in)	15cm (6in)
Broccoli	5°C (40°F)	5cm (2in)	60cm (24in)	60cm (24in)
Brussels sprouts	5°C (40°F)	5cm (2in)	60cm (24in)	1m (3ft)
Cabbage	5°C (40°F)	5cm (2in)	30cm (12in)	30cm (12in)
Calabrese	5°C (40°F)	5cm (2in)	25cm (10in)	30cm (12in)
Carrot	7°C (45°F)	2.5cm (1in)	8cm (3in)	15cm (6in)
Cauliflower	5°C (40°F)	2.5cm (1in)	45cm (18in)	60cm (24in)
Courgette (zucchini)	15°C (60°F)	2.5cm (1in)	1m (3ft)	1m (3ft)
Leek	7°C (45°F)	2.5cm (1in)	23cm (9in)	23cm (9in)
Lettuce	5°C (40°F)	1cm (½in)	30cm (12in)	30cm (12in)
Marrow (large zucchini)	15°C (60°F)	2.5cm (1in)	1m (3ft)	1m (3ft)
Onion	7°C (45°F)	1cm (½in)	4cm (1½in)	23cm (9in)
Parsnip	7°C (45°F)	1cm (½in)	15cm (6in)	30cm (12in)
Pea	5°C (40°F)	2.5cm (1in)	5cm (2in)	45cm (18in)
Radish	5°C (40°F)	1cm (½in)	1cm (½in)	15cm (6in)
Spinach	10°C (50°F)	1cm (½in)	15cm (6in)	30cm (12in)
Swede (rutabaga)	5°C (40°F)	2.5cm (1in)	15cm (6in)	30cm (12in)
Sweetcorn (corn)	10°C (50°F)	2.5cm (1in)	35cm (14in)	35cm (14in)
Tomato	15°C (60°F)	2.5cm (1in)	40cm (16in)	45cm (18in)
Turnip	15°C (60°F)	2.5cm (1in)	13cm (5in)	23cm (9in)

PLANTING MODULE SEEDLINGS

Cabbages and cauliflowers are often raised in modules so that the seedlings receive less of a shock when they are transplanted. Many modules are designed so that you can remove the plant by gently squeezing the base while gently supporting the plant at the top.

HOW TO MINIMIZE ROOT DISTURBANCE WHEN PLANTING PEAS

1 Start off the seeds in a length of old gutter. Block the ends and fill with soil. Sow the seeds about 5–8cm (2–3in) apart and cover with soil. Place the gutter in a greenhouse or cold frame, and water regularly to keep the soil moist.

2 When the seedlings are ready to plant out in their final position in the garden, make a shallow drill with a draw hoe. Carefully slide the peas out of the gutter and into the row. The seedlings will need to be thinned out as they grow.

Planting out vegetables

Hardy vegetables, such as cabbages, Brussels sprouts and other brassicas, that have been kept outside should be ready for planting out in the garden as soon as soil conditions allow. However, plants displayed under cover at the garden centre will need hardening off before being planted out. You will also need to harden off plants you have grown from seed in a greenhouse or a cold frame. It is important not to buy tender varieties too early in the season, otherwise you will have to keep them in a sheltered position until the risk of frosts has passed.

When planting out vegetables, try to minimize the root disturbance so that the plants don't suffer a check in growth. Water the seedlings before planting and set them out at the same depth as they were in the container. Use a garden line and cane marked with the correct spacing to make planting easier. Most vegetables are planted in straight rows, but sweetcorn (corn) should be planted in blocks of short rows because they are wind pollinated and need other plants growing on all sides to ensure a good set. Plant seedlings and container-grown plants at the correct distances apart.

If the weather is bad or the soil conditions prevent immediate planting, keep container plants well watered. If the delay is over two weeks, repot into the next size pot.

HOW TO TRANSPLANT SEEDLINGS GROWN IN A SEEDBED

1 Loosen the soil with a fork or trowel. It is best to lift each plantlet individually with a trowel, but if they have not been thinned sufficiently this may be difficult.

2 Plant with a trowel and firm the soil well. A convenient way to firm soil around the roots is to insert the blade of the trowel about 5cm (2in) away from the plant and press it firmly towards the roots.

3 Brassicas need to be planted firmly. Test this by tugging a leaf after planting. Always water in thoroughly after transplanting.

Growing legumes and onions

Beans, peas, onions and leeks are essential ingredients in the kitchen and can be very rewarding to grow in the garden.

Legumes

Treat most beans as half-hardy annuals and either sow them indoors in early spring, ready for planting out after the last frost, or sow direct outside into prepared soil in late spring. However, broad beans and peas can be sown direct outside in late winter or early spring.

Broad (fava) beans Sow 5cm (2in) deep and 15cm (6in) apart in a no-dig bed or 10cm (4in) apart in double rows spaced 50cm (20in) apart elsewhere. Sow an early crop in mid-winter under the protection of cloches, or in late winter, and a main crop in early spring. Pinch out 8cm (3in) of the growing tip as the first beans start to form to discourage aphids. Water well from this stage and provide support in exposed gardens using stout bamboo canes and string either side of the row.

Runner beans Sow indoors in deep pots in early spring and plant out after hardening off when the threat

HOW TO PLANT RUNNER BEANS

Runner beans should be planted against a wigwam of canes to provide support as they grow.

of frost has passed. Alternatively, sow direct outside against a supporting tent or wigwam of 1.8m (6ft) canes, spaced 15cm (6in) apart with 60cm (24in) between rows about a fortnight before the expected last frost. Sow spares to replace early losses. A second sowing in late spring will ensure a continuous crop until autumn. Mulch between rows and protect young plants from slugs. Do not allow pods to mature on the plant, otherwise cropping will be

Few things taste better than garden-fresh beans. Surpluses can be easily frozen for later in the year.

reduced. Grow over arches between no-dig beds for a decorative and productive feature.

Dwarf French beans (green beans) These tender plants need to be sown or planted out after the last frost. Sow beans 5cm (2in) deep in pots and then plant out in rows in mid-spring under the protection of cloches. Alternatively, the beans can

PINCHING OUT BEANS

Pinching out the tops of broad (fava) beans is good practice because it discourages aphids. The tops can then be boiled and eaten.

STAKING BEANS

Taller varieties of broad beans will need supporting with string tied to canes, which should be set at intervals along the rows.

SUPPORTING PEAS

Wire netting can be used to support shorter varieties of peas.

be planted 15cm (6in) apart in a no-dig bed or 8cm (3in) apart in rows. The rows should be spaced 45cm (12in) apart. A second crop of beans can be sown direct outside in mid-spring. Mulch between rows and protect young plants from slugs. Water well while pods are forming and provide support in exposed gardens with pea sticks or netting.

Peas Autumn sowings overwintered outside are often recommended for early crops of peas but are invariably disappointing. A more reliable method is to sow in lengths of guttering in early spring and plant out under cloches when about 8cm (3in) tall after hardening off. Later crops can be sown direct outside in a 15cm (6in) wide trench about 5cm (2in) deep, with staggered rows set 5cm (2in) apart. Make several sowings in succession every fortnight until early summer. Protect the peas from birds and mice. Mulch between rows to conserve soil moisture and water well while pods are forming. Taller varieties will need pea sticks or netting support.

The onion family

Bulbous vegetables including onions, leeks, garlic and shallots are very easy to grow and store, making them one of the most straightforward types of vegetables to provide a year-round supply for the kitchen. They can be raised from seed or grown from mini-bulbs (sets).

Onions Sow in early spring for a late summer harvest, or midsummer for a spring crop of Japanese varieties. Keep plants weed-free. There is no need to water unless the summer is particularly dry. Spring onions (scallions) should be sown in succession from mid-spring until early summer for a continuous supply throughout the summer

PLANTING OUT LEEK SEEDLINGS

Use a dibber to make a hole in the ground. The plant can then be dropped into the hole, and the earth firmed in around it.

months. In no-dig beds sow onions 5cm (2in) apart, or, elsewhere, sow in drills, that are about 1cm (½in) deep and 23cm (9in) apart. Thin out the plants to 4cm (1½in) apart once the seedling has straightened and later to 10cm (4in). Rows of spring onions need be only 10cm (4in) apart.

Onions raised in containers in the greenhouse should be planted out 10cm (4in) apart. Alternatively, plant onion sets in mid-spring about 10cm (4in) apart in rows that are spaced 23cm (9in) apart. Protect newly planted sets from birds. Hoe the soil carefully to keep the rows of onions free of weeds.

Leeks Sow in a well-prepared seedbed in drills about 1cm (½in) deep and 23cm (9in) apart, thinning the plants to 23cm (9in) apart. Pull up soil around the stems to blanch them. Make sure that you do not get soil between the leaves. Plant out greenhouse-raised plants and transplant seedlings raised in a seedbed when 20cm (8in) high. Plant into 15cm (6in) deep holes spaced 15cm (6in) apart in rows 30cm (12in) apart.

EARTHING UP LEEKS

As the leeks grow earth (hill) them up by pulling the soil up around the stems to blanch them. This will give the leeks a better flavour.

Shallots Sow as for onions, planting sets in early spring 15cm (6in) apart in rows 23cm (9in) apart during early spring. Keep the crop free from weeds, and water if necessary. Apply a mulch between the rows to conserve moisture.

Garlic Plant cloves during late winter or early spring about 2.5cm (1in) deep in rows spaced 15cm (6in) apart. Treat as described for shallots.

PLANTING OUT SHALLOTS

Once the shoots of container-grown shallots are about 10cm (4in) high, plant out in the garden, spacing them about 15cm (6in) apart, in rows that are 23cm (9in) apart.

Growing root crops

Root vegetables, which include crops such as carrots, parsnips and turnips, are reasonably easy to grow provided your soil is deep and not too stony. Root crops are biennials, which means that during their first year they build up reserves in a storage root to enable them to flower well the following year.

Cultivation

Most root crops prefer an open, sunny site. The soil should be light, and should not have been recently manured. Root crops prefer a moist soil, so you may have to water them in dry weather. They are usually hardy, and the vegetables can be left in the ground over winter, to be harvested as needed.

In very stony ground, root crops such as parsnips and carrots may fork and produce rather stunted growth. To avoid this, use a crowbar to make deep holes at the correct planting distance and fill them with potting compost (soil mix) so that the seeds can be sown in this.

A flourishing row of carrots coming to maturity.

HOW TO PLANT IN STONY SOIL

1 If the soil is very stony or of poor quality it is worth making improvements before planting. Use a crowbar to make a conical hole at the required planting distances.

2 Fill the hole with potting compost (soil mix). Sow the seed in the middle and then cover with more earth.

Beetroot (beets) Sow bolt-resistant varieties under cloches in early spring for an early summer crop, followed by a late spring sowing for a summer harvest. An early summer sowing will provide a crop in autumn and winter. Sow seed in a well-prepared seedbed in drills about 2.5cm (1in) deep and 15cm (6in) apart, spacing seeds 5cm (2in) apart. The seeds are in fact usually made up of a cluster of seeds and so produce several seedlings close together. Thin to leave the strongest plant at each station. When roots reach 2.5cm (1in) across, thin again by removing every other plant.

Carrots Sow carrot seeds under cloches in early spring for a crop by early summer. Sow maincrop varieties in succession every few

THINNING CARROTS

Thin carrots only if necessary as they resent disturbance. Choose a still, muggy evening to prevent the smell of carrots travelling and betraying their presence to carrotflies.

weeks from mid-spring for a midsummer crop to early summer for an autumn crop. A late sowing can also be made in late summer under cloches for a tender winter crop. Sow in a well-prepared seedbed in drills about 1cm (½in) deep and 15cm (6in) apart, thinning plants to 8cm (3in) apart when they are large enough to handle. Hand weed to keep the rows clear. Put up a 75cm (30in) high barrier of insect-proof

Beetroot growing in a raised bed. The bulk of the vegetable's swollen root sits on top of the ground so that you can watch its progress and determine when it is ready to harvest.

WATERING

Fennel plants, like root vegetables, need plenty of moisture. In dry periods you may have to water them to keep the crop healthy, but a good mulch should help.

mesh around the crop to prevent carrotfly. If necessary, cover the tops of developing carrots with soil to prevent them going green.

Parsnips Sow in mid-spring for a late summer harvest in a well-prepared seedbed in drills about 1cm (½in) deep and 30cm (12in) apart. Sow a few seeds together at 15cm (6in) intervals along the row, thinning seedlings to leave the strongest plant at each station.

Swede (rutabaga) Sow in late spring for an early autumn harvest in a well-prepared seedbed in drills about 1cm (½in) deep and 15cm (6in) apart. When large enough to handle, thin plants in stages until 30cm (12in) apart. Watch out for flea beetle.

Turnips Sow early varieties under cloches in early spring followed by crops sown in succession from mid-spring to early summer. A late sowing can also be made in late summer under cloches for spring greens. Sow in a well-prepared seedbed in drills about 1cm (½in) deep and 23cm (9in) apart, thinning to 13cm (5in) apart when they are large enough to handle.

Fennel Sow the seeds in early to midsummer in drills 1cm (½in) deep and 45cm (18in) apart. Thin the seedlings to 23cm (9in). When the bulbs begin to swell, draw up the soil around them to blanch, which will improve the taste.

Potatoes Although potatoes are relatively easy to grow, they take up a great deal of space and rewards are relatively low. However, they are worth growing if you particularly like an unusual variety or if you are fond of new potatoes, which are fairly expensive in the shops.

Place seed potatoes in the light to sprout (known as chitting) at a temperature of about 10°C (50°F). For an early crop, plant under cloches in late winter through a black polythene mulch, setting seed potatoes about 15cm (6in) deep and 30cm (12in) apart with 60cm (24in) between rows. Cover with a double layer of garden fleece to help insulate the crop.

Space later crops slightly wider and protect emerging shoots from frost by earthing up – pulling soil from between the rows to form a mound over the row. This will also eliminate weeds. You can also grow an early crop for a midwinter harvest in a large container, such as an empty plastic dustbin.

PLANTING POTATOES

Seed potatoes should be planted out after being placed in the light to sprout.

Growing leafy vegetables

Leafy vegetables such as cabbage, cauliflower and Brussels sprouts are all members of the brassica family and so can be treated in a similar way. They all suffer from the same range of pests and diseases, but these can largely be avoided if you use the right techniques.

Cultivation

Most brassicas do best in an open, sunny site in a soil that is fertile but free-draining. They do not like a soil that is too acid and it may be worth adding lime to bring the soil down to a pH of 6.5–7. You may have to protect Brussels sprouts, which grow fairly tall, from the wind. Some brassicas, such as savoy cabbages and Brussels sprouts, taste better after they have experienced a winter frost.

Brussels sprouts Sow under cloches in early spring for a late summer crop, wait until mid-spring for an autumn and winter harvest. Treat as for cabbages, except that the transplants should be 60cm (24in) apart in rows 90cm (36in) apart.

Stake tall varieties in winter and remove yellowing leaves. Firm soil around plants in winter if they are loosened by frost. There is a large amount of space between plants, so it may be worth intercropping with lettuces or radishes.

Cabbages By choosing the right combination of varieties you can have cabbages all the year round. Spring cabbages are sown in midsummer for cropping from early spring the following year, summer cabbages are sown under cloches in early spring for harvesting from midsummer onwards, while winter cabbages are sown in mid- to late spring for a crop from autumn until the middle of spring the following year. Sow in a well-prepared seedbed in drills about 1cm (½in) deep and 15cm (6in) apart, thinning plants to 8cm (3in) apart. When five leaves have developed on the seedlings they are ready for transplanting to their growing position. Space seedlings 30–45cm (12–18in) apart in the row and between rows depending on

Cauliflowers are sometimes scorched by the hot sun. Protect from discoloration by covering them with the inner leaves.

the variety. Make 15cm (6in) deep holes, firming well after planting. Place a 15cm (6in) square collar of carpet underlay, slit to the centre, around each seedling to protect against adult cabbage rootfly. Also cover with garden fleece or insect-proof mesh after planting to prevent butterflies from laying their eggs on your plants, and protect against birds. Keep weeds under control.

PLANTING IN A COLD FRAME

Cabbage plants can be started in a cold frame before moving to their final growing position.

This block of healthy Brussels sprouts has been inter-planted with red cabbages to create a highly decorative effect in the kitchen garden.

Cauliflowers More difficult to grow than other members of the cabbage family, cauliflowers are grouped into winter, summer and autumn varieties. All are sown from mid- to late spring to mature from early spring, early summer and early autumn respectively. Treat as for cabbages, but space the transplants 60cm (24in) apart both ways. It is important that the cauliflowers' growth is not checked because this causes irregular and undersized heads. Ensure the plants always have plenty of water.

Kale and broccoli Treat as for cabbages but space the transplants 45cm (18in) apart both ways. Stake tall varieties in winter and remove yellowing leaves. Firm soil around plants if they are loosened by frost. Kale should be kept steadily growing because it is slow to recover from any checks. Water during any dry spells.

Salad crops

These vegetables are the best crops for new gardeners to start with because they can be fitted in around other plants, even grown in flower beds and mixed borders. They grow

Lettuces grow relatively quickly and can be ready for harvesting from 5 to 12 weeks after sowing, depending on the variety. Start early sowings under glass; otherwise, sow directly into the bed.

and mature quicky and tend to suffer from fewer problems than many other vegetables.

Lettuces You can achieve a year-round harvest by selecting the right combination of varieties and sowing in succession. Sow undercover or under cloches in early spring for a crop in late spring and then follow this at intervals with further sowings made when the previous sowing has produced sturdy seedlings. Sow in a well-prepared seedbed in drills about 1cm (½in) deep and 30cm (12in) apart, thinning plants to 30cm (12in) apart when they are large enough to handle. Cover with insect-proof mesh to protect from insect pests (especially aphids) and birds. Slugs can also be a problem, so protect plants from these.

Radishes Site radishes between other slower-growing crops to make efficient use of space. Sow under cloches from early spring followed by crops sown in succession from mid-spring to early summer. A late sowing of winter radish can also be

made in late summer under cloches for a late autumn harvest. Sow in a well-prepared seedbed in drills about 1cm (½in) deep and 15cm (6in) apart in summer, or 23cm (9in) apart in winter. Thin seedlings if necessary to 2.5cm (1in) apart. Protect against birds and slugs and keep weeds under control.

HOW TO WEED

Weeding with a hand fork is often the best option when delicate plants are spaced very closely together.

HOW TO INTERCROP LETTUCES

Lettuces can be planted between slower growing plants. Here, they will be harvested before the cabbages overshadow them.

Protecting vegetables

The vegetable garden, with its rows of closely growing crops, is an ideal breeding ground for many pests and diseases. Always take preventative action before any problem gets out of hand.

Good garden hygiene

Most insect pests are fairly easy to control with chemicals, but in the vegetable garden it is always worth considering techniques that will help to prevent the pest from becoming a problem in the first place, making spraying unnecessary.

Plant debris and weeds will provide vital overwintering sites for pests and diseases and so must be cleared away to prevent problems persisting from one season to the next. Burn or throw away the material rather than composting to reduce the risk of the problem returning.

Most pests and diseases will not get a foothold if your plants are growing well at all times. Choose disease-resistant varieties whenever

A mixed garden that contains plenty of flowers will attract a host of welcome natural predators such as ladybirds (ladybugs) and hoverflies. They will attack any pests that arrive in the garden.

possible (see opposite) and, if you buy container-grown vegetables, choose healthy stock. It is essential that crops do not suffer a check in

growth due to lack of moisture or nutrients as this will weaken their ability to fight off an attack. Inspect vegetables regularly to spot pest and disease outbreaks early and take remedial action as promptly as possible. Caught early enough, most plants will recover from the pest or disease attacks.

USING NETS

Birds and butterflies can be kept at bay with fine-meshed nets.

USING WIRE NETTING

Wire-mesh nets can be used to guard your crops against rabbits and rodents.

PROTECTING BRASSICAS

Protect young brassicas from cabbage rootfly by placing a collar around the base of each plant. The collar can be made of plastic, felt or even a square of old carpet; the important factor is making a barrier.

Timing

Most pests have an annual life cycle, so if you understand when the pest is most likely to be a problem you can avoid it. For example, peas sown before early spring and after late spring will not be in flower when the pea moth is on the wing so cannot be attacked. Similarly, carrots sown by late spring will be harvested before midsummer to avoid carrotfly, and later sowings of brassicas can avoid the worst of the flea beetle attacks.

Barriers

Many pests can be out-smarted by using barriers. For example, after planting cabbage plants, place a 15cm (6in) square collar of plastic or carpet underlay, slit to the centre, around each seedling. This will prove to be an effective barrier to the cabbage rootfly adults as they try to lay their eggs. Similarly, seedlings that are susceptible to slugs and snails should be protected with individual cloches made from cut-down plastic drinks bottles.

Other pests, such as carrotfly and cabbage caterpillars, can be combated using physical barriers surrounding the crop. By putting up a 75cm (30in) high fence of insect-proof mesh around your carrots you can successfully prevent the low-flying carrotfly from reaching your plants. To deter cabbage caterpillars, cover susceptible crops with horticultural fleece or insect-proof mesh after planting to stop the adult butterflies from laying their eggs on your plants. Lay the crop cover loosely over the plants so that there is plenty of room for growth, burying the edges around the crop to prevent pests gaining access. These covers are also effective against other flying pests, including aphids.

Disease-resistant varieties

Brussels sprouts	powdery mildew	'Adonis', 'Cascade', 'Citadel', 'Cor', 'Icarus', 'Odette', 'Tavernos', 'Topline', 'Troika'
Cabbages	downy mildew	'Derby Day', 'Stonehead'
Calabrese	clubroot	'Trixie'
Courgettes (zucchini)	mosaic virus	'Defender', 'Supremo'
Leeks	rust	'Bandit', 'Conora', 'Poribleu', 'Poristo'
Lettuces	downy mildew	'Avondefiance', 'Challenge', 'Dolly', 'Musette', 'Soraya'
Marrows (large zucchini)	mosaic virus	'Tiger Cross'
Parsnips	canker	'Arrow', 'Avonresister', 'Gladiator', 'Javelin', 'Lancer', 'White Gem'
Potatoes	blackleg	'Kestrel', 'Maxine', 'Pentland Crown', 'Saxon'
	blight	'Cara', 'Maris Piper', 'Pentland Dell', 'Romano', 'Stirling', 'Valor';
	virus	'Pentland Crown', 'Sante', 'Wilja'
	nematode	'Accent', 'Cara', 'Concorde', 'Maris Piper', 'Nadine', 'Pentland Javelin', 'Sante'
	scab	'Accent', 'Carlingford', 'Nadine', 'Pentland Crown', 'Swift', 'Wilja'
	spraing	'Accent', 'Premiere', 'Romano'
Swedes (rutabaga)	mildew	'Marian'
Tomatoes	leafmould and wilt	'Blizzard', 'Counter', 'Dombito', 'Estrella', 'Shirley'

Pest-resistant varieties

Carrots	carrotfly	'Nandor', 'Nantucket', 'Flyaway', 'Sytan'
Lettuces	root aphid	'Avondefiance', 'Beatrice', 'Malika', 'Musette', 'Sabine'
Potatoes	eelworm	'Cara', 'Maris Piper', 'Pentland Javelin'
	slugs	'Pentland Dell', 'Romano'

USING HORTICULTURAL FLEECE

Physical barriers can be used to protect crops against pests. Here, fleece is used to cover brassicas to prevent butterflies from laying their eggs on the plants.

Harvesting vegetables

A well-planned kitchen garden will have a succession of crops that are ready to pick over a long period. The best time to harvest vegetables varies, of course, but the following guide will help you pick your vegetables in their prime.

Peas and beans

Pick peas when the pods swell and they have reached their full length. Harvest mangetout (snow) peas as soon as the blossom drops and pods are about 8cm (3in) long. Pick sugarsnap peas as the peas are just starting to form, but before the pods swell.

Pick over all pea plants regularly to ensure a continuous supply. After harvest is complete, put the plants on the compost heap.

Pick runner beans when they reach a usable size – say 15cm (6in). Pick French (green) beans when they have reached their full length, which is usually about 10cm (4in), but before the seed starts to swell. Both runner and French beans need to be picked regularly, before they get stringy, to ensure a continuous supply. Wait to harvest broad (fava) beans until the seeds have formed but before the stalk goes woody.

Root crops

Harvest beetroots (beets) when the roots are large enough to use but still tender, which is usually when the root starts to produce a square shoulder. Twist off the foliage but leave the stalks 5cm (2in) long to prevent bleeding.

Radishes and early carrots should be pulled as soon as they are large enough to use for the sweetest, most tender roots. Maincrop carrots should be lifted for storing at the end of the growing season. Cut off the leaves to prevent the root from going rubbery.

Turnips, parsnips and swedes (rutabaga) can be pulled as soon as they are large enough to use, or they can be left in the soil until needed and gently lifted with a fork. Twist off the leaves before storage.

Potatoes

Harvest early potatoes when the flowers open. The tubers should be the size of a large hen's egg and the skin should rub off easily. You do not have to dig up the whole plant, simply delve into the soil with your hands and remove tubers that have reached the right size, leaving undersized ones to develop further.

Maincrop potatoes should be harvested when the topgrowth (known as haulm) turns yellow and dies down and the skin on the tubers does not rub off. Remove the haulm and add it to the compost heap, then wait a week before lifting the potatoes. Remove all the tubers you find, even if they are too small to use, so they do not become a weed problem the next year.

Leafy vegetables

Spinach is harvested when the leaves are still young and tender; remove the fully developed outer leaves so that the younger inner ones can grow on. Repeat this process as the plant

HOW TO HARVEST VEGETABLES

Runner beans should be harvested regularly. Pick them over carefully to remove all maturing beans to ensure a continuous crop.

Harvest root vegetables such as carrots and parsnips by digging a fork well under the root and levering them out.

Lift maincrop potato tubers with a fork once the foliage has died down. You can leave them in the ground for longer if penetrating frosts are not likely to be a problem, but lift promptly if pests such as slugs appear.

grows to get a continuous supply. Harvest cabbages when the heads are firm and fleshy, and cauliflowers when the curds are firm and pure white but before they start to separate.

Vegetable fruits

Tomatoes should be harvested with a stalk when ripe and just starting to soften. At the end of the season you can pick unripe tomatoes to ripen off the plant. Place in a drawer with a banana skin to help the process.

Courgettes (zucchini) should be picked when young and firm and about 10cm (4in) long. Harvest regularly to ensure a continuous supply. Harvest marrows (large zucchini), squashes and pumpkins when they are large enough. At the end of the season remove all mature fruit before the first frost.

Pick sweetcorn (corn) when the tassels on the end of the cob turn brown and milky sap oozes from kernels when they are punctured with a fingernail. If the sap is watery the cob is not ready to be harvested.

HOW TO RIPEN ONIONS

1 Ripening can be hastened once onions near their maximum size by bending over their tops so the bulbs are exposed to as much sun as possible. As soon as the foliage has turned a straw colour and is brittle, lift the onions with a fork and leave them on the surface with their roots facing the sun for a week or two to dry off.

2 In wet seasons, finish off the hardening and ripening process by laying the onion bulbs on netting or wire mesh that is supported above the ground so that air can circulate freely. If the weather is very damp, cover the bulbs with cloches until you can store them.

The onion family

Harvest spring onions (scallions) as soon as they are large enough, before the bulb has started to form.

Maincrop onions should be harvested when mature. Loosen the soil under the bulbs when the tops topple over to speed the process. Lift completely about two weeks later. In wet years or on wet soils it may be necessary to lift the bulbs and dry them on mesh sheets or netting somewhere dry for a few weeks before storing.

Leeks can be harvested small or as mature vegetables. They can be left in the soil until needed, when they should be gently lifted with a fork.

Some vegetables are harvested by cutting through the stems as and when they are required. Swiss chard is a good example of this method of harvesting. The stem is cut close to the base. Some gardeners prefer to twist or snap the stems off at the base rather than cutting them.

Harvest cauliflowers by cutting the stem with a sharp knife just below the first ring of leaves.

Pick tomatoes as they become ripe, which will usually be when they turn red all over. Leave the stalk on.

Storing vegetables

If you have a glut of vegetables at the end of the season or want to have a continuity of supply throughout the winter, there are a number of techniques you can use to store them successfully.

Short-term storage

Although many vegetables can be stored in the freezer, it is best to save this method for crops that freeze particularly well and those that cannot be stored in any other way, because freezer space is usually limited. Some vegetables can be stored for short periods in the crisper drawer at the bottom of the refrigerator, where leafy crops such as lettuce can be kept for a fortnight or more – again, space will be limited. For longer term storage of most vegetables try the following methods. Store only perfect vegetables and make sure they are clean and dry before storage.

1 Carrots, like most root crops, can be stored in trays of just-moist sand or peat (peat moss or peat substitute). Place a shallow layer of peat in the bottom of a deep tray and then lay rows of carrots on top.

Packing in boxes

Many root crops, including carrots, parsnips, swedes (rutabaga), turnips and beetroot (beets), can be stored in boxes of sand in a cool, dark place, such as a garage or shed. Twist

2 Sprinkle peat over the carrots. Place another layer of carrots on top and cover these with more peat. Repeat with more layers until the tray is full, topping off with a final layer of peat.

off the foliage and pack the roots into sturdy boxes filled with moist sand, peat or peat substitute. Place the boxes in a frost-free area. This is a good method of storing root crops if you have particularly heavy soil that is difficult to work in winter or pest problems that might attack the roots if left outside in the ground.

Storing in sacks

Potatoes are best stored in purpose-made, double-thickness paper sacks (available from garden centres) because they keep out light and yet allow the movement of air that reduces the chances of rotting. Potatoes must be kept dark in a place where the temperature does not dip below 4°C (40°F); an insulated shed or garage is ideal.

Using nets

A few crops, including onions, shallots, garlic, marrows (large zucchini), pumpkins and cabbages, can be successfully stored in open-mesh nets. Hang up the nets in a well-ventilated, frost-free, dry place such as a garage.

It is essential that onions and shallots are completely dry before they are stored. Place them in trays or nets in a cool but frost-free place such as a cellar, shed or garage. Check the onions regularly, throwing away any that show signs of rot.

LEAVING CROPS IN THE GARDEN

Many root crops can be left in the ground insulated with straw.

Some hardy crops, including leeks, Brussels sprouts, cabbages and these red-topped turnips, can be left outdoors and harvested only when needed.

Storing dry

Onions, shallots and garlic also can be stored dry. Place them on trays, or twist string around the neck ends and hang up them up. Choose a dry and well-ventilated place such as a garage or shed to prevent rot. Peas and beans can also be stored dry. Lay the pods out to dry and remove the seeds when the pods are brittle. Put them in air-tight containers stored in a frost-free place.

Leaving in situ

Some root vegetables, such as carrots, swedes and turnips, as well as leeks and Brussels sprouts, can be left in the ground until needed. Root vegetables will go dormant in winter, but Brussels sprouts will continue to develop in milder spells. Cover root crops with an insulating mulch of straw or other insulating material to keep out the worst of the frost and use labels to indicate the ends of rows to help you find the roots when the topgrowth has disappeared. Lift extra supplies in advance of severe frosty weather because it is impossible to dig up root crops if the ground is frozen.

HOW TO STORE VEGETABLES

Place the largest potatoes in sacks and store them in a cool but frost-proof place. Paper sacks are best, but if you can't obtain them, use plastic sacks and cut some slits with a knife to provide some ventilation.

Many vegetables, such as marrows (large zucchini), can be stored in trays. Make sure that they do not touch each other.

A simple way of stringing garlic is to thread a stiff wire through the dry necks of the bulbs. The bulbs can also be tied on string and hung in a dry, airy place.

Herb gardening

The word "herb" is defined as a plant, some part of which – roots, stem, leaves, flowers or fruit – is used for flavouring food, or for medicine or scent. There is enormous variety in the types of plants understood to be herbs, and most gardeners find room for at least one or two. Beauty of foliage and flower, countless scents and tastes, cures for various ailments: herbs offer all these things and more.

You can grow herbs in special parts of the garden, creating separate beds for individual varieties for easy picking, or combining them with cottage-garden flowers to create a wonderful relaxed atmosphere. The beauty of herbs is that they blend perfectly with all kinds of design, from the strictly formal with neatly clipped box hedging to the cheerful informality of the cottage garden. This chapter will explain how to cultivate and harvest these rewarding and varied plants.

Alternating clumps of purple and green-leaved sage, *Salvia officinalis*, line a gravel path, giving a very decorative effect.

Buying herbs and designing a herb garden

Herbs are among the most popular garden plants, and room is usually found for them in any garden. Many gardeners prefer to grow herbs in a dedicated bed, while others like the convenience of a container of herbs by the kitchen door.

Selecting herbs

You can grow many herbs from seed or buy them as plants. Seed is the cheaper option, especially if you require a large number of plants, and it is the best way to grow specimens of basil and borage, which resent root disturbance. Some herbs, such as golden and variegated forms of marjoram, mint, sage and thyme, do not come true from seed.

Garden centres and other retail outlets offer a wide range of herbs in pots, and this is a good way of buying shrubby herbs, such as rosemary and bay, of which you will require just one or two specimens. Although it is a convenient way of buying herbs, it could prove costly for herbs that are used in larger quantities, such as chives and basil. Herbs can also be bought in pots from supermarkets. These have been

forced under cover and need to be hardened off carefully if you intend to plant them outside.

Grow the herbs that you like to eat and use most often in the kitchen. The most popular herbs are basil, bay, chervil, chives, dill, marjoram, mint, parsley, rosemary, sage, tarragon and thyme, but you might prefer to grow sorrel, fennel and savory if you like fish, or lemon grass, ginger, coriander (cilantro) and garlic chives for Asian dishes.

What to look for

Choose stocky, healthy-looking plants with plenty of leaves and a balanced shape. If you buy plants in early spring, make sure they have been hardened off properly before planting them out. Inspect plants carefully for signs of pests and diseases. Some problems are specific to different types of herbs. For example, check the undersides of mint leaves for tiny orange spots, which are the tell-tale sign of mint rust disease; inspect parsley plants for pale lines in the leaves, which are a sign of celery fly damage; while the stems of bay trees should be

checked for scale insect. Always look at the growing tips of all herbs for signs of aphids. As with other plants, buy specimens that are not showing signs of stress from over- or under-watering and avoid plants that are showing signs of neglect, such as weeds in the pot or roots growing through the pot's drainage holes.

Creating a herb feature

The best place to grow herbs is outside the kitchen door, where they will be close to hand when they are needed. Many herbs are drought-tolerant, so are ideal for growing in containers, but if you use a lot of herbs, a designated herb garden would be appropriate and useful.

Designing a herb garden

A dedicated herb garden can form a decorative focal point to a garden design. Formal gardens often look best in a traditional shape such as a wheel marked out using small unit paving or a knot garden surrounded by a low hedge of clipped dwarf box. Attractive contemporary designs include a chequer-board effect made using paving slabs.

BUYING HERBS

Two plants of verbena (vervain), one strong-growing and healthy, the other past its best and struggling.

This *Mentha* (mint) is becoming pot-bound with roots conforming to the shape of the pot and trying to escape out of the bottom.

For large orders of a single herb, buying rooted cuttings can be cost-effective. Here, purple sage and golden thyme have been propagated in plug trays.

HOW TO MAKE A RAISED HERB BRICK WHEEL

1 Use string and canes to mark a circle, then measure off equal points on the circumference for the spokes. Sink a length of earthenware (clay) sewage pipe in the centre.

2 Trace over the whole design with fine sand or line-marker paint.

3 Excavate a trench for the bricks and fill it with dry concrete mix to form a firm footing.

4 Build the outer circle and spokes with one or two courses of bricks, set in mortar. A herb wheel does not have to be very high; two or three courses of bricks should be sufficient.

5 Fill in the sections of the wheel and the earthenware pipe with rubble and gravel to provide drainage. Then add topsoil.

6 Plant up the herb wheel with a selection of culinary herbs, such as sage, thyme, rosemary and lemon verbena. Water in well and add an organic mulch. Continue to water until the herbs are established.

Herbs in containers

Many herbs used in the kitchen come from Mediterranean countries and like well-drained soil conditions. They are pretty drought-tolerant, making them ideal for container plants. Some herbs are even suitable for growing in hanging baskets. A few herbs require large containers if you choose to grow them this way, the main examples being deep-rooted herbs, such as fennel, which produce vertical taproots, and larger shrubby herbs, such as rosemary and bay. Moisture-loving herbs such as sweet cicely are suitable for growing bags.

Choose a reasonably deep container, at least 15cm (6in), to give them plenty of root run. You can either grow individual herbs in different pots or group herbs with similar cultural requirements in a larger pot. This will make looking after the herbs more straightforward. Short-lived herbs or those that are used up quickly, such as basil and chives, are worth growing in their own pot, which can be sunk rim-deep into the larger container holding the herb collection. The smaller container can be slipped out easily and replaced when necessary without disturbing the other herbs.

Interlocking containers are now available, and these allow you to grow the herbs separately, but they can be assembled so that they look like a single container.

Many of the most useful culinary herbs grow well in hanging baskets. Position the basket outside the kitchen door for convenience.

Growing herbs

The versatility of herbs is one of their great advantages in the garden. If you provide the right conditions, herbs are generally easy to grow, rewarding you with their colourful, fragrant flowers and foliage as well as their usefulness to flavour dishes in the kitchen.

Positioning herbs

Most herbs grow best in full sun with some protection from cold winter winds. The soil should usually be light and free-draining with plenty of organic matter forked in. Lavender, in particular, will not grow well in a very heavy clay soil. There are some herbs, however, that can cope with heavier soils and light shade. These include angelica, borage, chives, fennel, lemon balm, lovage and mint. It always makes sense to go with the conditions and not against them, so a hot, dry site will suit Mediterranean herbs, while

Companion planting

Many herbs have a reputation for repelling insect pests and are used as companion plants by organic gardeners for protecting vulnerable plants such as roses, fruit and vegetables from insect attack. Rue, cotton lavender, curry plant, tansy and southernwood are all strongly aromatic and are said to discourage many types of pest.

Camomile has a reputation for improving the health and vigour of surrounding plants.

Pennyroyal, planted in paving, is thought to keep ants away.

Summer savory, planted in rows next to broad beans (fava beans), provides them with some protection from aphids.

Chives and garlic are often planted to discourage the aphids that can damage roses.

Restricting invasive herbs

A few herbs, such as mint, are very vigorous and will quickly spread and overwhelm neighbouring plants if given free rein in the border. The easiest way to restrict their ambitions is to confine the roots by planting them in a large pot or bottomless bucket sunk into the border. As long as the rim of the pot is proud of the surface, the roots will be kept within bounds. However, it is still worth checking the plant from time to time to make sure that flopping stems have not rooted outside the pot.

a heavy moist soil suits plants that like streams and meadows. Looking at how a plant thrives in its natural habitat will tell you how best to grow it in the garden.

It is not essential to grow herbs in a specially designated herb bed. Individual herbs are delightful additions to flower borders and beds. Chives and parsley, for example, are useful edging plants, while stately bronze fennel will be an eye-catching addition to a mixed border. Low-growing herbs such as camomile and

thyme can be planted in cracks in paving in paths and on patios. Choose a variety that grows well in these conditions.

Growing herbs from seed

Raising your own plants from seed is not only very rewarding, it is also the best way to stock your herb garden economically. Sow seed thinly in seed compost (soil mix), using plug trays. The advantage of using these trays is that when the plants are transferred to a pot, there is little

HOW TO PLANT A HERB GARDEN

1 Newly planted box trees line this wooden-edged herb bed and provide a framework inside which the herbs will be laid out. First prepare the site by thoroughly weeding and forking over to break up the soil, then rake the ground level.

2 Work out the eventual spread of the herbs and decide how much room to give each plant. A helpful method is to "draw" on the soil with sand trickled out of a pot. If you make a mistake, it can be easily erased and the design begun again.

Choosing herbs

Hanging baskets	Borders
Basil	Angelica
Marjoram	Artemisia
Sage	Bay
Thyme	Catmint
Winter savory	Chervil
	Chives
Containers	Curry plant
Basil	Fennel
Bay	Hyssop
Camomile	Lavender
Marjoram	Marjoram
Parsley	Mint
Rosemary	Parsley
Sage	Rocket (arugula)
Summer savory	Rosemary
Thyme	Sage
Winter savory	Thyme

Planting herbs in the garden

Prepare the site by eliminating all weeds, especially perennials. Dig the soil well and rake it over. If you are creating a dedicated herb garden, with each plant allocated to a certain space, plan out the design before you start. Transferring a design to the soil can be made simple by using sand poured from the hole in the bottom of a container. If you make a mistake it is easy to rake the soil over and start again.

Thoroughly water all pot-grown plants several hours prior to planting, then knock them out of their pots by giving a sharp rap on the bottom of the container. Plant the herb at the same depth it was in the pot, firming the soil well around the roots afterwards. Water generously and label unless you are quite sure of the names of the different herbs.

A herb garden from container-grown plants can be created at any time of year, provided it is kept well-watered, but early spring is probably the best time as it will give the plants a full season to establish before the trials of winter.

Bay prefers a sheltered, sunny position. They are evergreen, frost hardy plants, so are ideal for growing in a container close to the house for year-round interest. Protect from severe weather, however. This specimen has been grown by plaiting (braiding) three stems.

root disturbance, so the growth of the herb is not checked. This method of sowing suits borage, dill and chervil in particular.

Alternatively, you can sow seed into a well-prepared seed bed in spring. Parsley must only be sown when the soil has warmed up in spring, and trying too early can result in poor germination.

3 Remove the herbs from their pots and plant them carefully, at the same level as they were in the container. If you want to keep the pots for reuse, then scrub them well with soap and water.

4 Water each plant thoroughly and keep them watered in dry weather until they are established. Avoid planting on a hot day; just before rain is ideal.

5 The newly planted herb garden looks rather bare, but it won't be long before the plants grow to fit their allocated space. It can be tempting to plant too close together for a more immediate effect, but this will lead to overcrowding later.

Aftercare of herbs

Most herbs are easy to grow, requiring little maintenance and generally remaining free from pests and diseases. There are, however, a few seasonal tasks that will ensure you get the most from your plants.

Watering

Herbs in pots need regular watering in summer and even in well-drained beds and borders annual herbs may need the occasional watering during prolonged drought. Make watering pots easier by leaving the compost (soil mix) 2.5cm (1in) below the rim of the pot and cover the surface with gravel to help reduce water loss through evaporation.

Do not use a high-nitrogen inorganic fertilizer on herbs because this encourages soft sappy growth, prone to aphid infestation and unable to stand the stress of droughts. The herb will also lack fragrance and aroma.

HOW TO PRUNE COTTON LAVENDER

1 Keep cotton lavender (*Santolina rosmarinifolia*) neat and compact by regular pruning. Use a pair of shears to clip the bush into shape. Do not prune back as far as the older, woody stems; there should be plenty of greenery below the cut stems.

2 When the plant has been pruned into a dome shape it will quickly put on new growth. Clipping about twice a year will keep the bush compact and neat.

Weeding

In the border it is essential to keep on top of weeding throughout the growing season. Weeds not only compete with the herbs for light, moisture and nutrients, but they also harbour pests and diseases. Hand weed or hoe annual weeds and use a hand fork to dig out perennial weeds complete with their roots to stop them re-sprouting. If it is impossible to remove the weeds completely because they are growing among the herbs, cut the leaves of the perennial weeds back to ground level and repeat the process each time they sprout. This weakens the weeds and may even kill them.

Mulching

In spring each year top up the loose mulch to prevent weed seeds from germinating and to help reduce moisture loss from the soil surface. Use an organic mulch, such as bark chippings, around herbs, such as lovage and sweet cicely, and those that like a moist root run, and a gravel mulch around herbs, such as thyme and marjoram, which prefer well-drained conditions.

Pruning

Remove any all-green shoots from naturally variegated plants because these will be more vigorous and will outgrow the variegated foliage. Some herbs are also worth pruning annually to keep them looking neat and to prevent them from self-seeding and becoming a weed problem. Use shears to trim small flowering plants, such as thyme and chives, and secateurs (pruners) on woody shrubby herbs, such as

Mint is an extremely vigorous plant once established, but keep an eye on young plants during hot spells and water if necessary.

Mulching helps to keep beds and borders weed-free. Gravel is a good choice for herbs that like free-draining soil.

rosemary and bay, to keep them in shape. Some herbs, such as fennel, become coarse in stem and leaf if left unpruned. Cut back early to make plenty of young growth for cooking. Use secateurs (pruners) to cut the stems almost to ground level.

You don't have to let pruning go to waste; healthy leaves can be used in the kitchen or frozen for later use.

Overwintering herbs

Summer is the usual time for harvesting herbs, but the normal growing season can be extended by covering selected plants with cloches in early autumn to keep them growing for a few more weeks. To get year-round supplies of herbs, you can lift and pot up a few plants of perennial herbs, such as mint and marjoram, in autumn and move them indoors where they will sprout new leaves.

You can also maintain a supply of annual herbs, such as basil and parsley, by sowing in late summer in pots and keeping plants on a sunny windowsill or in a heated greenhouse or conservatory.

HOW TO PROTECT HERBS IN AUTUMN

Protect late-sown herbs, such as parsley, with cloches to ensure a supply of fresh leaves.

HOW TO POT UP HERBS FOR WINTER USE

1 Mint is an easy plant to force indoors, or in a cold frame or greenhouse. Lift an established clump to provide a supply of roots to pot up.

2 Select only pieces with healthy leaves (diseased leaves are common by the end of the season). You can pull pieces off by hand or cut through them with a knife.

3 Plant the roots in a pot if you want to try and keep the plant growing indoors for a month or two. Three-quarters fill a 20cm (8in) pot with compost (soil mix), then spread out the roots and cover with more compost.

4 If you want a supply of tender fresh leaves early next spring, cut off the tops of the mint plants and put the roots in seed trays (flats) or deeper boxes. Cover with soil. Keep in a cold frame or the greenhouse for an early harvest in spring.

5 Chives also respond favourably to lifting for an extended season. Lift a small clump to pot up. If it's too large you should be able to pull it apart into smaller pieces.

6 Place the clump in a pot of soil, firm well and water thoroughly. The pot of chives, if kept indoors, should continue to provide leaves after those outdoors have died back, and will produce new ones earlier next year.

Harvesting and storing herbs

Herbs need to be picked regularly to maintain a continuous supply of fresh, young leaves. If you want to store herbs for winter use, however, you should make sure that you harvest them at their best.

When to harvest herbs

The best time to harvest herbs for later use varies depending on the part of the plant you are harvesting. Large leaves should be picked individually, but smaller-leaved herbs can be picked in sprigs and stripped before processing.

Most herbs are best harvested in early summer, just before they come into flower, although leafy herbs, such as mint, are best cut back to near ground level to encourage a second flush of young, aromatic leaves later in the season. If you are storing flowers, pick them at their peak as soon as they have opened. Again, smaller flowers can be picked on sprigs, ready

WHEN TO HARVEST HERBS

Harvest herbs when they are at their peak, usually before they flower. Cut them on a dry day, avoiding times when they are wilting in the heat. Harvest the best leaves, not the older leaves lower down the plant.

for processing in the kitchen. If you are collecting seeds, cover seedheads with a paper bag as they are becoming ripe, then cut off the seedheads and

keep them somewhere warm and dry until the seeds are released. Root herbs, such as horseradish, should be harvested in autumn.

Harvesting herbs for storage

Choose a fine, dry day when the sun is out but before the foliage starts to wilt to capture the essential oils that give herbs their distinctive flavour and aroma. The foliage must be dry when it is harvested, so wait until any dew has evaporated before you start. This will help to prevent the herbs from going mouldy while they are drying. Choose only the best material for storing, avoiding leaves that show signs of age or pest and disease attack. Cut the herbs with sharp garden snips or secateurs (pruners) so that the plant tissue is not crushed. Pick little and often because herbs that are processed quickly will retain their flavour. Handle the herbs as little as possible.

HOW TO HARVEST MARJORAM FOR DRYING

1 Small-leaved herbs, such as marjoram, are easily air-dried. Cut bunches of healthy material at mid-morning on a dry, warm day.

2 Strip off the lower leaves, which would otherwise become crushed and damaged when the stems are bunched.

3 Twist a rubber band around a few stems to hold them tightly together. Gather as many bunches as you need.

HOW TO STORE HERB SEEDS

1 Pick seedheads just as they are ripening. At this stage the seeds should readily come away from the stalks. Place on a tray and leave the seeds for a few days in a warm, dry place until they have completely dried.

2 Once the seeds are thoroughly dried, tip them into a glass jar with an airtight lid. Store in a cool, dry, dark place.

HOW TO FREEZE HERBS

The best method of storing soft-leaved herbs, such as parsley and mint, is to freeze them. Chop up the herb and place in ice-cube trays. Top up with water and freeze. This has the advantage of keeping the herb's colour.

Storing herbs

Some herbs, such as thyme, can be dried with no loss of flavour, but others are best stored in infusions to retain their distinctive taste. Soft-leaved herbs can be frozen.

Drying Hang up sprigs of individual herbs in bunches in a well-ventilated, warm, dry, dark place, such as an airing cupboard (linen closet). Root herbs should be cleaned and cut into small pieces and dried in the oven at a low temperature on a baking tray. Store dry herbs in airtight containers. Herbs should be kept in the dark, so store in a cupboard (closet) or, if herbs will be kept on open shelves, place them in opaque containers.

Freezing Whole leaves can be placed in clearly labelled plastic bags and then kept in the freezer. Alternatively, the leaves can be finely chopped and frozen with water in an ice-cube tray. Individual frozen cubes can be added to dishes as required.

Infusions A popular method with some cooks is to create infusions using good-quality olive oil or wine vinegar. The infusion can be of a single herb, such as basil, or two or three different herbs, and used to add flavour to dishes, such as pizzas and salads.

DRYING HERBS

Bunches of herbs can be dried by hanging them in a dry place where they are out of direct sunlight.

Herb mixtures

Different herbs can be combined in a number of distinctive mixtures. Bouquet garni, for example, is a combination of several herbs, such as bay, parsley, marjoram and thyme. Sprigs of the herbs are tied together or placed in a muslin (cheesecloth) bag, which is cooked with the dish and removed before serving.

Greenhouse gardening

A greenhouse offers many gardening opportunities and challenges. It can transform your gardening activities, extending the season and increasing the range of crops you can grow. The enclosed environment means you can give plants exactly the conditions they need to grow fast and well, but unfortunately it is also the ideal environment for pests and diseases.

The health of the plants in the greenhouse will depend on your management skills, and a productive greenhouse requires almost constant attention. Fortunately, there are many products to help you, including thermostatically controlled heaters to keep the greenhouse warm in winter and automatic vent openers to keep it cool in summer. There is also a range of special equipment for automating the time-consuming task of watering. Careful planning of the layout of the greenhouse and of the cropping programme will help make efficient use of your time and space.

A greenhouse enables you to grow a far wider range of plants than would otherwise be possible.

Controlling the greenhouse environment

The temperature inside a greenhouse can quickly rocket out of control on sunny days in spring and summer, sometimes soaring to over 50°C (120°F). Equally, in winter it can drop low enough to cause damage to frost-tender plants. Use the following strategies to keep the temperature in the greenhouse under control.

Providing ventilation

There are three basic methods you can use to prevent overheating in the greenhouse: ventilation, shading and damping down.

Providing ventilation is the best way to control temperatures during the early days of spring. Opening a roof vent and a vent in the side of the greenhouse will allow the hot, humid air that has risen to the top of the greenhouse to escape, while at the same time drawing cooler, dryer air through the side vents. This is known as the chimney effect, and it is an extremely effective cooling technique until the temperatures outside start to rise in late spring. You can take the hard work out of opening the vents by installing automatic vent-openers throughout

CHECKING THE TEMPERATURE

A maximum/minimum thermometer is ideal for keeping track of the temperature inside a greenhouse, warning you to adjust the conditions before the plants start to suffer.

the greenhouse. This mechanism opens the greenhouse windows as soon as a specific pre-set temperature is reached.

You can increase the flow of air through the greenhouse by opening more and more vents – and even the door – but eventually, in the hottest weather, this method alone will not be sufficient to cool your greenhouse to the correct temperature.

INCREASING HUMIDITY

Splashing or spraying water over the greenhouse floor helps to create a humid atmosphere. This traditional technique is known as damping down. It is especially beneficial for crops, such as aubergines (eggplant), and cucumbers, but most plants appreciate a moist atmosphere on hot days. Carry out damping down frequently on very hot days as the humidity helps to reduce the temperature.

Providing shade

The second strategy to avoid overheating is to prevent the sun's rays, which heat up the greenhouse, from entering. The easiest way to do this is to put up greenhouse shading. There are three main types: indoor shading fabric, which is fixed to the inside frame of the greenhouse; roller blinds, which are attached to the outside of the greenhouse; and a special whitewash paint, which is applied to the glass in spring and removed in autumn when light levels decline.

Roller blinds are best because they prevent the sun's energy from entering the greenhouse, but they are most expensive and awkward to adjust. Shading fabric is cheap and easy to adjust, but it absorbs some

VENTILATING

It is vital not to let greenhouses overheat. Opening the windows at the right time is not always possible if you are not at home during the hottest part of the day, but automatic vent-openers will do the job for you.

SHADING

It is important to keep the sun out of the greenhouse during the hottest part of the year. Shading, in the form of temporary netting, helps to keep the temperature down and also protects the plants from the scorching effects of the sun.

of the sun's energy and so is less effective. Shading wash is both cheap and effective, but once applied it is on for the whole season regardless of the weather. However, there is a type, called Varishade, which turns opaque when it gets wet, so allowing more light into the greenhouse when it rains. In a greenhouse used to grow a variety of plants, use sun-loving plants, such as tomatoes, to shade other plants by growing them on the sunny side of the greenhouse.

Damping down

During the long, hot days of summer, especially if there is little air movement outside, the greenhouse temperature can still rise too high. You can help cool things down using the traditional technique of damping down. This is where all surfaces, including the floor and staging, are sprayed with water in the morning. As the temperature increases, energy will be absorbed by the water as it evaporates and is carried out of the greenhouse in the form of water vapour.

Protecting from cold

During the winter it is important not to let your greenhouse get too cold, as this could damage any tender plants or seedlings. One of the best ways to heat a greenhouse is to install an electric heater. A thermostat will ensure that no heat (or money) is wasted, because the appliance only comes on when the temperature drops below a certain point. Heating bills can be reduced with insulation. A cheaper alternative to double glazing is to line the greenhouse with sheets of clear polythene (plastic) containing air bubbles. If you have just a few plants, a heated propagator may be sufficient for your needs.

An unusually shaped greenhouse with a steeply pitched roof not only looks different from conventional greenhouses but has the advantage that the steep sides absorb the low winter sun more easily, making heating the greenhouse more economical.

HEATING

Electric fan heaters are very efficient. When equipped with thermostats, they come on only when extra heat is required. They can also be used to circulate the air on still, damp days, reducing the risk of fungal disease caused by stagnant air.

INSULATING

Insulating the greenhouse is important during the cold winter months, helping to keep heating costs down as well as preventing any violent fluctuations in temperature. Polythene (plastic) bubble insulation is cheap and efficient and easy to install.

Watering and feeding

In the greenhouse plants are especially vulnerable to a shortage of moisture and nutrients. Establishing a routine of providing both water and fertilizer will ensure that your plants remain healthy.

When to water

Watering is probably the most difficult technique to get right in the greenhouse because it depends on such variable factors as the time of year, the plants chosen and their stage of growth, light levels, where the plants are growing and the temperature in the greenhouse.

Do not wait until a plant starts to wilt before you water it since this means it is already under stress, leading to reduced growth and yields. It is essential to check plants regularly to make sure they do not run short of water, and this may mean more than once a day in summer. The best way to judge the moisture is to

Plants in growing bags, whether they are grown outside or in a greenhouse, quickly use up the moisture and nutrients available in the compost (soil mix). They will require regular watering and feeding throughout the growing season.

push your finger into the compost (soil mix) of each pot. If the compost about 2cm (¾in) below the surface is dry, it needs watering; if it is moist, leave it for another day.

Making watering easier

If you have a greenhouse full of plants checking individual pots is clearly impracticable. Fortunately, there are a number of ways you can

HOW TO WATER GREENHOUSE PLANTS

Plants should be watered before they show obvious signs of distress, such as wilting. With bushy plants it is not possible to judge by the appearance of the potting compost (soil mix), and you really need to feel below the surface, but this is time-consuming if you have many plants.

Moisture indicators for individual pots can be helpful for gardeners who find it difficult to judge the soil or if there are just a few plants, but they are not practicable if you have a whole greenhouse full of plants.

Capillary matting is an ideal way to water most pot plants in summer. You can use a proprietary system fed by mains water or improvise with a system like this one, which uses a length of gutter for the water supply. You can keep it topped up by hand, with special water bags or from a cistern.

take much of the hard work out of watering. First, by planning the layout and positioning of plants carefully you can make watering a lot easier, for example, by grouping together containers with similar requirements. Second, it is worth investing in simple watering devices.

Capillary watering If you have a lot of small containers a sandbench is worth considering. It is fairly simple to make out of a strong wooden box about 15cm (6in) deep. Line it with heavy-duty polythene (plastic) and place a 2.5cm (1in) layer of pea gravel on the bottom. Add a further 10cm (4in) of horticultural sand on top of this and stand the pots and trays on the sand. When the sand is wet the plants in the containers will draw up as much moisture as they require via capillary action.

A similar system involves using capillary matting. Cover a flat surface with heavy-duty plastic and

If you are watering by hand, use the can without a rose unless you are watering seedlings. This will enable you to direct water more easily to the roots rather than sprinkling the leaves. Use a finger over the end of the spout to control the flow, or stick a rag in the end to break the force.

HOW TO FEED GREENHOUSE PLANTS

A liquid fertilizer is applied at the same time that you water, but you must remember to do it regularly. There are both soluble powders and liquids, which can be diluted to the appropriate strength.

then lay the matting on top. Drape one end of the plastic sheet and matting into a reservoir, such as a trough or a short piece of guttering fitted to the end of the bench. When the reservoir is filled with water it will soak the matting so that the containers placed on it can draw up all the moisture they require. Remember to keep the reservoir topped up with water.

Drip watering Another option is to install a drip irrigation system. You can buy bladder bags that supply a single drip nozzle (similar to a medical drip) or a micro-bore drip irrigation system, or make your own out of a large plastic drinks bottle. Cut the bottom off the bottle and make a small hole in the bottle top. Fix a galvanized screw into the hole and insert the upended bottle into the compost. When the bottle is filled, water will slowly leak out, past the screw, keeping the compost moist between waterings. Keep an eye on the reservoir and top up as necessary. This method is ideal for watering larger pots and growing bags.

Fertilizer sticks and tablets that you push into the container are a convenient way to administer fertilizer if you don't want to apply liquid feeds regularly. Most release their nutrients over a period of several months.

Automatic watering Both capillary and drip systems can be made completely automatic by plumbing them into the mains. You can either use a water timer or computer to regulate the watering periods or install a header tank with a ballcock valve to act as a reservoir.

Feeding

The amount of food a plant requires depends on how fast it is growing. Fast-growing crop plants grown in containers will need feeding once a week from about six weeks after potting up. Use a high-potash liquid feed, such as tomato fertilizer, for all flowering and fruit-bearing crops and a high-nitrogen feed for leafy vegetables. Follow the manufacturer's instructions for application rates. Vegetables in the greenhouse are gross feeders that quickly deplete the nutrients in the compost (soil mix). To save time, mix slow-release fertilizer granules into the compost for ornamental and foliage plants. This will provide sufficient food for several months.

Troubleshooting

The greenhouse offers the perfect breeding ground for many pests and diseases. Many can be prevented by growing the crops so that they are vigorous enough to withstand most problems, but some insects and diseases will need to be controlled.

Avoiding problems

There are many things you can do to prevent pests and diseases taking over. Keep the growing environment as clean and uncluttered as possible, clearing away rubbish and washing and sterilizing used pots.

In the winter, clear out the greenhouse and give it a thorough clean. Wash down the insides with a garden disinfectant and scrub all the surfaces, including the path, benches and frame. Clear any algae that is trapped between glass overlaps and clean out the awkward mouldings of an aluminium frame. As you bring plants back inside, inspect them for signs of pest and disease attack. Always use sterilized pots and

If you have had an infestation of pests or diseases, fumigation is a good way to rid the greenhouse of the problem. You may be able to keep the plants in while you carry out the process, or you may have to fumigate in an empty greenhouse. Check the label.

compost (soil mix) when sowing and planting. If you buy plants make sure they are free from pests and diseases so that they do not introduce problems into your greenhouse.

Make sure that you provide the right environment for your plants so that they are growing strongly and do not suffer a check in growth. Use your time while watering to inspect plants closely, especially the growing tips and undersides of leaves, for any early signs of pest or disease activity and take action promptly when necessary. If you are vigilant you should be able to avoid having to use chemical controls.

Some infestations can be prevented by covering vents with insect-proof mesh. If there are insects in the greenhouse, use sticky traps, which consist of sheets of yellow plastic covered with a non-drying glue. This form of non-chemical control is becoming popular for a wide range of flying pests, and works particularly well in a greenhouse.

If a pest or disease attack is severe make sure you select the right chemical for the problem and follow the manufacturer's instructions given on the label.

HOW TO CONTROL PESTS IN THE GREENHOUSE

If vine weevil grubs destroy your plants by eating the roots, try controlling them with a parasitic nematode. A suspension of the nematodes is simply watered over the compost (soil mix) in each pot.

A number of greenhouse pests can be successfully controlled with other insects. The beneficial insects are released, here from a sachet, on to the susceptible plant in order to attack the pests. There are predatory wasps and mites that will attack whitefly larvae, spider mite, soft scale insects and thrips.

Biological controls

Most plants in the greenhouse are grown to eat, so avoid spraying them with insecticide as far as possible. Fortunately, there are a number of biological measures to control pests.

Several common garden pests can be controlled by other insects, which either eat or parasitize the pest. For example, the small wasp, *Encarsia formosa*, will control whitefly, while a predatory mite, called *Phytoseiulus*, can be used against spider mite attacks, and nematodes can be used to attack vine weevils.

Introduce the biological control as soon as the first signs of attack are noticed, remove yellow sticky traps and do not use chemicals that might kill the biological controls. Be patient, and accept there will be some damage before the biological agent takes effect.

Common pests and diseases

Identifying the problem is the first step to eradicating it.

Spider mite This pest can attack a wide range of greenhouse crops throughout the summer. Leaves become speckled, eventually turning yellow, and later webbing can be seen. The tiny insects are visible. Prevent problems by thoroughly cleaning your greenhouse in winter and increase the humidity in the greenhouse by damping down and misting the plants because this pest likes a dry atmosphere.

Whitefly This pest attacks a wide range of plants, especially tomatoes, peppers and aubergines (eggplant). Small white flies congregate on the undersides of leaves and fly up in a cloud when disturbed. Use a car vacuum to suck up flying pests or hang up yellow sticky traps.

Damping off This disease affects all types of seedlings, causing them to

French marigolds have been planted with a row of tomatoes in this greenhouse. They are thought to ward off whitefly from the tomatoes, a technique known as companion planting.

keel over like felled trees. It is a particular problem in the spring. Apply a suitable fungicidal drench before sowing, use sterile pots and compost, and space seedlings to improve air flow. Water from below.

Grey mould Velvety patches appear on leaves, fruit and stems of most crops, especially tomatoes, cucumbers and lettuces. Prevent outbreaks by keeping the greenhouse

well ventilated and clear away yellowing foliage and other debris.

Powdery mildew A white powdery coating forms on leaves of many crops, including cucumbers, especially during the summer months. Keep the compost (soil mix) moist but keep the atmosphere dry by careful ventilation, and avoid wetting the leaves. Try growing mildew-resistant varieties if the problem recurs.

Growing tomatoes

There is nothing quite like the flavour of a freshly picked, home-grown tomato. To get the best crops, choose a good variety and don't neglect it at any stage.

Growing methods

Tomatoes are easy to raise from seed but need to be sown early in the year and require a high temperature to germinate. This means you will need a propagator set to 18°C (65°F) to get them started and somewhere heated to 21°C (70°F) to grow them on. On the other hand, you could buy plants that are ready for planting out much later in the year saving you time, trouble and money. Make sure that you choose a healthy-looking, stocky plant, showing no signs of yellowing leaves or pest or disease attack. Plant tomatoes out when they are showing colour (the flowers are beginning to open) in their first truss.

Greenhouse tomatoes can be grown in two main ways: in the greenhouse border and in containers, such as pots or growing bags. A third method, called ring culture, is also used by some growers but it has never gained popular appeal, despite the lower maintenance it requires.

HOW TO RAISE TOMATOES

1 With ring culture, the water-absorbing roots grow into a moist aggregate and the feeding roots into special bottomless pots filled with a potting compost (soil mix). Take out a trench about 15–23cm (6–9in) deep in the greenhouse border and line it with a waterproof plastic to minimize contamination by soil-borne diseases.

2 Fill the trench with fine gravel or coarse grit, then place the special bottomless pots ("rings") on the aggregate base. Fill them with potting compost and plant the tomatoes into the rings. Water into the rings at first. Once the plant is established and some roots have penetrated the aggregate, water only the aggregate and feed through the pot.

3 Planting directly into the greenhouse border gives the plants' roots a chance to spread out, making it less likely that the plants will suffer from a lack of water or nutrients. You will need a cane or string to support the plant as it grows.

4 Growing bags are less trouble than ring culture to set up, but you will have to feed plants regularly and watering can be more difficult to control unless you use an automatic system. Insert a cane through the bag or use a string support.

5 String makes a simple and economical support. Fix one length of wire as high as practicable from one end of the greenhouse to the other, aligning it above the border. Fix another wire just above the ground, attaching it to a stout stake at each end of the row. Tie lengths of string between the top and bottom wires, in line with each plant.

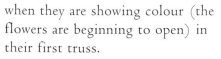

6 There is no need to tie the plant to its support. Loop the string around the growing tip so that it forms a spiral.

Tomatoes in the border This is the best method of growing tomatoes for the beginner or anyone else who finds routine watering a chore. The plants will have a lot more space for their roots to roam, so they will be less dependent on you for food and water. You will need to improve the soil with well-rotted organic matter before planting and to incorporate a general fertilizer at the rate recommended by the manufacturer. You will still need to water the plants thoroughly every couple of days during the height of summer.

The main drawback of border planting is that soil-borne problems build up after a few years, so once every few years it is a good idea to dig out the soil and replace it with fresh from the garden.

Tomatoes in growing bags This convenient method is now probably the most popular way of growing tomatoes. Clean, fresh compost (soil mix) is used each year, which means there is no carry-over of soil-borne pests and diseases. Using growing bags also means the greenhouse can be cleaned out properly in winter to eliminate any overwintering pests. However, bags cost money, and plants will need regular feeding and watering at least once a day during the hottest weather.

The other option is to pour the contents of the growing bag into a large pot or bucket with drainage holes drilled in the base. This means that the compost (soil mix) is much deeper, with more volume per plant, so that the plants can last longer between waterings.

Training tomatoes

Cordon tomatoes are trained with a single main stem. They will need to be supported by canes or pieces of string tied to strong overhead wires. Strings are either tied to the bottom of the plant or looped under the rootball when planting. If plants are in growing bags, consider buying one of the special metal supports now available from garden retailers. Tie the plant loosely to the support straight after planting, then tie in any extension growth each week as the plant grows.

Remove any sideshoots that grow from the leaf joint with a sharp knife or simply break them off using your finger and thumb. If you accidentally break the main leader of the tomato plant while you are training it, leave the top sideshoot to train up in its place. When the tomato plant reaches the top of the support or has produced seven trusses, pinch out the growing tip so that the plant puts all its energy into producing fruit. Remove leaves from the base of the plant as they start to yellow. Pick the tomatoes when they are fully coloured.

Reliable tomato varieties

Standard	Plum
'Ailsa Craig'	'Super Roma'
'Alicante'	
'Moneymaker'	**Cherry**
'Red Alert'	'Cherry Wonder'
'Shirley'	'Gardener's Delight'
Beefsteak	'Mirabelle'
'Big Boy'	
'Dombello'	**Striped**
'Dombito'	'Golden Sunrise'
'Golden Boy'	'Tigerella'

TRAINING CORDON PLANTS

Use a sharp clean knife to remove large sideshoots. Small ones can be pinched between thumb and finger.

RIPENING TOMATOES

At the end of the growing season, tomatoes grown outdoors can be ripened in the greenhouse. Strip off the lower leaves and hang the plants upside down.

Growing cucumbers and peppers

In most years in temperate climates, cucumbers and (bell) peppers can be grown successfully only under the protection of a greenhouse. Plant in mid-spring for an early crop that will last all summer long. Both will be a welcome sight in summer salads.

Cucumbers

Choose seeds of an all-female variety, as the cucumbers are less likely to be bitter. Sow two seeds on their sides in pots or modules in early spring in a heated greenhouse or in mid-spring in an unheated one. Provide a temperature of around 25°C (80°F) for speedy germination.

When the seeds germinate discard the weaker seedling. After about a month, the cucumber seedlings should be planted out, with as little root disturbance as possible. It is important to maintain a temperature of 16°C (60°F) thereafter.

Cucumbers are best grown as cordons, with a single stem tied to a vertical supporting cane or piece of string tied to an overhead wire. Tie in the plant as it grows using plant ties. Pinch out any sideshoots, flower buds and tendrils that appear until the seventh leaf. Thereafter, leave the flowers and tendrils and pinch out the sideshoots.

When the plant reaches the top of the support, pinch out the growing tip and leave the top two sideshoots to grow. These can be trained along the top wire and then down towards the floor.

Water the cucumbers regularly, keeping the soil moist at all times and throwing water on the floor of the greenhouse to keep the atmosphere humid.

Once the fruit starts to develop, feed the plants with a high-potash liquid feed once every two weeks.

Many modern cucumbers produce only female flowers, but some greenhouse varieties produce both male and female blooms (the female flowers have a small embryo fruit behind the petals). Pinch out male flowers before they have a chance to pollinate the female ones, because the resulting cucumbers will taste bitter.

Maintain a temperature of about 21°C (70°F). Harvest the cucmbers when they are large enough, which is usually when their sides are parallel. Cut the fruit with a short length of stalk. Pick cucumbers frequently to encourage the development of more fruit.

The most popular sort of cucumber is long with a smooth skin, and can only be grown under glass. It is a climbing variety.

There has been a recent rise in the popularity of both growing and eating (bell) peppers. Green peppers are the unripe fruit, yellow peppers are the first stage in the ripening process, and the final stage is red peppers. All peppers can be eaten raw, or cooked.

Chillies

Related to (bell) peppers, the fiery flavour of chillies is indispensable in many cuisines including Indian, Thai and Mexican. Chillies are sometimes grown as house plants, but they will do better if grown in a greenhouse, following the same growing technique as used for peppers. Remember to water the chillies often and feed with a liquid fertilizer about once a fortnight.

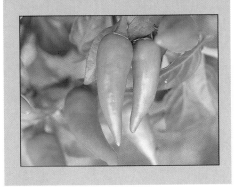

Peppers

Sow seeds for (bell) pepper in spring at 21°C (70°F) in seed trays or modules. Keep at a temperature of 18°C (65°F) after germination. Prick out seedlings into individual pots when they are large enough to handle. Once established, lower the temperature to 16°C (60°F) to grow on. As soon as they are big enough, transfer the young plants to the greenhouse border, growing bags or large pots. If you use growing bags, plant two or three peppers to a bag.

Pinch out the tops of young plants when they get to 15–20cm (6–8in) to make them bush out. If the plants get above 45–50cm (18–20in) they may need to be supported with canes or string. Tie plants in loosely.

Water the peppers as necessary and feed every fortnight once the fruit starts to swell using a tomato fertilizer. Peppers can be harvested from midsummer onwards. The fruit

Some plants, such as (bell) peppers, are usually grown in a greenhouse although they can be grown outside in the open air. The plants will do much better in a greenhouse as they are assured of a constant temperature and humidity. You will find the plants have an increased yield of fruit and will continue producing fruit over a longer period.

is ready when the skin turns glossy, usually when it is about the size of a tennis ball. Pick the first fruit when green to encourage more to develop. Subsequent fruits can be picked at the green or coloured stages.

Peppers enjoy the same kind of growing conditions as tomatoes, so they make ideal companions. If you do decide to grow both, make sure you grow the peppers on the sunny side of the greenhouse so they are not shaded by the faster growing and much taller tomato plants.

Good cucumber and (bell) pepper varieties

Cucumbers	Peppers
'Brigit'	'Ace'
'Carmen'	'Ariane'
'Fenumex'	'Bell Boy'
'Femspot'	'Canape'
'Flamingo'	'Golden Bell'
'Pepinex 69'	'Gypsy'
'Petita'	'Luteus'
'Telegraph'	'Rainbow'
'Telegraph	'Redskin'
Improved'	'Yellow Lantern'

Growing other greenhouse crops

Many other crops, including aubergines, melons, salad vegetables and herbs, can be grown in a greenhouse. Combine crops that need a similar growing environment for the best results.

Lettuces

Sow seed in trays from late winter to early spring at 13°C (55°F). Prick out when the seedlings are large enough to handle into individual pots. Plant out in the border or growing bags (old ones used for a previous crop of tomatoes are ideal), spacing them 15cm (6in) apart in the border and planting 12 to a standard growing bag. Lettuces grow relatively quickly and will be ready from 5 to 12 weeks after sowing, depending on the variety. Make a succession of sowings every fortnight or so through the spring and early summer for a continuity of supply throughout the summer.

Melons

Sow seed singly on edge and place in a heated propagator set to 18°C (65°F). Once germinated, grow them on at 16°C (60°F). When each seedling has four true leaves plant them out two plants to a growing

Melons can be grown very successfully in a greenhouse; the plants are supported on a wire frame and the ripening fruit is held in a net. Harvest the fruit when the flower end gives slightly when pressed gently.

Greenhouse flowers

A wide range of flowers can be raised in the greenhouse, both to populate beds and containers outdoors and to provide colourful pot plants for the house. *Abutilon, Browallia, Calceolaria, Celosia, Cuphea, Gerbera, Gloxinia, Hibiscus,* various primulas, *Schizanthus* and *Streptocarpus* are all good choices. They can be raised from seed in a propagator and grown on at around 13°C (55°F), or bought as small plants from a garden retailer and grown on.

bag or singly in large pots filled with growing bag compost (soil mix).

Plant the seedlings shallowly, with 2.5cm (1in) of the rootball proud of the surface to prevent stem rot. The plant will need support as it grows. Use plastic netting, or erect a series of sturdy horizontal wires, spaced 30cm (12in) apart, and tie the melon loosely to a vertical cane secured to the wires. Continue to tie in the plant as it grows and remove any sideshoots until it reaches the first wire. Allow two sideshoots to develop and tie these to the horizontal wire either side of the main stem. Repeat this process as the plant grows until there are shoots trained along all the wires.

Pinch out the growing point of the main stem when it reaches the top wire. Also pinch out the growing

point of each of the sideshoots when they have produced five leaves. New shoots will be produced from the leaf joints of the sideshoots, and these should be pinched out after the second leaf has formed.

When there are female flowers (those with a slight swelling behind the flower) on all the sideshoots, use a male flower to pollinate them by dabbing pollen from the male flower into the female ones.

Keep plants well fed and watered and the atmosphere humid thereafter. Remove any further flowers and sideshoots as they develop. Support the fruit in an individual net as it grows. Harvest melons when the fruit is ripe. A good indication is when the melon smells sweet and it gives slightly when pressed at the flower end of the fruit.

Aubergines

This plant is sometimes called eggplant due to the white, egg-shaped fruit produced by some varieties. The aubergine is an extremely versatile vegetable and is widely used in Mediterranean cooking.

Aubergines are related to tomatoes, and are just as easy to grow. However, they do need a long growing season to get reliable crops. This means sowing in late winter in a propagator set to 21°C (70°F). Soak the aubergine seeds overnight before sowing. Prick out seedlings individually as soon as they are large enough to handle, then grow them on at a temperature of 16°C (60°F). Plant out the seedlings three in a growing bag or singly in large pots filled with growing bag compost (soil mix). Use canes or string to support the plants once they get to about 45–60cm (18–24in) high. Tie the stems in loosely.

Keep the plants well fed and watered and keep the atmosphere in the greenhouse moist. Pinch out the tips of the plants when they reach about 38cm (15in) high to encourage the formation of fruit. Pick when shiny and about 15cm (6in) long, which should be from midsummer onwards.

Herbs

It is worth ensuring you have a good supply of herbs to use throughout the winter. Pots of herbs can be kept growing throughout the autumn by moving them into the greenhouse before the first frost. Keep them well watered but do not wet the foliage.

Herbs, such as clumps of chives and mint, which have been growing in a border, can be potted up and moved into the greenhouse in late autumn so that they are ready to harvest in spring.

Both parsely and basil require a high germination temperature of 18°C (65°F) and benefit from starting off in a greenhouse in mid-spring, before being potted up into a large container and moved outside for the summer.

This swelling fruit shows the glorious purple colour of the most common aubergines (eggplant). Only harvest when the fruit is fully ripe and shiny, otherwise the aubergine will taste bitter and not be worth eating.

GROWING AUBERGINES OUTDOORS

Aubergines (eggplant) can be grown in pots indoors and moved to large containers in a sheltered position outside when the weather is warmer. Plants that are not grown under glass take longer to mature, and the fruit will not be ready for harvesting until the autumn.

PINCHING OUT AUBERGINES

You will have bushier plants if the growing tip is pinched out when the aubergine plant is about 30cm (12in) high. Allow only one fruit to develop on each shoot. Pinch out the growing tips of these shoots three leaves beyond the developing fruit.

Reliable greenhouse varieties

Lettuces	Aubergines
'Cynthia'	'Black Beauty'
'Kellys'	'Black Bell'
'Kwiek'	'Black Enorma'
'Marmer'	'Black Prince'
'Novita'	'Bonica'
	'Dusky'
Melons	'Easter Egg'
'Amber Nectar'	'Long Purple'
'Charentais'	'Moneymaker'
'Classic'	'Short Tom'
'Honeydew'	'Slice Rite'
'Galia'	
'Ogen'	
'Superlative'	
'Sweetheart'	
'Venus'	

Fruit gardening

You do not need a large garden to grow a few fruit trees and bushes. It is possible to train trees in many styles against walls and fences or use them as garden dividers. There are even dwarf forms of popular fruits that are small enough to grow at the edge of a border or in containers.

Once established, fruit trees and bushes are able to compete with other plants for soil moisture and nutrients and so can be accommodated all around the garden. Make sure that they are planted in a sunny spot and that there is sufficient access to carry out essential maintenance tasks such as pruning, spraying and harvesting.

If you want to grow a lot of fruit, you would be better off allocating a separate area of the garden where the fruit trees, bushes, canes and vines are easier to manage and protect. Before planting any fruit it is essential to prepare the ground thoroughly because most plants will occupy the same spot for many years.

This pear tree has been beautifully trained into a fan, which is supported on wires, but it could also be grown against a wall.

Planting a fruit garden

When choosing which fruit to grow in your garden, consider the position you are intending to plant them in. Select good specimens of reliable and trouble-free varieties that you like to eat.

Buying fruit trees

It is important to choose healthy and vigorous specimens when you are buying fruit. Whether you buy bare-root or container-grown plants is a matter of personal preference: most varieties are available as both. Garden centres usually offer a limited range, but for the best choice and for unusual varieties or for trained forms you will probably find that you need to visit a specialist nursery.

When choosing a fruit tree, look for one with a sturdy, straight main trunk and several well-spaced branches that are not too vertical. This is important because the angle between the branch and the trunk will determine how strong the branch will be in later years and, therefore, how much fruit the tree can bear.

An apple tree that has been well cared for when young will fruit for many years, needing little maintenance once it is established.

Fruit tree varieties are all grafted on to a rootstock, and it is essential that you choose a type to suit your particular needs (see box below). It is also important to check that the union between the fruiting variety and rootstock is well healed and strong – look for a bulge about 15cm (6in) above the ground. When you buy plum or cherry trees you should also check the branches for rough areas of bark and oozing sap (a sign of canker disease) as well as foliage with a silvery sheen (a sign of silver leaf disease). Avoid buying suspect plants.

Buying bush and cane fruits

Look for varieties that have been "certified", which means they have been inspected and approved as being of a certain quality.

Currants All types should have three or four equally strong, well-spaced branches of about pencil thickness so the plant forms a well-balanced bush. Many redcurrants and white currants are sold on a short, clear stem, about 10cm (4in) long, but all blackcurrants shoot from the ground.

Choosing a rootstock

Fruit tree varieties are grafted (joined) on to a range of different rootstocks, which vary in their vigour. If you choose a dwarfing rootstock you will get a slower growing, smaller tree, but if you choose a vigorous rootstock you will get a much faster growing, larger fruit tree.

Dwarf rootstocks are good for planting in restricted spaces and produce trees that are easy to manage. Vigorous rootstocks are worth considering if you want a larger tree, if your soil is very poor, or if the tree will get a lot of competition from surrounding plants.

The rootstocks of apples and pears have been given codes; those of cherries and plums have names.

Rootstock	vigour	eventual size
Apples		
M27	very dwarf	1.8m (6ft)
M9	dwarf	2.4m (8ft)
M26	semi-dwarf	3m (10ft)
MM106	semi-vigorous	4.5m (15ft)
MM111	vigorous	5.5m (18ft)
Cherries		
Colt	semi-dwarf	4.5m (15ft)
Pears		
Quince C	semi-dwarf	3m (10ft)
Quince A	semi-vigorous	3.5m (12ft)
Plums		
Pixy	semi-dwarf	3m (10ft)
St Julien A	vigorous	5.5m (18ft)

PLANTING A FRUIT TREE OR BUSH

When you are planting a fruit tree or bush, always make sure that it is planted at the same depth as it was in its container or in its nursery bed.

Gooseberries These plants are also sold on a short stem about 10cm (4in) long. Choose one with a balanced head of three or four well-spaced and equally strong branches.
Raspberries When choosing, look for single, strong canes, each of about pencil thickness.
Blackberries and other hybrid berries Choose plants with at least two shoots of pencil thickness. Do not buy plants that have split stems or uneven colouring to the stems because this is a sign of neglect and possibly disease.

Planting fruit trees and bushes

Prepare the ground thoroughly before planting fruit trees and bushes, ensuring that you remove all perennial weeds. Dig in plenty of organic material.

As long as the weather is neither too wet nor too cold the best time to plant is between late autumn and mid-spring. If bare-rooted plants are delivered when you cannot plant

TYING IN A NEWLY PLANTED TREE

Make sure that a newly planted fruit tree is anchored to a stake. Attach the tie firmly, but not too tightly, approximately 30cm (12in) above the ground.

them, heel them in (plant in a shallow trench, with their stems leaning at an angle close to the ground) temporarily until they can be planted in their permanent position. Container-grown plants can be planted at other times of the year, but they need more attention to make sure that they survive.

Fruit trees and bushes should be planted to the same depth as they were in their pots or nursery bed when you purchased them. If a tree needs staking, place the stake in the ground before planting. Water the plants in thoroughly and keep them watered in dry weather until they are well established. Apply a mulch around the base of the plant in order to help preserve moisture as well as to keep the weeds down. Remove any weeds that do appear. You may also find it necessary to use wire guards around the trunks or netting over the branches to protect fruit trees and bushes from pests such as rabbits, deer or birds.

PROTECTING TRAINED FRUIT

Fruit trees and bushes that are trained against a wall can be protected against birds with netting over a home-made frame. A similar frame can be covered with plastic sheeting to protect the blossom from frosts.

PROTECTING BARK

Damage to trees from rabbits and deer can be prevented by using wire guards.

Growing trained fruit trees

Although free-standing fruit trees look lovely, the best way to grow fruit trees in a small garden is as trained forms against boundaries and as garden dividers. Not only do they take up less room, but there are practical advantages to the method.

Siting trained fruit trees

A sunny wall or fence offers several advantages for training fruit. The trees are well supported and branches well spaced. Walls and fences help to protect the blossom from cold winds and frosts in early spring, and encourage rapid ripening of fruit in late summer. Another advantage is that all parts of the tree are within reach, making maintenance straightforward. It will be easier to protect against birds in summer, frost in spring and cold in winter, as well as diseases, such as the dreaded peach leaf curl disease.

The best option for training fruit trees is to buy a ready-trained tree in a container from a fruit specialist, but you can do it yourself using a single-stemmed (maiden) tree.

PRUNING A CORDON

In summer, cut back any new sideshoots to three leaves and new growth on existing sideshoots to the first leaf.

Supporting fruit trees

If you do not have a sturdy wall or fence to grow the tree against, make a free-standing support from fence posts high enough for the form you are training. Space the posts 1.8m (6ft) apart and set them in concrete, with the end posts braced with an angled strut (also set in concrete). String heavy-duty fencing wire horizontally between the posts, using

In winter, thin out any of the older spurs if they have become congested, then cut back the main stem's new growth to 15cm (6in).

screw-in, galvanized vine-eyes and tensioning bolts at either end. The first wire should be 30cm (12in) above the soil, with subsequent wires 45cm (18in) apart. When growing a tree against a wall, have the first wire 30cm (12in) above the soil and subsequent wires 15cm (6in) apart.

Training and pruning cordons

Cordons have a single stem trained at an angle of 45 degrees. After planting at the correct angle, tie a bamboo cane behind the main stem and to the top wire. Prune sideshoots to just above the third bud. In the first summer, tie extension growth to the cane and prune back any new shoots from the main stem to above the third bud. New shoots produced from the stubs of sideshoots produced last year should be pruned to their first leaf. Each winter, thereafter, cut back the main stem's new growth to within 15cm (6in). Once the tree reaches the top of its support, cut any extension growth to the first bud. Each summer all new shoots produced from the stubs cut back the previous year should be pruned to the first leaf.

HOW TO FIX SUPPORTING WIRES TO A WALL

1 To support trees against walls, use wires held by vine eyes. Depending on the type of vine eye, either knock them into the wall or drill and plug before screwing them in.

2 Pass heavy-duty galvanized wire through the holes in the eyes and fasten to the end ones, keeping the wire as tight as possible.

PRUNING A FAN-TRAINED TREE

The main aim when pruning a fan tree is to maintain the fan shape. In spring, cut out any new sideshoots that are pointing towards or away from the wall. If necessary, reduce the number of new shoots to about one every 15cm (6in).

In summer cut back all new shoots to about six leaves, leaving any that are needed to fill in gaps in the main framework. In autumn, after cropping, further cut back the shoots to three leaves.

Training and pruning fans

Fan-trained trees have up to ten equally spaced ribs radiating from the main stem. It is a good way of training fruit trees because the fan produces a large number of fruit-bearing stems.

After planting, cut back the main stem to just above the first bud which should be about 5cm (2in) above the bottom wire. Tie in two bamboo canes to the supporting wires either side of the tree at angles of 45 degrees. The following summer select two sideshoots and tie them into the canes as they grow. Remove all others. During the dormant season cut back sideshoots to about 45cm (18in). The following summer, untie the first pair of canes and lower the canes, with branches attached, to the lowest horizontal wire each side of the tree. Tie in another pair of canes at 45 degrees and tie two new suitably placed shoots to them. Remove any unwanted shoots to their first leaf.

Repeat the process each year to create a symmetrical, fan-shaped tree. Once established, it will still need regular pruning to remove unwanted or badly positioned new shoots and to keep it fruiting well, because the fruit is borne on one-year-old wood. Always prune in summer to avoid silver leaf disease.

Training and pruning espaliers

Espalier trees have three or four horizontal tiers of branches trained along the supporting wires. Follow the method described for pruning fans, except the main stem is retained and trained vertically. Each winter the main stem should be pruned back to just above the horizontal wire, and the sideshoots are trained along canes held at 45 degrees in their first year, then lowered to the horizontal wire in their second. Each summer all unwanted new shoots should be pruned to the first leaf and suitably placed new shoots tied into the next pair of canes. Once the tree covers the support, cut back the extension growth of the main stem to one bud above the top wire and treat each branch as described for a cordon.

Growing a fan-trained peach tree against a wall creates an ideal environment for the tree and looks attractive. All parts of the tree are within reach and so maintenance is easier.

Growing apples and pears

Apples and pears can be grown in a variety of ways, ranging from free-standing specimens for the middle of a lawn or border to neatly trained types for growing against a fence or a wall or other type of supporting framework.

Planting

If you are growing more than one tree, in an orchard for example, you will need to space the trees according to their eventual size, which is dependent on the rootstock. Trees on dwarfing rootstocks can be planted 1.5m (5ft) apart, while trees on vigorous rootstocks should be up to 7m (25ft) apart.

Container-grown fruit trees can be planted at any time of the year, but they will establish more quickly and be easier to look after if they are planted in spring or autumn when the soil is moist and warm, which encourages rapid root growth and so establishment.

Bare-root specimens, however, have to be planted during the dormant season, which is between autumn and spring. The planting technique for fruit trees is the same as that described for ornamental trees and shrubs.

Good apple and pear varieties

Eating apples	'Grenadier'
'Discovery'	'Howgate
'Fiesta'	Wonder'
'Greensleeves'	
'James Grieve'	**Pears**
'Jonagold'	'Beth'
'Katy'	'Concorde'
'Sunset'	'Conference'
	'Doyenné du
Cooking apples	Comice'
'Bramley's	'Williams' Bon
Seedling'	Chrétien'

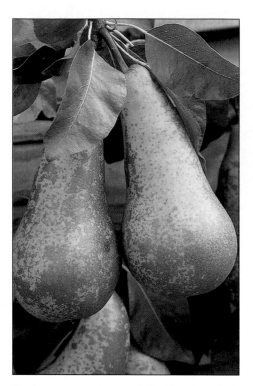

Conference pears have a distinctive elongated shape. These healthy specimens are ripe for picking and enjoying.

Malus 'John Downie' is one of the best varieties for making crab apple jelly.

Pruning free-standing trees

Despite a popular belief that apple and pear trees are difficult and time-consuming to keep in shape, if you buy trees that have been well trained, they will require the minimum of care. Pruning is best carried out in mid- to late winter. First, cut out dead or diseased stems and any new shoots that are crossing or touching. Also cut out any very upright-growing shoots. Then shorten about half of the remaining new growth to maintain a well-balanced overall shape. Every few years you may have to remove one or two larger branches so as to maintain the balanced shape and keep the tree from becoming congested in the centre.

General care

Three or four years after planting, start feeding all fruiting trees as a matter of course each spring. Apply a general fertilizer at a rate recommended by the manufacturer, on the ground under the canopy of the tree. Then top up the loose organic mulch so that it is about 8cm (3in) thick over the same area. Established trees do not need watering, although a thorough soaking every couple of weeks during a prolonged drought will ensure that crop yields are not affected. Spraying garden trees against pest and disease attacks is not normally worthwhile.

Harvesting and storing

Fruits are ripe when they separate from the tree with their stalk intact. Gently twist the fruit in the palm of your hand: if it comes away it's ready to pick. In general, the fruit on the sunny side of the tree will ripen first.

Not all varieties of apples and pears store well. Early varieties of eating apples should not be stored. Choose only perfect fruit of average size. Small fruit tend to shrivel and large fruit tend to rot. Separate

PRUNING A FREE-STANDING TREE

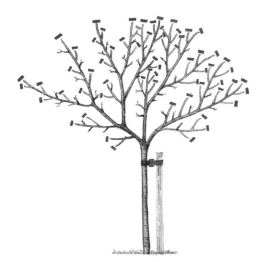

After planting cut back the leader to about 75cm (30in) above the ground. Leave any sideshoots that appear just below this cut and remove any others lower down. The following year reduce all new growth by about half. This will form the basic framework. Subsequent pruning is restricted to reducing the length of new growth by about a third and removing overcrowded growth.

different varieties because they store for different durations. Keep the fruit in moulded paper trays in ventilated cardboard boxes, both of which are often available free from supermarkets. Place boxes in a cool, dark, frost-free place and check at least once a week to remove deteriorating fruits.

Apples are not only delicious when they are picked straight from the tree, many varieties also retain their qualities when stored. This crop of ripening apples will make for a successful harvest.

HOW TO HARVEST APPLES AND PEARS

Apples and pears are removed from the tree with a twist of the wrist. The stalks should remain attached to the fruit.

HOW TO STORE APPLES AND PEARS

Apples, pears and quinces can be stored in trays in a cool, dry place. It is best if they are laid in individual screws of paper or moulded paper trays so that the individual fruits do not touch. The length of storage time depends on the variety.

Growing other tree fruit

Plum and cherry trees can be grown in a number of ways, ranging from full-sized standards to pyramid bushes. They can also be trained as fans against walls and fences.

Choosing a site

Fruit trees grow best in a moisture-retentive but free-draining soil, so it is worth digging in plenty of well-rotted organic matter before planting. Cherries, in particular, do not do well on dry or shallow soil. All need full sun to thrive, although acid cherries are more tolerant of shady conditions.

General care

Apply a general fertilizer at the rate recommended by the manufacturer, under the canopy of each peach and nectarine tree. Plums and cherries respond to a slightly higher rate of feed, so apply a general fertilizer at approximately double the rate that you would use for other trees. Fruit trees should be mulched each spring with loose organic material, such as well-rotted garden compost, so that it is about 8cm (3in) thick. Water in prolonged dry spells. Wall-trained trees should also be watered regularly while fruit is swelling.

Reducing vigour

You can keep young plum trees small and fruiting well using a technique called festooning. During the summer pull down the main stems into a horizontal position by tying strings to their tips and tying the other ends to the trunk. This reduces sap flow. During the following summer prune back the main shoots and tie down in the same way the new shoots that are produced. In time, you end up with a smaller, slightly weeping tree that fruits well.

Eat damsons fresh when they are fully ripe. Surplus fruit can be frozen whole or used to make jams and jellies. Damsons are suitable for cooking once they have coloured.

PRUNING A SOUR CHERRY FAN

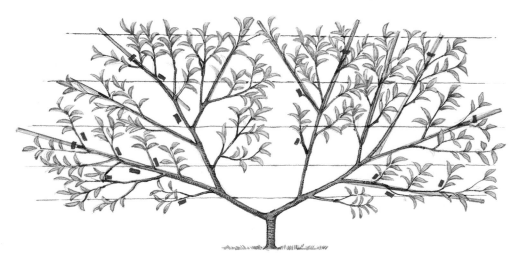

Once established, there are two purposes to pruning a cherry fan: to keep the fan shape and to ensure that there is a constant supply of new wood. When you are pruning to keep the shape, remove any shoots that are pointing in the wrong direction. For renewal pruning, cut back in summer one-third of the shoots that have fruited, preferably as far back as the next new shoot. Tie these new shoots to the cane and wire framework.

Peaches and nectarines blossom early in the year, when only a few pollinating insects are about, so it is worthwhile hand-pollinating the blossom with a soft paintbrush to ensure a good set of fruit.

During cold spells in early spring, it is worth covering fruit trees with insulating hessian (burlap) or a double layer of horticultural fleece to protect the blossom from frost. Later in the year, use netting to protect ripening fruit from the birds.

Peach leaf curl disease distorts leaves and can eventually weaken the tree. You can prevent new leaves from becoming infected by clearing away infected leaves once they fall and by covering the tree from early winter until late spring so that rain cannot wet the foliage. The fungal disease is spread by rain splash.

Pruning and training

Plums should be pruned in summer to avoid silver leaf disease. Once the basic shape of the tree has been established, cherries and plums need little pruning apart from the removal of dead, diseased or congested growth. Sour cherries are produced on one-year-old wood and should be pruned after the fruit has been harvested. Cut back about one-third of the fruiting stems to the first new shoot lower down the stem.

Plum and sweet cherry trees, on the other hand, produce most of their fruit at the base of one-year-old and older shoots. This means that they are not suitable for training as cordons or espaliers but can be trained as fans. After formative pruning of a fan-trained tree has established the framework, you need to make sure there is a constant supply of new growth that will bear the fruit. In summer cut back all shoots that have fruited to a

PRUNING A FRUIT TREE

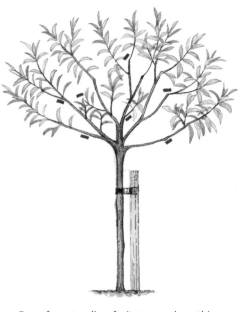

For a free-standing fruit tree such as this peach, not a great deal of pruning is required. In spring cut back some of the older barren wood as far as a new replacement shoot. Remove any awkwardly placed branches and keep the bush open and airy. Avoid making large cuts, because this is likely to allow canker to infect the tree.

new shoot lower down. Then tie in this new shoot to the supporting cane as a replacement for the one you have removed. Also prune out any unwanted growth to maintain the overall shape of the fan.

Peaches and nectarines can be grown as free-standing trees, but they are most successful when grown as a fan against a south-facing wall or fence. Not only does the support provide protection during early spring when the blossom is susceptible to frost damage, but it also captures more of the sun's energy during the summer, improving the chances that the fruit will ripen successfully.

Harvesting and storing

Pick fruit as soon as it is ripe. You can also pick plums slightly under-ripe for storage in the salad drawer of your refrigerator for a couple of

weeks. Sweet cherries, nectarines and peaches do not continue to mature after picking, so do not harvest until they are ready. Ripe fruit is best eaten straight away, although it will last a few days if kept somewhere cool. Gluts of fruit can be made into jam and preserves, or plums and sweet cherries halved and stoned (pitted) and then frozen whole.

Good fruit tree varieties

Plums	'Garden Anny'
'Cambridge	'Garden Lady'
Gage'	'Garden Silver'
'Czar'	'Garden Gold'
'Marjorie's	'Peregrine'
Seedling'	'Rochester'
'Merryweather'	'Terrace Amber'
'Oullins Gage'	'Terrace
'Victoria'	Diamond'

Cherries	**Nectarines**
'Morello' (acid)	'Early Rivers'
'Stella'	'Garden Beauty'
'Sunburst'	'Golden Glow'
	'Lord Napier'
Peaches	'Nectarella'
'Bonanza'	'Terrace Ruby'
'Duke of York'	

Patio peaches and nectarines

Dwarf peaches, such as 'Bonanza', and those in the Garden and Terrace series, as well as dwarf nectarines, such as 'Nectarella' and 'Golden Glow', are suitable for growing in pots on the patio. Use a large container filled with soil-based compost (soil mix). Hand-pollinate with a soft brush and keep frost free (in a conservatory or heated greenhouse) until late spring when the plant can be moved outside. Feed with a high-potash liquid feed, such as tomato fertilizer, every fortnight throughout the growing season. Net ripening fruit against birds.

Growing bush fruit

Gooseberries and currants are more tolerant than many other fruit and can be grown in partial shade, although better crops and earlier harvests will be achieved in full sun. Red- and white currants need a well-drained site, but blackcurrants can tolerate poorly drained soil.

Planting

For best results plant bush fruits in a moisture-retentive but free-draining soil that does not get waterlogged in winter. They can be grown as free-standing bushes, novelty hedges or as trained forms against a fence or other support. On an exposed site, a wall or fence will provide protection, especially in spring when late frosts can reduce yields considerably.

Gooseberry bushes should be spaced 1–1.5m (3–5ft) apart, depending on the vigour of the variety. Blackcurrant bushes should be spaced 1.5m (5ft) apart. Red- and white currants, grown as bushes, should be spaced 1.2m (4ft) apart or, as cordons, should be spaced 45cm (18in) apart.

HOW TO PRUNE A GOOSEBERRY BUSH

On an established gooseberry bush, cut back the new growth on the leaders in winter by about half and reduce all other new growth to two buds. In summer, remove any damaged wood, crossing branches, suckers and basal growth to keep the centre of the bush airy and prevent it becoming congested.

Pruning and training

Gooseberries and currants can be grown as airy, open-centred bushes or as cordons against a supporting framework. Gooseberries and blackcurrants are produced on shoots that are one or more years old, so bushes will produce a crop even if you do not prune them. However, the stems will soon become very congested and picking will be difficult.

Gooseberry bushes After planting, prune back three or four well-spaced sideshoots by about half to an upward-facing bud. Remove all other shoots. In the following winter cut back two new shoots on each sideshoot by about half to form the main framework of the bush and at the same time remove any shoots congesting the centre. Cut back any other new growth to two buds so that they form fruiting spurs. Thereafter, prune in summer to keep the centre of the bush open and healthy. In winter, cut back any growth from the framework branches by about half and all other new growth to two buds.

Gooseberry cordons After planting, cut back the main shoot by about half and tie it in to an upright bamboo cane fixed to the support. Prune off any sideshoots to leave two buds. Thereafter, prune in late summer, cutting back new sideshoots to 10cm (4in) from the main trunk. In winter cut back the leading shoot by a third. Once the cordon has reached the top of its support, cut it back to one bud instead.

Blackcurrant bushes This fruit can only be grown on bushes. Prune established blackcurrants in winter, removing one-third of the stems starting with the oldest, cutting back to 2.5cm (1in) above the ground. Alternatively, they can be pruned when harvesting.

Red- and white currant bushes After planting, select three or four well-spaced sideshoots and cut them back by about half to an upward-facing bud. All other shoots should be removed. The following winter cut back two new shoots on each sideshoot by about half to form the main framework of the bush and remove any shoots congesting the centre. Cut back any other new growth to two buds so that they

Gooseberries can be grown as single cordons. This is achieved by tying them into canes, which are supported by horizontal wires.

Blackcurrants and redcurrants are delicious when ripe, picked fresh from the garden.

form fruiting spurs. In subsequent years, prune in summer to keep the centre of the currant bush open and healthy. In winter, cut back extension growth from the framework branches by about half and other new growth to two buds.

Red- and white currant cordons

After planting a cordon, cut back the main shoot by about half its length and tie it in to an upright bamboo cane fixed to the support. Prune back any sideshoots to leave two buds. Thereafter, prune in late summer but cut back new sideshoots to leave about five leaves. In winter cut back the leading shoot by a third. Once the cordon has reached the top of its support, cut it back to one bud instead.

Good bush fruit varieties

Gooseberries	Blackcurrants
'Careless'	'Baldwin'
'Greenfinch'	'Ben Lomond'
'Invicta'	'Ben Nevis'
'Lancashire Lad'	'Ben Sarek'
'Leveller'	'Black Reward'
'Whinham's	'Boskoop Giant'
Industry'	
	White currants
Redcurrants	'White Dutch'
'Laxton's No. 1'	'White Grape'
'Red Lake'	'White Versailles'

General care

Apply a general fertilizer at the rate recommended by the manufacturer around each fruit bush annually in spring. Mulch each spring with loose organic material, such as well-rotted garden compost.

Bush fruits are largely trouble-free, although American gooseberry mildew disease can be devastating if it is allowed to take hold. If your bushes show symptoms (powdery patches on young leaves), prune back affected branches by about a third before spraying the rest of the bush with a suitable fungicide. The variety 'Invicta' is resistant to mildew.

Sawfly caterpillars can strip leaves from gooseberries in late spring; pick off any caterpillars by hand and kill them. You may also need to protect bushes with netting from bud-stripping bullfinches in winter and the ripening fruit from other birds in summer.

Harvesting and storing

Gooseberry bushes that are developing a lot of fruit can be thinned in late spring and the unripe fruit used for cooking, allowing the

HOW TO PRUNE BLACKCURRANTS

After planting, cut blackcurrants back to a single bud above the ground. The following winter, remove any weak or misplaced growth. Subsequent pruning can take place either in winter or when harvesting. Remove dead and diseased stems and cut out up to a third of two-year-old or older wood.

The simplest method of preserving bush fruits is to freeze them.

rest to swell and ripen to be eaten fresh. Gooseberries will not all ripen at once, so you will have to pick over the bushes several times. The fruit can be kept for a few weeks in a cool place or made into preserves.

Blackcurrants can be picked and pruned at the same time. Simply cut back all fruiting stems to 2.5cm (1in) from the ground above a plump bud and then take the laden stems to the kitchen for stripping. Pick or prune off sprigs of red- and white currants while the fruit is well coloured but still shiny. All currants can be kept for a couple of weeks in a cool place, or frozen or made into preserves.

HOW TO PRUNE OTHER CURRANTS

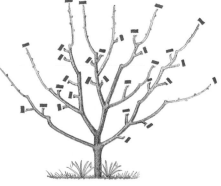

After planting a red- or white currant bush cut back each main shoot by about half. During subsequent pruning, in summer, aim to form an open bush. In winter, cut back all new growth on the main shoots and reduce the new growth on all sideshoots to two buds. Remove any dead and diseased stems.

Growing cane fruit

Raspberries, blackberries and hybrid berries such as loganberries are easy to grow. Blackberries will even produce a decent crop if they are grown against a north-facing wall.

Raspberries

This crop needs a sunny, sheltered spot and a well-drained but moisture-retentive soil to do well. Raspberries dislike winter wet, so grow them on a ridge of topsoil if your soil is heavy. Space plants 38–45cm (15–18in) apart in the row. After planting, cut back the stems to about 30cm (12in), cutting just above a bud. The following spring cut back the old stem to ground level as new shoots emerge.

Raspberries can be grown against a free-standing support or alongside a fence. The easiest form of support consists of stout posts at 3m (10ft) intervals along the row with horizontal fencing wire strung between the posts and held taut with tensioning bolts. Only two wires are needed, one running about 60cm (24in) from the ground and the second at a height of about 1.2m (4ft).

There are two types of raspberry: summer fruiting and autumn fruiting. By far the most common are the summer-fruiting varieties, which bear fruit on canes produced the previous year. Autumn-fruiting raspberries, on the other hand, produce their fruit at the tips of the canes produced during the current season. Prune summer-fruiting raspberries in early autumn by removing all shoots that have fruited back to ground level and tying in new shoots to the support. If there are too many shoots to space about 8cm (3in) apart on the support, cut out the weakest. Autumn-fruiting raspberry canes should be cut back to ground level after harvesting. New shoots produced from below ground in spring will bear fruit in the following autumn.

Blackberries and hybrid berries

Although blackberries prefer a sunny spot, they are much more tolerant than other types of fruit and can be grown in shade and on any type of soil. Space plants 1.8–3m (6–10ft) apart depending on the vigour of the variety. Do not plant blackberries too deeply; the soil should only just cover the roots. Blackberries and most hybrid berries need a support. This can be constructed as described for raspberries, but the horizontal wires should be spaced just 30cm (12in) apart, with the lowest wire 1m (3ft) from the ground and the highest wire at about 1.8m (6ft).

The easiest way to train blackberries and hybrid berries is to use a fan method. Select one new cane to be trained along each wire on one side of the plant, then tie in the canes as they grow. The following

HOW TO ERECT POSTS AND WIRES

1 Knock a stout post well into the ground at the end of the row of cane fruit. It may be easier to dig a hole and insert the post before backfilling and ramming down the earth.

2 Knock another post at an angle of 45 degrees to the vertical to act as a support to the upright post. Nail firmly using galvanized nails so that the upright post is rigid and will support the tension of tight wires.

3 Fasten the wires around one end post and pull tight along the row, stapling it to each vertical post. Keep the wire as taut as possible. If necessary, use eye bolts on the end posts to tension the wire.

4 Fasten the canes – in this case raspberry canes – to the wire with string or plant ties. Space the canes out evenly along the wire so that the maximum amount of light can reach the leaves.

year do the same on the other side of the plant. Once canes have fruited in autumn, cut them back to ground level and tie in new ones to replace those that have been cut out.

General care

Hand-weed around the plants rather than using a hoe so that you do not damage their shallow roots. Every spring, apply a general fertilizer, at the rate recommended by the manufacturer, on either side of the row. Mulch each spring with loose organic material, such as garden compost, and remove any suckers that appear away from the row.

HOW TO PICK CANE FRUIT

Small cane fruit, such as raspberries and blackberries, should be carefully picked between thumb and finger. The fruit should be placed in small containers so that they are not squashed or bruised.

Good cane fruit varieties

Autumn raspberries	Blackberries
'Autumn Bliss'	'Ashton Cross'
'Fallgold'	'Bedford Giant'
	'Fantasia'
	'Loch Ness'
Summer raspberries	'Oregon Thornless'
'Delight'	
'Glen Clova'	Hybrid berries
'Glen Moy'	'Loganberry LY59'
'Glen Prosen'	
'Julia'	'Loganberry L654'
'Leo'	'Sunberry'
'Malling Admiral'	'Tayberry'
'Malling Jewel'	'Vietchberry'

TRAINING BLACKBERRIES: ALTERNATE BAY

There are several methods of training blackberries. One method is to tie all the new growth to one side of the wirework. After fruiting, remove the previous year's growth from the other side and then tie next year's new growth on that side. Repeat each year.

TRAINING BLACKBERRIES: ROPE

A second way to train blackberries is temporarily to tie in all new growth vertically to the wirework and along the top wire. The current fruiting canes are tied in groups horizontally. These are removed after harvesting and the new growth is tied into their place.

TRAINING BLACKBERRIES: FANS

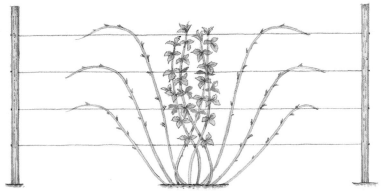

The new blackberry canes are temporarily tied vertically and along the top wire, while the fruiting canes are tied in singly along the horizontal wires. Any excess canes are removed. After fruiting, these canes are taken out and the new growth is tied into their place.

TRAINING RASPBERRIES: POSTS AND WIRES

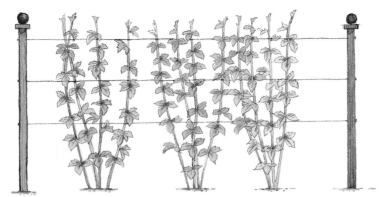

Raspberry plants are set at intervals of 38–45cm (15–18in). Each year, new raspberry canes are thrown up. When fruiting has finished on the old canes, these are cut out and the new canes are tied to the wires in their place. This sequence is followed every year.

Growing strawberries

To get a reliable crop of strawberries it is important to choose a good variety and grow them well. There are several excellent varieties, which can give a succession of fruit over a long period.

Planting strawberries

Strawberries should be planted into soil that has not been used for growing them for at least the last five years. Choose a sunny, sheltered site with well-drained soil and add plenty of well-rotted manure before planting. Plant bare-root strawberries on a slight ridge at the same depth as they were in the field. Container-grown strawberries should be planted slightly deeper so that the rootball is just covered with soil. Space plants 45cm (18in) apart, with 75cm (30in) between rows.

Plant through a mulch of black polythene (plastic) to prevent weeds. Lay over the prepared bed where the soil has been ridged slightly in the centre and plant through cross-shaped slits. Bury the edges of the polythene to keep it in place.

On this plant a succession of stages can be seen, from flowers to ripe fruit. Strawberries eaten immediately after picking taste best.

Succession of strawberries

Because different varieties of strawberry are ready to harvest at different times, if you choose the right combination you can achieve a succession of fruit through the early summer. Very early varieties, such as 'Pantagruella', can be brought on even earlier under cloches to give you a garden crop in late spring – or even earlier if grown in pots or a growing bag in an unheated greenhouse. Follow this with an early variety, such as 'Idil', and a mid-season variety, such as 'Tenira', and finally a late variety, such as 'Bogota', for a continuous harvest until late summer. You can extend the season

MULCHING WITH STRAW

Place a layer of straw under the leaves of the strawberry plants in order to prevent the developing fruit from getting muddy or covered with dirt.

MULCHING WITH MEMBRANE

Strawberries can be grown through a polythene (plastic) mulch. This not only protects the fruit from mud splashes but also reduces the need for weeding and watering.

Good strawberry varieties

Summer-fruiting strawberries	'Royal Sovereign'
	'Tamella'
'Bogota'	'Tenira'
'Cambridge Favourite'	
	Perpetual-fruiting strawberries
'Cambridge Vigour'	
'Cambridge Rival'	'Aromel'
'Domanil'	'Gento'
'Hapil'	'Ostara'
'Honeoye'	'Red Rich'
'Idil'	'St Claude'
'Jamil'	**Alpines**
'Korona'	'Alexandria'
'Pantagruella'	'Delicious'
'Redgauntlet'	'Yellow Wonder'

Replacement crops

Strawberries produce their best crops in the second or third year after planting, then yields tend to fall and the health of the plants deteriorates as pests and diseases take a hold. Therefore, it is a good idea to replace the whole strawberry bed every few years with new, vigorous plants set in fresh soil. The cheapest way to do this is to raise your own plants by rooting runners from healthy, heavy-cropping plants.

Strawberries can be protected against frost with cloches.

A tunnel of wire netting can be used to protect the fruit from birds. The netting can be in short sections for easy removal and storage.

further by planting a perpetual strawberry variety, such as 'Aromel', which will continue to produce fruit into the autumn provided it is given the protection of cloches if cold weather threatens. Even winter and early spring crops can be achieved in a heated greenhouse.

General care

Keep strawberry beds free of weeds at all times. Hand-weeding is best, so as not to disturb the roots. Keep plants watered until they are

established. Water strawberry plants as necessary when the fruits are swelling and in the autumn when the following year's flower buds are formed. Apply a general fertilizer, at the rate recommended by the manufacturer, either side of the row in midsummer.

Strawberries are vulnerable to a number of pests and diseases. If you do not wish to use chemical controls you will need to remain vigilant at all times and clear fading foliage and rotting fruit as soon as they are

noticed. Aphids and slugs are the main pests, but watch out for botrytis if the season is moist. Protect ripening fruit from birds by covering the rows with nets held off the crop on wire hoops.

Harvesting and storing

Check ripening strawberries every day and pick when the fruits are red all over. Eat fresh straight away or keep somewhere cool for a few days. Surpluses can be frozen for purée or made into jam.

After summer-fruiting strawberries have produced their fruit, cut off all the leaves and burn or compost them, along with the straw mulch, to help prevent the spread of diseases.

1 After fruiting, the strawberry plant sends out a series of runners that root along their length to produce new plants. This method of propagation is called layering.

2 The layered plants can be dug up once they have rooted and used to start a new bed.

Propagation

The thrill of seeing your first seeds germinate or your first cutting take root is often when the gardening bug really gets a grip on a beginner. There are many ways you can increase your stock of plants, and the method you choose will depend on the type of plant you are growing, although some plants can be propagated using a variety of techniques.

All annual flowers and vegetables are raised from seed, and this is a useful way of growing some perennials and shrubs that you want a lot of – for ground cover or for a hedge, for example. But perennials, shrubs, climbers and trees can also be reproduced vegetatively by taking cuttings or by layering, and this might be more appropriate if you want just a few plants of a particular variety.

You do not need elaborate equipment, but your success rate will increase if you can provide the right environment. So, if you want to raise a lot of new plants, you should consider investing in a thermostatically controlled propagator.

The white, fragrant flowers of *Lilium regale* make it a popular plant. It can be propagated by seed in early autumn.

Sowing seed

Raising plants from seed has got to be one of the most satisfying aspects of gardening and is probably the easiest way of growing a lot of the same plant within a tight budget.

Collecting seed

If you want a lot of one particular plant or are propagating plants for sale at a plant fair, for example, many flowers can be raised successfully from seed collected from your own garden. Bear in mind, however, that seed from a named variety may not grow into a plant that is exactly the same as its parent.

To save your own seed, simply cut the seedhead just before it is fully ripe and place it in a paper bag in a dry, airy room where it will finish ripening. For plants that eject their seed, you will need to cover the seedhead with the paper bag before you remove it from the plant.

Sowing techniques

To raise plants successfully early in the season you will need to keep the sown seeds somewhere warm, such as in an airing cupboard (linen closet) or a thermostatically controlled propagator, and have somewhere frost-free, such as a windowsill or heated greenhouse, to grow them on.

Seed is available in various forms, and the method of sowing varies according to the type you are growing. Always check the seed packet for details such as whether the seed needs light to germinate, its sowing depth, germination and growing-on temperatures, and use this information as a guide before you start.

Many seeds are now available pre-treated for more reliable germination (known as primed, chitted or pre-germinated seed). Such seeds are more expensive, but they are worth

considering for expensive and difficult-to-germinate subjects. Some seed suppliers also offer coated or pelleted seed, which is larger and easier to space when sowing. This eliminates the need for pricking out, and will reduce the wastage from discarding seedlings.

Planning ahead

It makes sense to plan ahead if you intend to sow a lot of plants from seed. This will not only make the most efficient use of your time, equipment and available space, but it will also help even out the workload.

The best way to organize a programme is to decide when you want the plants and to work backwards to decide on a sowing date. Make sure that you have the time and growing space at each stage of development. It's a good idea to make a seed organizer out of an old

COLLECTING SEED

1 Most self-sowing flowers will drop their seed without need for assistance but to make sure that seed does fall on the soil, tap ripe seedheads to dislodge and scatter the seed before discarding the dead flowers.

2 Seed can also be collected by tapping the seedhead over a sheet of paper. Remove any bits of seed case and pour the seed into a paper bag, labelled with the plant's name, until it is required. Store in a cool, dry place.

Germinating seed

A few types of seed will not germinate reliably unless given a special treatment before sowing – check the seed packet for details. The seeds of sweet peas, for example, have a particularly hard coat that needs to be softened by soaking in water for 24 hours before sowing or breached by nicking the seedcoat with a sharp knife or rubbing it with sandpaper.

Other types of seed need a period of cold (known as stratification) before they will germinate. In nature this is the winter period, and the easiest way to provide this is to sow the seed in autumn and overwinter it in a cold frame. However, you can mimic the process at other times of the year by mixing seed with moist sand and placing it in a refrigerator for one to three months, depending on the type of seed.

shoebox with weekly dividers to help you keep track. If you need to sow several batches of the same seed over a period of time (such as with many salad crops) move the seed packet after sowing to the next date in the organizer. In general, sow twice as much seed as you need mature plants to allow for erratic germination and losses along the way.

The best way to sow most seed is in a seed tray (flat) using a sowing compost (soil mix) because you can control the conditions accurately and so achieve more reliable germination. However, it is worth sowing some types of seed, such as hardy annuals and many vegetables, in their final position, direct into a specially prepared seedbed.

HOW TO SOW IN THE GARDEN

1 Sow the seed along the drill, taking care not to sow too thickly, to reduce the amount of thinning that will be necessary.

Sowing small seed

Some plants, such as lobelias and impatiens, have dust-like seed that is very difficult to sow thinly and evenly. You can make the job a lot easier by mixing the seed with a

2 Rake the soil into the drill over the seed. Gently tamp down the soil along the row with the flat of the rake and lightly rake over.

little dry silver sand before sowing. The sand will effectively "dilute" the seed, making it easier to sow, and, because it is light in colour, you will be able to see which areas of compost have been sown.

SOWING IN CELLULAR BLOCKS

Fill the blocks with compost (soil mix) and tap on the table to settle down. Sow one or two seeds in each cell. Cover lightly with compost. Remove the weaker seedling after germination.

HOW TO SOW IN TRAYS

1 Fill the seed tray (flat) with seed compost and tamp down the compost lightly to produce a level surface. Sow the seed thinly across the compost.

2 Cover with a thin layer of compost (unless the seed needs light to germinate), lightly firm down and label the tray. Labelling is very important as many seedlings look the same.

SOWING IN POTS

Fill the pot with a good sowing compost (soil mix), tap it lightly on the bench and sow from one to three seeds in each pot. Once germinated, the weaker seedlings can be removed, leaving one to grow on.

HOW TO USE A PROPAGATOR

1 Place the seeds in a propagator. Adjust the temperature of heated propagators as required – seed packets should indicate the best temperature, but you may need to compromise if different seeds need different temperatures.

2 This propagator is unheated and should be kept in a warm position in a greenhouse or within the house. Start opening the vents once the seeds have germinated to begin the hardening-off process.

Pricking out and aftercare

Once the seeds have germinated, they need to be given the perfect growing conditions to produce independent, healthy and vigorous plants suitable for planting in their permanent position.

Pricking out

Poor seedling care is the most usual reason for failure when raising new plants from seed. The aim is to provide a suitable growing environment where the plants can establish and develop without receiving a check in growth. This means that the seedlings indoors

need to be spaced (pricked) out either into seed trays (flats) or other containers, and those raised outside need to be transplanted or thinned out to the correct spacing.

As soon as they are large enough to handle safely, space seedlings into prepared seed trays (flats) or modules or into individual pots filled with fresh compost (soil mix). Gently lift each seedling individually, holding it by a leaf (never the stem), and support the root system with a dibber, plant label or pencil. Position the seedling at the correct spacing at the same depth as it was before,

spreading its delicate roots carefully. Water the tray of seedlings from below by standing it in a bowl of water until the surface of the compost darkens. Place the seedlings somewhere bright but shaded from direct sunlight and mist occasionally if they threaten to flag. Maintain the correct growing-on temperature (depending on the type of plants you are growing) until they are ready to plant out.

If conditions outside are not suitable, you may have to keep the plants growing in limited amounts of compost for several weeks. If they

HOW TO PRICK OUT SEEDLINGS INTO MODULES

1 Choose a module that suits the size of plant. A small seedling, such as ageratum, will not need such a large cell as, say, a dahlia. Fill the cells loosely with a suitable potting mixture (soil mix). Strike the compost off level with a straightedge but do not compress it. It will settle in the cells once the seedlings have been inserted and watered.

2 Loosen the seedlings in the tray or pot you are pricking out from and if possible lift them one at a time by their seed leaves. Never hold seedlings by their stems as this can damage them. The seed leaves are the first ones to open, and they are usually smaller and a different shape from the true leaves.

3 Use a tool designed for the purpose, or improvise with a pencil or plant label, to make a hole large enough to take the roots with as little bending or disturbance as possible. Gently firm the compost around the roots, being careful not to press too hard. Water thoroughly, then keep the plants in a well-lit spot but out of direct sunlight.

HOW TO PRICK OUT SEEDLINGS INTO POTS

1 Fill small pots with potting mixture (soil mix) and firm it lightly, using the base of another pot. Loosen the compost around the seedling to be transplanted with a small dibber or transplanting tool. Hold the seedling by its leaves, not the stem.

2 Make a hole in the centre of the pot, deep enough to take the roots. While still holding the seedling by a leaf, gently firm the potting mixture around the roots, using a small dibber or a finger. Do not press too hard, as watering will settle the mixture around the roots.

3 Water carefully so that the soil settles without washing the plant out. Keep in a warm, humid place out of direct sunlight. Labelling individual pots is tedious, so you may prefer to group individual varieties into trays, and use just one label.

begin to show signs of starvation (yellowing lower leaves) water them with a dilute liquid feed. Also space plants as necessary so that the leaves do not touch.

About two weeks before you want to plant out, they will need to be weaned off the cosy temperatures found inside the greenhouse to the harsher environment outdoors. This is known as hardening off.

Transplanting

A few flowers, such as wallflowers, and vegetables, such as cabbages and Brussels sprouts, are best sown in specially prepared nursery seedbeds and then transplanted to their final growing position when they are large enough to move. This allows you to grow the plants in an out of the way spot until they are large enough. Water the seedbed well before you intend to transplant the seedlings and lift them carefully, holding the plant by the leaf rather than the stem. Replant them as quickly as you can, firm well and water thoroughly once more.

Thinning

Seedlings sown directly outside should be thinned in two stages. When the majority of the seedlings have emerged and are large enough to handle, thin the rows to half their final spacing. Then allow the partially thinned seedlings to grow on before thinning again to their correct spacing. In this way you are more likely to get the final spacing right. Choose a fine day when the soil is moist to thin the plants. Re-firm any seedlings loosened while thinning and water the row well afterwards. With some plants you can use thinnings to fill any gaps in the rows, while some vegetable thinnings can be used in the kitchen.

HOW TO TRANSPLANT SEEDLINGS

1 Water the row of seedlings, the previous night if possible, but at least a few hours before transplanting. This will soften the earth and make transplanting easier. It will also reduce the stress the seedlings are under.

2 Using a hand fork, dig up, rather than pull out, the plants to be moved. Only dig up the plants as you need them. Do not dig them up all at once and leave them lying around or they will dry out.

3 Using a garden line to keep the row straight and a measuring stick to make sure that the distances are equal, replant the seedlings using a trowel.

4 Gently firm in each plant and rake the soil around them in order to tidy it up and to remove footprints and uneven soil. Water the seedlings carefully.

There is really nothing to surpass the delicate paper-tissue flowers of the *Papaver somniferum* (opium poppy), which are followed by large, grey-green seedheads. It is fairly easy to collect the seeds for propagation and grow them up, ready to plant outside in the spring.

Spring cuttings

Many plants, including shrubs and herbaceous plants, can be propagated easily from cuttings. Spring is a good time to take cuttings as the young plants will grow quickly. It is always worth experimenting if there is a plant that you want to propagate but are not sure if a softwood or basal cutting is suitable. The chances are that some will root.

Different types of cuttings

There are several types of cuttings that make use of plant material in its different stages of development at various times of the year. Softwood and basal cuttings are taken in spring from the new, soft growth. In summer, semi-ripe and heel cuttings can be taken from material that is starting to ripen and go woody at the base. Hardwood cuttings are fully ripe shoots, and these cuttings are taken in winter.

Softwood cuttings

Although softwood cuttings are usually taken in spring, while the plant is putting on new growth that is soft and green, material can also

Pelargoniums such as this 'Little Gem' propagate well from softwood cuttings. A cutting taken early in spring will be sufficiently mature to flower by the summer.

be taken from tender perennials in late summer. These cuttings are then overwintered as rooted cuttings as an insurance against winter losses. Choose healthy, non-flowering shoots that are typical of the plant and cut off material just above a leaf joint using a sharp knife or pair of

secateurs (pruners). Collect the cuttings early in the day while they are turgid (firm, not wilted) and keep in a plastic bag to prevent them wilting. Prepare the cuttings by trimming the stem just below a leaf joint to make a cutting 2.5–8cm (1–3in) long depending on the type

HOW TO TAKE SOFTWOOD CUTTINGS

1 Take cuttings from non-flowering shoots. A good guide to length is to cut the shoot off just above the third joint below the growing tip. Here a softwood cutting is taken from a pelargonium.

2 Remove the lowest pair of leaves with a small sharp knife. Trim straight across the base of each cutting, just below the lowest leaf joint. You can dip the ends in a rooting hormone, but the cuttings usually root quite readily without.

3 Insert about five cuttings around the edge of a 13cm (5in) pot containing a cuttings mixture (soil mix) and firm gently. Keep in a light, warm position but out of direct sun. Be careful not to overwater, otherwise the cuttings will rot. Pot up individually when rooted.

of growth that the plant produces. Remove the lowest pair of leaves and the growing tip from longer cuttings and insert them around the edge of a pot filled with moist, fresh cuttings compost (soil mix). The success rate for some types of plant can be increased by using a rooting hormone. Some types of rooting hormone also contain fungicide, which may be worth buying if the plant you are propagating is particularly vulnerable to disease.

It is important that the softwood cuttings are not allowed to wilt, so either place them in a covered propagator or cover the pot with a clear plastic bag held off the cuttings by short canes and secured by a rubber band. Place in a well-lit spot shaded from direct sunlight. Puncture the bag or ventilate the propagator when the cuttings start to root. Pot up into containers when they have sufficient roots.

Basal cuttings

Some plants, such as asters, chrysanthemums and dahlias, produce almost no woody growth, and can be propagated from new shoots produced at the base of older stems in spring and early summer. These are called basal cuttings.

When the new shoot reaches about 5–10cm (2–4in) long, with the first leaves starting to unfurl, use a sharp knife to cut it off cleanly from the crown. Insert it in a pot filled with cuttings compost. Several more cuttings can be placed around the edge of the pot.

Cover the pot with a plastic bag, held in position with a rubber band, and place the pot on a shady windowsill. Alternatively, use a heated propagator for quick results. After a few weeks, rooted cuttings can be potted up individually.

HOW TO TAKE BASAL CUTTINGS

1 Take short cuttings from the new growth at the base of the plant. Place the cuttings in a plastic bag until they are required so that they don't wilt.

2 Trim the base of the cuttings. Cut through the stem just below a leaf joint and then remove all the leaves, except for a few right at the top.

3 Place the cuttings in a pot of well-drained compost mix (soil mix) with added grit, perlite or vermiculite. You can root several in the same pot.

4 Label the pot, including the date on which you took the cuttings. Water the pot and place it in a propagator. You can use a plastic bag, but ensure that no leaves touch the bag. Seal with a rubber band.

Rooting hormones

You can increase your chances of success with most stem cuttings, particularly those that are reluctant to root, by using a rooting hormone. When applied to the cut surface at the base of the cutting, the hormone encourages root formation and increases the speed of rooting. Rooting hormones are usually formulated as powders, but you may also come across liquids and gels.

To avoid contaminating the hormone, tip a small amount into a saucer. Dip the cutting's cut end into the hormone, shaking off excess if you use powder, and insert into the compost (soil mix). After treating the batch of cuttings, discard any powder that is left over in the saucer. Rooting hormone deteriorates rapidly, so buy fresh stock every year to make sure of its effectiveness.

Apply a rooting hormone to plants such as this fuchsia to help increase the chance of successful propagation.

Summer cuttings

During the summer months you can increase your stock of many shrubs, climbers and perennials using semi-ripe and heel cuttings. This is one of the easiest ways to propagate plants and is usually successful.

Timing

When plant growth begins to slow down in summer, new shoots start to ripen and turn woody at the base, and are suitable for semi-ripe cuttings.

To test that the plant is at the correct stage of development, hold the main stem steady and bend the shoot over. If the shoot breaks it is either too soft and sappy or too hard and woody, but if it is springy and returns to its original position when you let go, it is at just the right stage of development.

Semi-ripe cuttings

During late summer, select non-flowering, healthy shoots that are typical of the plant and cut off material just above a leaf joint using a sharp knife or a pair of secateurs (pruners). Prepare the cuttings by trimming the stem just below a leaf joint to make a cutting 2.5–10cm (1–4in) long, depending on the type of growth the plant produces. Then treat as for softwood cuttings.

Heel cuttings

The cuttings of some plants, notably conifers, root better if taken with a small sliver of wood pulled from the main stem, known as a heel cutting. This is because the plant produces more hormones at this point and so the propagation is often more

successful. Select material of a suitable length, depending on the growth of the plant, and carefully pull it backwards up the stem so that it rips a small piece of older wood with it (known as a heel). Use a sharp knife to trim the heel to neaten up any rough edges so that it is 1–2cm (½–1in) long. Then dip the cut end of the prepared cuttings in rooting hormone before inserting the cuttings around the edge of a pot of cuttings compost (soil mix) or evenly spaced in a seed tray, then water well.

Making a border propagator

Summer cuttings are easy to root and need no special equipment. You can root most types in a simple border propagator in the garden.

HOW TO TAKE SEMI-RIPE CUTTINGS

1 Cut a length of the current season's growth. Trim each cutting just below the second or third leaf beneath the terminal leaves at the stem tip. Cut off the lowest one or two leaves from the base of each cutting.

2 Remove a sliver of bark about 1–2.5cm (½–1in) long from the base of each cutting, opposite the lowest leaf bud.

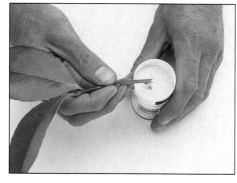

3 Dip the base of each cutting into hormone rooting powder and then tap it gently on the side of the tub to remove any excess.

4 Insert the cuttings into pots of well-drained compost mix (soil mix) with added grit, perlite or vermiculite.

5 Water well and mist the leaves with water to prevent the cuttings from wilting.

6 Label the cuttings and tent them in a clear plastic bag supported on canes.

Wounding cuttings

If you have had problems rooting cuttings from a particular plant, try increasing your chances of success by removing a sliver of stem from the base of the cutting while you are preparing it. Apply rooting hormone to the wound before inserting into the compost (soil mix).

Choose a position in a sheltered spot in light shade for most of the day. Dig a trench 5cm (2in) deep about 25cm (10in) wide and fill it with sharp sand. Make hoops 50–62cm (20–25in) out of stiff wire (old coat hangers work well). Insert the prepared cuttings into the sand and water well. Push wire hoops every 15cm (6in) along the trench and cover with a piece of opaque or white plastic, such as a plastic bag, which should be buried in the soil on one side and held down with bricks at the ends and along the other side. Check periodically to see if the cuttings need watering and to remove any that are starting to rot. When most of the cuttings have rooted carefully slash the cover for ventilation, then after a couple of weeks remove it and plant out or pot up the rooted cuttings.

Like other camellias, *C. transnokoensis* can be propagated by semi-ripe cuttings taken in late summer. Take the cutting from a healthy looking stem to increase the chances of success.

HOW TO TAKE HEEL CUTTINGS

1 Select a strongly growing, non-flowering sideshoot from the parent plant and grasp it near its point of origin. Pull it sharply away from the main stem, tearing off a tail (heel) of bark from the main stem.

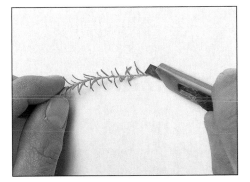

2 Trim the heel of the cutting with a small sharp knife, if necessary, cutting at an angle. Carefully strip off the foliage from the bottom half of the cutting with your finger and thumb.

3 Immerse the cutting in a fungicide solution to prevent disease problems. Dip the base of the cutting in hormone rooting powder and tap off the excess.

4 Insert the cuttings in a pot of cuttings compost (soil mix) to half its length using a fine dibber or skewer. Water well to seal the surface of the compost and leave to drain.

5 Blow up a plastic bag large enough to hold the tray and seal the tray inside. Place in a cool, shady spot outdoors. The bag should fog over. Water again if it dries out, then reseal until the cuttings have rooted.

Autumn and winter cuttings

When plants go dormant in winter some can still be propagated from hardwood cuttings and a few from root cuttings. This is the easiest way of propagating some deciduous trees and shrubs.

Root cuttings

There are a few popular plants that are difficult to propagate by other methods. Some of these can be raised successfully from root cuttings, which are taken during the dormant season. You can either lift a whole plant or leave it in the ground and dig around the edges to find suitable cuttings material. Select vigorous, healthy roots of about pencil thickness if possible and cut from the parent plant. Prepare the cuttings so they are about 5–10cm (2–4in) long, making a straight cut nearest the crown and an angled cut furthest away (so that you can tell which way up the cutting is). Dip the cutting in a fungicide powder before inserting vertically around the edge of a pot filled with a well-drained mixture of equal parts of grit and compost (soil mix), so that the straight cut is just proud of the surface. Top up with a thin layer of grit so that you can still see the top of each cutting and water well. Place in a cool, sheltered spot such as a cold frame or under a cloche in the garden.

If the roots are thinner than pencil thickness, lay them horizontally on the surface of the compost, before covering with grit.

Hardwood cuttings

These cuttings are taken from current year's shoots of deciduous woody plants that are fully ripe. When the plant has lost its leaves, select vigorous and healthy stems of around pencil thickness. Trim them off the

HOW TO TAKE ROOT CUTTINGS

1 Lift a young but well-established plant for the cuttings. If you don't want to use the whole plant for cuttings, and prefer to leave the parent plant largely undisturbed, remove soil from one side so that you can get to the roots. If the plant has large, fleshy roots, cut some off close to the main stem or crown.

2 You should be able to make several cuttings from each root by cutting it into lengths about 5–10cm (2–4in) long. To help you remember which way up they are, cut them horizontally at the top and diagonally at the bottom.

3 Fill a pot with a gritty potting mixture (soil mix) and insert the cuttings using a dibber or pencil to make the hole. The top of the cutting should be just above the top of the potting mixture.

4 Sprinkle a thin layer of grit over the surface, leaving the cuttings just visible. Label the pot so that you don't forget what it contains. Place in a cold frame or greenhouse and keep the potting mixture just moist.

5 Some plants, such as border phlox, and rock plants, such as *Primula denticulata*, have thin roots. These can be laid horizontally, so don't make sloping cuts to indicate the bottom. Just cut into 2.5–5cm (1–2in) lengths.

6 Fill a seed tray with a gritty compost and firm it level. Space the cuttings out evenly over the surface, then cover them with a layer of the gritty potting mix. Keep moist but not too wet in a cold frame or greenhouse.

Suitable plants for autumn and winter cuttings

Root cuttings	Hardwood cuttings
Acanthus	Aucuba
Bergenia	Berberis
Campanula	Buddleja
Dicentra	Buxus
Echinops	Cornus
Eryngium	Cotoneaster
Gaillardia	Escallonia
Geranium (hardy	Forsythia
varieties)	Hebe
Gypsophila	Kerria
Monarda	Leycesteria
Papaver orientale	Ligustrum
Phlox	Lonicera nitida
Primula	Philadelphus
denticulata	Ribes
Pulsatilla vulgaris	Rosa
Romneya coulteri	Salix
Stokesia laevis	Sambucus
Symphytum	Spiraea
Trollius	Weigela
Verbascum	

plant using secateurs (pruners) just above a bud or pair of buds. Prepare the cutting so that it is about 25–30cm (10–12in) long, making a horizontal cut at the bottom and an angled cut at the top. Wound difficult-to-root subjects and dip the cut ends in hormone rooting powder.

Hardwood cuttings are usually rooted outside in a sheltered spot. After preparing the soil by digging and weeding, make a 15–20cm (6–8in) deep, V-shaped slit trench, with one side vertical, using a spade. Fill the bottom 5cm (2in) of the trench with sharp sand and then insert the cuttings about 8–10cm (3–4in) apart along the trench. Refill the rest of the trench with soil, firm lightly and water well. Leave the cuttings *in situ* for the whole of the following season, watering and weeding as necessary. Then plant out rooted cuttings the following autumn, one year after taking the cuttings.

HOW TO TAKE HARDWOOD CUTTINGS

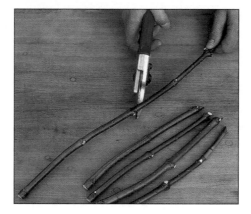

1 Choose stems of pencil thickness that are firm and hard but not too old. With shrubs such as *Cornus* you should be able to make several cuttings from one shoot. Make the first cut straight across the stem, just below a node, and a second, angled cut about 25cm (10in) above the first.

2 A rooting hormone is not essential, but it should increase the success rate. Moisten the bases of the cuttings in water then dip them into a rooting powder. You can use liquid or gel rooting hormones, in which case there is no need to dip the end in water first. Treat only the base end of each cutting.

3 Make a slit trench by pushing a spade into the ground and levering it backwards and forwards. The trench should be a little shallower than the length of the cuttings. Choose an unobtrusive spot in the garden to leave the cuttings undisturbed for a year.

4 Sprinkle some grit or coarse sand in the base of the slit trench if the ground is poorly drained. This will help to prevent water-logging around the cuttings.

5 Insert the cuttings 8–10cm (3–4in) apart, making sure that they are upright against the back of the slit and leaving about 5–10cm (2–4in) above the ground.

6 Firm the soil around the cuttings, to eliminate the pockets of air that would cause the cuttings to dry out. Water and label. Remember to water in dry weather.

Layering

This easy method of propagation is a useful way of increasing some shrubs and climbers that cannot readily be propagated from cuttings.

Simple layering

Layering is a method of getting a growing shoot to produce roots while it is still attached to the "parent" plant. There are several variations on the technique, and the one you use will depend on the plant and the type of growth it produces.

To make a simple layer choose a strong, actively growing shoot that is representative of the plant and showing no signs of pest or disease attack. It should also be low down on the plant and flexible enough to bend down to the ground without snapping. If there are no suitable stems, prune the parent plant back during the dormant season to encourage the production of suitable material next year.

Carefully dig over the area of ground next to the plant where the layer is to be rooted, removing weed roots and improving the soil with grit and well-rotted organic matter. Trim any sideshoots from the stem to be layered, leaving the growing point intact. Then bend down the stem to the soil and mark where it touches the ground about 30cm (12in) behind the growing tip. Use a trowel to dig a shallow trench along the line of the stem at this point. Carefully bend the stem to form a right angle about 20cm (8in) behind the growing tip and secure it into the bottom of the hole using a piece of stiff wire. Tie the growing tip vertically to a short bamboo cane.

More difficult-to-root plants will benefit from a slit cut on the underside of the stem. Dust the wound with rooting hormone and peg into position. Replace the soil around the layer, firm lightly and water well. Leave for 6–18 months until the layer has rooted well, then cut it from the parent and plant it elsewhere in the garden.

Serpentine (compound) layering

Some plants, especially climbers such as clematis, wisteria and honeysuckle, produce long, flexible shoots that can be layered several times along their length. The stem is buried at several points along its length, with the growing tip out of the ground, as for simple layering (see above). Make sure that each loop of the stem exposed above the soil has at least one bud. Separate and plant out the layers once rooted.

French layering

Some multi-stemmed shrubs, such as *Cornus* (dogwood) and acers, can be layered by burying the entire stem just below the surface of the soil. First, peg down the stem on to the soil surface in early winter so that all the buds break at the same time in spring. Once new sideshoots are about 5cm (2in) long, lower the stem into a shallow trench and cover with soil, taking care not to damage

HOW TO LAYER

1 Find a low-growing shoot that can easily be pegged down to the ground. Trim off the leaves just from the area that will be in contact with the soil.

2 Bend down the stem until it touches the ground. Make a hole about 10cm (4in) deep, sloping toward the parent plant but with the other side vertical.

3 Twist or slit the stem slightly to injure it. Peg it into the hole with a piece of bent wire or a peg, using the vertical back of the excavation to force the shoot upright.

4 Return the soil and firm it well. If you keep the ground moist, roots should form, and within 6–18 months you may be able to sever the new plant from its parent.

HOW TO AIR-LAYER

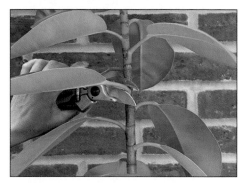

1 Air-layering is a useful technique to propagate plants whose stems cannot easily be lowered to ground level. Begin by using secateurs (pruners) to remove a few leaves from the point on the stem where you want to make the layer.

2 Using a sharp knife, carefully make an upward slit about 2.5cm (1in) long, below an old leaf joint. Do not cut more than halfway through the stem, otherwise it may break.

3 Cut a piece of plastic that is large enough to wrap around the stem of the plant, making a wide sleeve with space to add a thick layer of moss. Fix the bottom of the sleeve a short distance below the cut with a twist-tie or adhesive tape.

the shoots and leaving the tops exposed. As they grow, carefully earth up the sideshoots – leaving at least 5cm (2in) of shoot exposed – until a ridge of soil about 15cm (6in) high has been created. Separate and plant out layers once rooted.

Tip layering

A few plants, notably blackberries and hybrid berries, can be easily propagated by tip layering. This is a process whereby the tip of a suitably placed shoot is pegged into prepared soil and left until it roots.

4 Brush a small amount of rooting hormone compound (powder or gel) into the wound to speed rooting. Then pack a little sphagnum moss into the wound to keep it open.

5 Pack plenty of damp sphagnum moss around the stem to enclose the wound, then cover with the sheet of plastic and secure at the top with another twist-tie or tape. Make sure that the moss is kept moist, and carefully check for roots after a month or so. When well rooted, sever from the parent to pot up.

Mound layering

Some small bushy shrubs, such as heathers, can be propagated by mound layering (also known as stooling or burying). This is where the whole plant is covered with soil – a useful technique for replacing old woody specimens that have gone bare at the base.

First, thin out the shoots so that soil can be pushed between those that remain. Carefully pile a free-draining soil mixture on in layers, making sure there are no air pockets, until just 5–10cm (2–4in) of each shoot is above the mound of soil. Keep well watered throughout the summer. Separate and plant out layers once they are rooted.

1 Prepare a sandy, friable mixture of garden soil, sand and compost (soil mix). Mound this carefully around the stems of the plant, spreading the stems apart with your fingers if necessary. Cover the stems to within 5–10cm (2–4in) of their tips.

2 Keep the mound well watered during dry spells in the summer. You may need to replenish the mound if heavy rainfall washes away some of the soil. The shoots should have rooted by late summer, when they can be separated from the parent plant and potted up or planted out.

Division

Many fibrous-rooted plants, including a few shrubs and most perennials and aquatic plants, can be propagated by division. It is also the best way to keep them growing strongly and flowering well.

Timing

Division is best carried out straight after the plant has flowered so that you do not miss the display the following year. However, most experts recommend dividing plants in spring or autumn, depending on how much time you have to spare in each season. Dividing in spring is probably better for plants of borderline hardiness, so that they have time to settle in before they have to face their first winter, while autumn is best for hardier types, because the soil is still warm and moist – ideal for quick establishment.

Some perennials, such as astilbe, liriope and solidago, respond to regular division. Others, such as agapanthus, alstroemeria, eryngium and helleborus, do not like being disturbed and can take several years to recover from the process.

Techniques

The precise technique used to divide a fibrous-rooted plant will depend on the type of root system it produces and how long it has been since the plant was last divided, but the principle is the same. For most perennials you should be able to ease the crown apart using two border forks pushed and pulled while back to back. This method avoids damaging the roots. For old, neglected plants that have produced a solid mass of roots you will need to use a sharp spade to slice the crown into sections. Some plants, such as asters and campanulas, produce a loose mass of roots that

Propagate *Caltha palustris* (kingcup or marsh marigold) by division in spring or autumn.

HOW TO PROPAGATE PLANTS BY DIVISION

1 Water the congested plant to be divided during the previous day. Dig up a clump of the plant, in this case the Michaelmas daisy, *Aster novi-belgii*.

2 Insert two forks back-to-back into the plant and lever apart by pushing the handles together and apart. Keep on dividing until the pieces are of the required size.

3 A few of the most vigorous pieces of the plant can be replaced in the bed, but dig over the soil first, removing any weeds and adding some well-rotted organic material.

4 Alternatively, small pieces of the plant can be potted up individually. After watering, place these in a closed cold frame for a few days, before hardening off.

HOW TO DIVIDE PLANTS WITH TANGLED ROOTS

1 Many plants, such as these kniphofias, have very tangled roots or grow in heavy soils that will not easily fall away.

2 Shake the plants in a bucket of water so that the soil is washed from the roots. Wash with a hose if the soil is very difficult to remove.

3 Once the soil is washed away, most plants break up surprisingly easily into individual sections, each with a growing point.

4 Some plants do not come apart very easily. If this is the case, separate the sections with a sharp knife, making certain that each section has a bud.

5 Once the plants have been cleaned and divided, they can be potted up individually and then kept in a shaded cold frame until they have recovered.

can be teased apart by hand. Others, such as hostas and red-hot poker, are so compact you will have to use an old kitchen knife or pair of secateurs (pruners) to divide them up.

Dividing perennials

Choose a dry day when the soil is still moist but workable. Lay out a plastic sheet in a clear space, such as on the lawn or nearby patio, to work on. Then clear as much old foliage from the plant to be divided as possible so that you can clearly see what you are doing. Use a garden fork to loosen the soil around the plant, then carefully move it on to the plastic sheet. Choose your tool – spade, border forks, old kitchen knife or secateurs (pruners) – and split the old crown into smaller chunks – each will need a proportion of the shoots and roots. Replant the young and vigorous outer sections into well-prepared soil and discard the exhausted woody core. Firm all divisions after replanting and water well until established.

Plants with horizontal rhizomes, such as bergenias and irises, can be cut into sections with a sharp knife or secateurs. Cut back leaves of tall plants by half to prevent wind-rock and then replant the rhizome at the same depth as it was before.

HOW TO DIVIDE RHIZOMES

1 Divide plants grown from rhizomes, such as this flag iris, when they get congested. Lift the clump and cut away the oldest parts. Replant only the newest growth.

2 Trim the leaves by about half to prevent wind-rock. Replant the pieces of rhizome on a slight ridge of soil, covering the roots but leaving the tops exposed.

Propagating bulbs

Bulbs look best planted *en masse* in borders or naturalized in grass, where they will increase naturally if left undisturbed. Some types, however, may become congested and need dividing or you may wish to propagate them to grow elsewhere.

Dividing bulbs

Bulbs increase naturally once they are planted in the garden and will form clumps. The easiest method of propagation is, therefore, simply to lift an established clump and divide it up before replanting. Daffodils, for example, can be lifted about six weeks after flowering when the foliage has started to die down. Clear soil from the bulbs and pull off any offsets to be replanted along with the healthy parent bulbs. The offsets of bulbs such as *lachenalia* are best removed when growth is just beginning. Lilies produce offsets, but these are joined firmly to the parent and should be severed with a sharp knife. The new corms of crocuses and colchicum are produced on top of the old ones, which are dead and should be separated and thrown away. A few bulbous plants, including anemones, form knobbly tubers with several growing points. These can be lifted and cut up with at least one growing point on each division, before being dusted in fungicide and replanted.

Stem bulbils, bulblets and pips

A few types of lily bulb, including the tiger lily, produce small bulbs called bulbils or bulblets at the leaf axils up the stem. These should be removed about a fortnight after the plant has flowered and planted out or potted up. The largest will reach flowering size within a year.

Bulbs can be encouraged to produce bulbils by burying about half the ripened stem at a 45-degree

1 Lift the clump when flowering has finished, but before the leaves have died back completely, using a fork to reduce the risk of damage. Try to avoid spearing the bulbs. Loosen the soil all round, then insert the tines of the fork beneath the bulbs to lift them.

2 Unless you require a large number of individual new bulbs, prise apart the clump into three or four pieces and then replant the pieces immediately. They will produce good-size clumps that will look well established next season.

3 Replant the bulbs straightaway, before they can dry out. Plants that produce small bulbs can be replanted with a trowel; a spade may be better for larger ones.

4 Firm the soil after planting, making sure that there are no large air pockets where the roots may dry out. Water well if the weather is dry. Carefully fork in a general fertilizer around the plants.

angle in a bed of leafmould after flowering. Bulbils will form on the underground portion. Stem-rooting lilies produce bulbils underground if they are mulched with a thick layer of loose organic material. The bulbils can be separated when the lily stem dies down in autumn.

On some types of ornamental onion and leek, pips are formed at the top of the flowering stem as the flowers go over. To propagate, simply remove these from the plant and pot up the healthiest looking pips. The largest should reach flowering size within two years.

It is easy to propagate lilies, such as *Lilium martagon*, to create a spectacular summer display of flowers.

Scaling and chipping

Each scale of a lily bulb can be separated from an established plant and encouraged to produce one or more bulblets. This is a relatively simple technique that is best carried out in late summer or early autumn, before the roots have begun to grow. Similarly, some bulbs, including daffodils, hyacinths and snowdrops, can be propagated by chipping – a technique whereby the bulb is sliced into sections, each of which has a proportion of the basal plate. The cut surfaces are then dusted in fungicide and allowed to dry before planting. Each separate piece should produce a new plant.

HOW TO PROPAGATE LILIES FROM SCALES

1 Take a clean, dormant bulb and snap off some outer scales, as close to the base as possible. Be careful not to damage the scales as you remove them from the bulb.

2 Put the scales in a bag of fungicide, and gently shake to coat them. Prepare a mixture of equal parts peat (or an alternative) and perlite or vermiculite in a plastic bag.

3 Dampen the mix. Shake the scales free of excess fungicide and place them in the bag. Store in a warm, dark place for 6–8 weeks and plant up when bulblets appear on the scales.

Basic techniques

There are a range of basic gardening techniques, such as weeding, watering and feeding, that are common to most if not all parts of the garden. They are all easy to understand and take little skill to master, so it is worth spending some time getting these techniques right because they can have a considerable impact on the rest of your gardening.

Carrying out simple tasks correctly can often save you hours of time later. Weeding, for example, is best carried out before you plant up a bed. Once the flowers and shrubs have been planted and a thick layer of mulch added, the bed will need very little weeding.

Once the basic tasks have been mastered, you will have the time to carry out more elaborate and challenging techniques. Do remember to take sensible safety precautions to prevent injury and ensure gardening remains a pleasure.

As well as being the ideal place to store your tools, equipment and other gardening materials, a shed can be an attractive retreat in its own dusty way.

Essential tool kit

You don't need a shed full of
tools to be able to garden
successfully, but you will find
some items indispensable and
can build up your kit as you go.

Choosing tools

If tools are going to be used
they need to be effective,
convenient and comfortable to
use, and it is always worth
trying out new tools before
making your selection. Always
buy the best you can afford,
because well-made and well-
maintained garden tools will
last a lifetime.

Tools for digging You will need
some form of digging tool, such
as a spade or fork. A spade is
perhaps the more versatile but a
fork is better on stony ground
or if you find digging particularly
hard work. Smaller, easy-to-use
border forks are also available.
Whatever digging tool you select,
choose a make that is strong,
with a comfortable handle that is
long enough to prevent you
stooping when you dig; long-
handled versions are available to
suit taller gardeners. Make sure

Rosa 'Zéphirine Drouhin', *Clematis* 'Lady Betty Balfour' and *Vitis coignetiae* need regular pruning
to keep them in good shape. Use secateurs (pruners) or long-handled loppers to cut them back.

Lawn care equipment

If you have a lawn you will need a
range of specialist equipment,
including a mower with a cutting
width to suit the size of your lawn, a
pair of shears or a nylon-line trimmer
to keep the edges in trim and a
spring-tined (wire or lawn) rake with
springy, wire-like tines set at an angle
for combing through grass to remove
dead leaves, moss and thatch.

the grip of a D-shaped handle is wide enough to be comfortable when you are wearing gloves. Stainless steel tools are more expensive but might be worth the investment if your soil is particularly heavy. If you intend to do a lot of digging choose tools with a tread (a flat area on top of the blade to put your foot on) because this will be more comfortable and be less damaging to your footwear.

Tools for weeding Most gardeners will find a hoe of some kind invaluable. The style you choose is a personal matter, but Dutch and draw hoes have stood the test of time. Again, choose one with a handle that is long enough for your height and make sure the head is securely fastened to the shaft. The Dutch hoe is the easier to master and more versatile, using a simple push and pull action to chop off weeds just below the soil surface. The shape of a draw hoe makes it easier to draw up soil around plants and to use among plants in existing borders.

Tools for levelling soil There are several types of rake, each designed for very specific purposes, but for most gardeners a soil rake is most frequently used. It usually has about a dozen, equally spaced, solid metal, vertical teeth and is used for levelling soil and removing stones before planting or sowing.

Tools for cutting These are also an essential element in the basic gardening tool kit. A well-made, straight-bladed, all-purpose knife is top of the list because it has a multitude of uses around the garden. A sturdy pair of secateurs (pruners) for deadheading and most types of pruning is also essential, but if serious pruning is contemplated, a pair of long-handled loppers or a pruning saw will be needed, too.

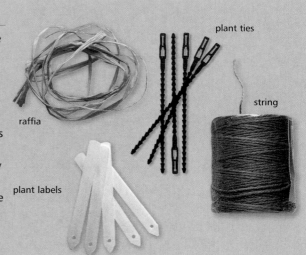

Labelling and tying

When you are working in the garden, it is useful to have a tray of odds and ends, such as string, raffia, plant ties and labels. You never know when you might need them. For example, wayward shoots of climbers may need fixing to their supports, or you may be sowing seeds or planting seedlings that you need to be able to identify.

raffia

plant ties

string

plant labels

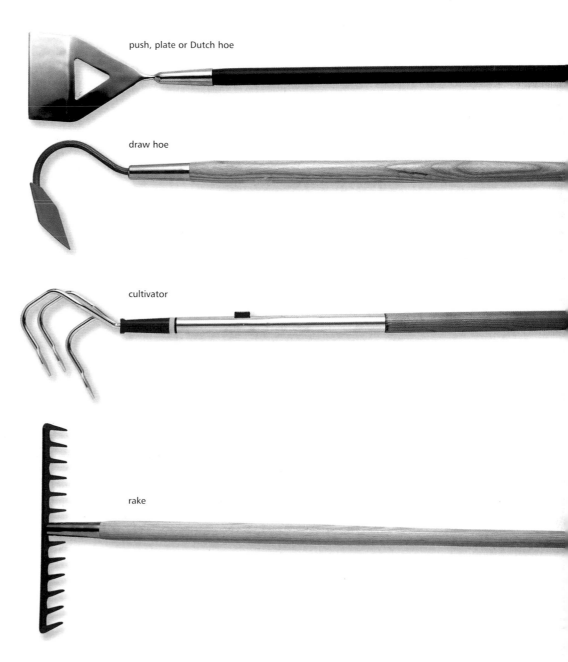

push, plate or Dutch hoe

draw hoe

cultivator

rake

Weeding

Weeds are nothing more than plants growing where they are not wanted. There are several techniques you can adopt to reduce the number of weeds in the garden and, therefore, the time spent weeding.

Controlling weeds

There are two types of weeds: annual weeds, such as groundsel and chickweed, which grow from seed, flower and set seed again in one season; and perennial weeds, such as dock, bindweed, couch grass and thistle, which survive for more than two growing seasons and often many years. It is important to remove all weeds before they flower and set seed, otherwise you will be weeding for many seasons to come – after all, a single weed can scatter many thousands of viable seeds near and far.

Weeds will be able to grow only if there is bare soil waiting for them to colonize, so you can go a long way to preventing weeds by covering all the bare soil in your garden: by planting up your borders and filling any gaps with ground cover plants or mulches. Alternatively, you can use a special chemical between established woody plants, such as trees and shrubs, to inhibit the germination of weed seeds. Such products will also damage the new growth of desirable plants, so they are not suitable for mixed borders containing herbaceous perennials or bulbs.

The best way to tackle weeds depends both on the type of weeds you have and where they are growing. In general, annual weeds are easy to control by using a hoe in open spaces between plants and by hand to remove weeds among ornamental plants. Perennial weeds are more difficult to eliminate because you have to remove the entire root as well as the topgrowth, otherwise the weed is likely to re-sprout. This can be hard work with some weeds, such

HOW TO WEED

Deep-rooted perennial weeds that have long, penetrating roots are best forked up. Loosen the roots with a fork, and hold the stem close to its base as you pull up the whole plant. If you don't get all the root out, the plant may re-grow.

Hoeing is one of the best forms of annual weed control, but it needs to be done fairly regularly. Slice the weeds off just beneath the soil, preferably when the soil is dry. Keep beds and borders as well as the vegetable garden hoed throughout the growing season.

Contact chemical weedkillers are useful if you need to clear an area of ground quickly and easily. Some types, which normally kill only the top growth so are better for annuals than problem perennial weeds, leave the area safe to replant after a day.

Systematic weedkillers kill the whole plant. Large areas can be sprayed, but some formulations can be painted on the leaves so will not harm other plants. Some types break down immediately in the soil.

Mulches are an effective method of controlling weeds. In the vegetable and fruit garden various forms of matting and plastic sheeting are a cost-effective method.

Where appearance matters, use a mulch of an organic material, such as chipped bark or garden compost. If the ground is cleared first a mulch at least 5cm (2in) – ideally 8cm (3in) – thick will suppress most weeds.

USING CHEMICAL WEEDKILLERS

A chemical weedkiller is best used to kill persistent weeds when first preparing a bed. Avoid using chemicals near fruit, vegetables or herbs. Always follow the manufacturer's instructions on the packet.

as dandelions and thistles, which produce a carrot-like taproot, and for brittle-rooted weeds, such as couch grass and bindweed, which send out roots in all directions, it can be close to impossible. Indeed, if these weeds have become established in your garden, you may have to dig up the entire border and painstakingly remove every weed root you can find before replanting the ornamental plants. If this is not a practical option you could try exhausting the weeds into submission by removing all the topgrowth and repeating the process every time it re-sprouts.

Your final option is to use a chemical weedkiller, which should be applied according to the instructions on the pack. There are two main types: contact weedkillers, which kill the parts of the weed they touch; and systemic formulations, which are transported around the plant, killing all parts. Which you choose will depend on personal preference and where the weeds are growing.

Beds and borders

Hand-weed mixed borders and use a hoe to clear annual weeds from bare soil between plants. Perennial weeds can be removed by hand where practicable or killed with a spot treatment weedkiller. Large weeds are easier to treat with a glyphosate-based, ready-to-use spray, but cover all nearby ornamental plants with a plastic sheet before spraying and leave the sheet in position until the spray is dry.

Lawns

Remove isolated weeds by hand using an old knife or a special weeding tool. Alternatively, kill them using a spot weedkiller. If the weed problem is more widespread, it is more efficient to use a specially formulated lawn weedkiller.

Where moss is also a problem it is a good idea to use a combined moss and weedkiller treatment in spring.

Patios and paths

Remove individual weeds by hand using an old knife or a special weeding tool. Alternatively, kill them with a spot weedkiller. Where the problem is widespread use a path weedkiller, which will kill existing weeds and prevent further weed problems for the rest of the year.

Neglected areas

If there are no ornamental plants, dig over the entire area, hand-weeding as you go. If this is not practicable, remove all the topgrowth and cover the area with black plastic or old carpet for a few years. A glyphosate-based weedkiller is another option. Stubborn weeds, such as bramble, may need several applications, or you could use the more potent chemical, sodium chlorate, although you will not be able to plant the treated area for at least six weeks afterwards.

The close planting of vigorous perennials, such as *Dictamnus albus* (dittany), prevents weed seedlings from germinating and surviving.

Ground cover

Weeding is a time-consuming task, and it is best to prevent weeds from germinating in the first place if you can. Carpeting the ground with a mass of attractive foliage, which also makes an effective foil for other plants and may produce flowers itself, makes good gardening sense.

What is a ground cover plant?

To make a suitable ground covering, a plant needs to establish quickly and cover the ground with a dense layer of leaves, without any gaps where weeds could germinate. The principle is that the plant is so dense that little light can reach the ground and any weed seedlings that do manage to germinate are starved of light, become sickly, and soon die.

The ground cover plant should also be low growing, so as not to detract from the ornamental plants,

The dense ground cover subshrub *Lithodora diffusa* makes a vivid carpet of blue in spring.

and not so invasive that it swamps the whole bed. Although a wide variety of plants are labelled and described as suitable, relatively few make ideal ground cover.

Choosing the right ground cover

Low-growing ground cover plants are an ideal way of covering the soil between shrubs and trees in the border. Choose plants that are ground-hugging and can cope with the occasional trampling; you will need to tread on them to carry out maintenance to other plants.

Try to select plants with foliage that will contrast with the other plants, so that they set one another off. An underplanting of bulbs will provide seasonal variation and interest: tulips, spring-flowering dwarf narcissi and autumn-flowering colchicums are suitable. Some plants, such as heather or *Hypericum calycinum*, also have flowers to enhance their appearance.

Ground cover is also useful for areas where grass is not practical. For example, *Hypericum calycinum* is useful on slopes that are difficult to mow,

while *Vinca minor* is good for awkward areas at the bottom of a fence or alongside a driveway. Ground cover plants also make a low-maintenance option in the front garden.

A few ground cover plants, such as cotoneaster and prostrate junipers, produce stiff spreading foliage, which lends itself to covering eyesores such as manhole covers or ugly tree stumps.

Planting and aftercare

Although ground cover will prevent weeds from establishing, they do need to be planted into weed-free ground to start with. The best time to plant is autumn.

Prepare the ground by digging thoroughly and removing weeds, including the roots of perennial weeds. Incorporate well-rotted manure and a handful of bonemeal per square metre (yard). Take care not to damage the roots of existing plants if you are planting between or under them. When planting ground cover, do so either through a mulch matting or mulch after planting with an 8cm (3in) thick layer of loose

DIVIDING GROUND COVER

If you buy large ground cover plants in containers, they can be divided before planting for maximum cover. Gently knock the plant, such as this *Pachysandra terminalis*, out of its pot without damaging the roots. If the crown is too tough to pull or prise apart, try cutting through it with a knife. Replant larger pieces with several shoots and plenty of roots immediately. Smaller pieces can be potted up and grown on for a year before planting out into the garden. Keep new plants well watered until they are established.

HOW TO PLANT GROUND COVER

1 Clear the ground of weeds first, and be especially careful to remove any deep-rooted or persistent perennial weeds.

2 Add plenty of garden compost or rotted manure, then rake in a slow-release fertilizer or bonemeal. This will help the plants establish successfully.

3 Cover the area with a weed-suppressing mulching sheet. The special semi-permeable membrane allows water and air to penetrate to the soil.

4 Make crossed slits through the mulching sheet where you want to plant. Avoid making the slits too large.

5 Excavate holes and plant the ground cover, firming in well. If necessary, tease a few of the roots apart first.

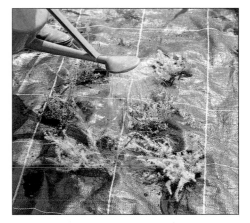

6 Water thoroughly, and keep well watered. In prominent positions you could disguise the mulching sheet with a thin layer of soil.

organic mulch to prevent weeds from germinating before the ground cover can do the job. The distance between each of the ground cover plants will depend on the vigour of the plant you have chosen and how long you are prepared to wait for complete cover. Obviously, the closer the spacing the more plants you will need and the costlier it will be.

Good ground cover plants should remain pest and disease free and require little maintenance, other than an annual tidy up. This is best done in late autumn when deciduous leaves that have become trapped in the stems can be collected.

Good ground cover plants

Shrubs	Perennials
Berberis thunbergii 'Atropurpurea Nana'	*Ajuga reptans*
Calluna vulgaris cultivars	*Alchemilla mollis* (lady's mantle)
Ceanothus thyrsiflorus var. *repens*	*Bergenia* (elephant's ears)
Cotoneaster dammeri	*Convallaria majalis* (lily-of-the-valley)
Cotoneaster x *suecicus* 'Coral Beauty'	*Epimedium perralderianum*
Erica carnea cultivars	*Geranium*
Euonymus fortunei 'Emerald Gaiety'	*Heuchera*
Gaultheria procumbens	*Hosta sieboldiana*
Genista lydia	*Houttuynia cordata*
Hebe pinguifolia 'Pagei'	*Lamium maculatum*
Hypericum calycinum	*Lysimachia nummularia* (creeping Jenny)
Juniperus horizontalis Glauca Group	*Nepeta* 'Six Hills Giant'
Juniperus squamata 'Blue Carpet'	*Pulmonaria* (lungwort)
Mahonia aquifolium	*Rodgersia*
Vinca minor	*Symphytum* (comfrey)

Mulching

A mulch is a layer of material laid on the soil surface to discourage weeds from germinating and to prevent moisture loss. Organic mulches also improve soil fertility.

Types of mulch

The most natural mulch is loose organic material laid over the surface of the soil in a layer 8cm (3in) deep. In nature autumn leaves provide a blanket of organic matter, but in the garden we can use anything from chipped bark or cocoa shells to garden compost, leafmould or grass clippings. Non-organic mulches are used too, such as stone chippings and pebbles, or manufactured sheet mulches, as well as old carpet and black polythene.

A mulch helps to retain moisture in the soil by preventing water evaporating from the surface layer. Dark coloured mulches can also help warm the soil early in the season and promote rapid root growth in spring.

Organic mulches

These are popular because they are easy to use, adaptable and help to improve soil fertility as they slowly decompose and are incorporated into the soil by earthworms and other soil-dwelling creatures. Some, such as bark chippings, composted bark and cocoa shells, are attractive to look at and provide a useful foil for low-growing border plants and bulbs. Bear in mind that loose organic mulches, such as grass clippings, that have not been composted will deplete the levels of nitrogen in the soil surface as they decompose. They are suitable for use only between established plants or alongside a hedge.

Inorganic mulches

Loose inorganic mulches are particularly useful in certain areas of the garden. Pea gravel, for example, is ideal around alpines, which like well-drained conditions and would rot if surrounded with a loose

Applying mulches

Mulches are best applied to weed-free soil in spring when the soil is moist. Loose organic mulches need to be at least 5cm (2in) deep, preferably 8cm (3in) deep to be effective, and will need to be topped up each spring.

organic mulch. Similarly, stone chippings are often the best choice for covering the soil in planting pockets and between paving slabs in and around the patio. Pebbles, on the other hand, are ideal for mulching around plants, such as clematis, which like to have a cool root run, or as an attractive finishing touch to containers.

If you are planting a new bed or a specimen tree or shrub, specially made sheet mulches are an option worth considering. This material, also called mulch matting, is permeable and weed-proof. Lay the sheet over the prepared soil before

DIFFERENT TYPES OF MULCH

A border without any kind of mulch on the soil is prone to weed infestation and to loss of moisture.

Grass cuttings are readily available in most gardens. They are not attractive but can be used effectively between established plants at the back of borders, where they are not highly visible. Do not heap them on thicker than 5cm (2in) or they may heat up too much as they decompose, harming the plant.

Composted bark is an ideal material for mulching, being both effective and attractive. Do not use bark that is fresh, however, or the resin may harm the plants. Hedge and shrub prunings can be shredded and used after they have been composted for a couple of months.

This bright border has been well tended, resulting in the vigorous growth of healthy plants. An organic mulch of well-rotted garden compost was applied early in spring to return nutrients to the soil and to prevent weed seeds from germinating.

planting up a bed and simply cut cross-shaped slits in the sheet at each planting position. For larger plants, place a sheet over the soil around the specimen after planting, covering an area of at least 1sq m (1sq yard) around each plant. Sheet mulches are more effective weed barriers than loose organic mulches and do not need to be reapplied every spring. They do not, however, improve soil fertility and are unattractive. They are best disguised with a thin layer of soil or a mulch if used in prominent positions.

Semi-permeable mulching membrane, which has small holes in it to allow water and air to pass through to the soil, is available from many garden retailers. Measure out how much you will need, then cut the membrane to shape and lay it on the surface of the soil.

Mulching membrane is fairly unattractive so, in prominent positions, it is worth disguising it with a layer of gravel to improve the appearance of the border. Make sure that the membrane is flat and completely covered with stones.

Material mulches are not suitable to cover areas planted with bulbs or dormant herbaceous plants. In such positions, a loose organic or inorganic mulch such as gravel would be a better option.

Watering and feeding

Watering and feeding are among the most time-consuming tasks in the garden, especially if you have a lot of containers or own a greenhouse. Use the following techniques to help you work efficiently.

Watering

The ground must be thoroughly soaked after watering: a sprinkling will do little other than lay the dust. Effective watering should supply the equivalent of 2.5cm (1in) of rain.

Every gardener should have a watering can fitted with a fine rose, and this may be all that you need if your garden is small or if you do not grow many plants in containers. Most gardeners, however, will benefit from installing an outside tap (faucet) fitted with a hose on a reel. This will make transporting water around the garden straightforward, and the reel will keep your hose neat and tidy.

Ideally, the hose should be long enough to reach all parts of the garden, but if this is not possible it should certainly reach the areas that require the most frequent watering, such as the patio, greenhouse and kitchen garden. An adjustable nozzle at the end of the hose is a good idea as this will eliminate the need to keep returning to the tap to regulate the supply. If you have a lot of hanging baskets, window boxes or other out-of-the-way containers a hose lance (hose wand) that directs the water is a good investment.

A hose-end sprinkler is worth considering for large areas. Choose an oscillating or rotary type for the most even coverage. However, most garden plants do not need regular watering, even during a drought, and because the water is applied indiscriminately over the entire area a great deal is wasted. It is, moreover, tempting to leave the tap running for longer than is really necessary.

If you cannot afford the time to water all your plants on a regular basis, you can buy systems that will do the job for you. For most gardeners, the best option is a system of micro-bore tubes that carry water to individual plants. These networks usually have an adjustable nozzle fitted to regulate the correct amount of water. Such systems can be used for watering all types of container, including hanging baskets, and can also be linked to lengths of leaky pipe (sometimes called a seep hose or drip hose) for watering plants in

WATERING SYSTEMS

Most automatic watering systems have a control system to reduce the water pressure, and some act as a filter to prevent nozzles becoming clogged.

Drip-feed systems can be used for beds, borders and containers. T-joints allow tubes to be attached for individual drip heads.

The delivery nozzle of this drip-feed system is held in position with a pipe peg, so that the head can deliver water to an individual plant.

A seep or drip hose can be laid along a row of plants and will water only the immediate area. The water slowly seeps out of the pipe and soaks into the soil.

A timing device will turn water on and off automatically. You can preset the timing, so this is an ideal way of watering your plants while you are away on holiday.

HOW TO APPLY FERTILIZER

If it is necessary to pep up a flagging border towards the end of a long season, add a liquid feed to a watering can. Follow the instructions given by the manufacturer.

If you want to apply a foliar feed to a large number of plants, use a special applicator fitted to the end of a garden hose so that a measured amount is applied.

Dry fertilizer can simply be scattered on the soil around individual plants that need feeding, so there is no waste.

rows, such as in fruit and vegetable gardens. Plumbing the system to an outside tap (faucet) and including a water timer or watering computer will give a completely automatic watering system.

Feeding

The other regular task facing the gardener during the summer is feeding. Plants in containers will quickly deplete the fertilizer present in the potting compost (soil mix) unless a slow-release fertilizer was added at the planting time. You will need to feed weekly from about six weeks after planting.

Some fertilizers are formulated for specific plants – tomatoes, roses and lawn grass are the best known – but most gardeners will also find a general fertilizer of some kind useful. These fertilizers are supplied in powder or liquid form and may need to be diluted or made up according to the manufacturer's recommendations. Alternatively, you can add a slow-release fertilizer to the compost in the form of pellets or granules. These will usually provide sufficient nutrients for a growing season.

When planting permanent borders of trees and shrubs, add a slow-release fertilizer, such as bonemeal, and improve the soil with well-rotted organic matter.

In a very small garden or in the greenhouse, a watering can is probably the most efficient way to deliver the appropriate amount of your chosen feed to individual plants. In a large garden a special attachment for a garden hose can be used to deliver fertilizer over a large area.

Collecting your own water

Place a water butt beneath the gutter of a greenhouse, shed or garage to catch the water as it runs off the roof. Rain water is slightly acidic so ideal for watering acid-loving plants, especially if you live in a hard-water area. It will also save water and money spent on metered water.

You can easily collect sufficient water in a water butt to keep a collection of acid-loving plants happy all summer long. If you are more ambitious you can now get kits to link water butts together to create a serious garden water storage system.

The butt should be easy to use, so make sure there is room to get a watering can under the tap. Keep the butt covered at all times so that the water remains sweet and clean.

You can also recycle water that has been used for washing or bathing in the house. Known as "grey-water", it is suitable for applying to established plants in borders and on lawns, but is best used immediately not stored.

Pests and diseases

The best way to control pests and diseases is to maintain a healthy garden environment and grow plants well so that they are able to shrug off or recover quickly from most attacks. It is also worth seeking out problem-free varieties that are naturally resistant to attack.

Deterring pests and diseases

Good garden hygiene is the most important factor in the battle against pests and diseases. Clear all debris from around the garden and put suitable material on the compost heap. Consign the rest to the dustbin or bonfire as soon as you can. Clean containers once you finish using them. Stay vigilant for the first signs of attack and take necessary remedial action as soon as possible. Keep weeds under control, including during the winter, because they can provide a convenient overwintering site for some problems.

Nectar-rich plants

Shrubs and trees	Iberis
Buddleia	Limnanthes
Crataegus	Lunaria
Viburnum	Matthiola
	Sedum
Flowers	Solidago
Arabis	
Aubrieta	
Erysimum	

Encouraging natural predators

A well-managed garden will be a dangerous place for pests because it is full of natural predators including birds, small mammals, amphibians, spiders and insects. You can increase the numbers of these natural predators by providing them with food, shelter and suitable places to breed. Frogs and toads, for example, are voracious eaters of slugs and will happily take up residence if you provide suitable places for them to

Natural predators

Introducing or encouraging beneficial insects can have a dramatic impact on the number of pests in your garden. Check which pests your plants are vulnerable to, and encourage their natural predators into your garden.

Ladybirds (ladybugs) and larvae – eat aphids, scale insects, mealy bugs and caterpillars

Hoverflies and larvae – eat up to 50 aphids a day

Lacewings – eat aphids, woolly aphids, spider mites, scale insects and caterpillars

Ground beetles – eat slugs, flat worms, cabbage and carrot rootfly (eggs and larvae), vine weevils and spider mites

Anthocorid bugs – eat vine weevil larvae, caterpillars, midge larvae and spider mites

Centipedes – eat slugs and snails

PREVENTING DISEASE

Thoroughly wash and clean pots, trays and equipment after use to get rid of loose soil that may harbour pests and diseases.

There are many beautiful garden plants that have the added advantage of attracting the natural predators of pests into the garden. This wallflower (*Erysimum*) is nectar-rich and will attract bees and butterflies, as well as hoverflies and lacewings.

WEEDING

Continue to weed vegetable and flower beds during the winter. Weeds can harbour pests and diseases that will attack plants later.

HOW TO TREAT MILDEW

1 Mildew is common in humid conditions, so apply a mulch to keep the roots moist but do not water the leaves.

2 Remove leaves affected by mildew. Severely damaged plants can be sprayed with a suitable fungicide.

hide and a pond where they can breed. Similarly, useful insects, such as hoverflies, can be lured into your garden by nectar-rich plants and a supply of insect pests. You can even provide a "hotel", made from bundles of bamboo, where they can safely hibernate.

Controlling pests and diseases

Stay one step ahead of the pests by sowing and planting at appropriate times and putting up traps and barriers. Protecting plants with suitable netting is probably the only solution to prevent damage caused by mammals such as rabbits. Isolated

attacks of snails and caterpillars can be picked off by hand and destroyed, while small colonies of aphids can be rubbed out between finger and thumb. Similarly, isolated disease symptoms can be pruned out and the affected material put in the dustbin or burned. Do not put any material that looks as if it has been attacked by disease in the compost bin, as this may spread the disease to other plants in the garden.

It is worth having a few chemicals to hand for the most intransigent pests and diseases. Slug pellets, for example, can be used sparingly around vulnerable plants, notably

hostas, when they are planted out, and each spring thereafter, before the new leaves emerge.

If you have problems with aphids, choose a selective treatment based on piricarb, which is specific to aphids. A systemic insecticide is also useful for all other insect pests. Choose one based on permethrin or dimethoate or a spray based on pyrethrum if you garden organically.

Combined chemical treatments can be very quick and effective. Many rose growers, for example, like to use a combined treatment to combat the three main rose diseases of blackspot, mildew and rust.

HOW TO DEAL WITH CATERPILLARS AND SLUGS

The best way to get rid of caterpillars, such as these on *Polygonatum odoratum*, is to pick them off by hand.

When slugs and snails eat holes in hosta leaves, the holes remain visible throughout the growing season. If you do not mind using slug pellets, scatter them around the plants.

Dishes and jars half-filled with beer or sweetened water and sunk into the ground will attract slugs and snails, which can be collected up and disposed of.

Safety in the garden

The garden can be a dangerous place if you are careless. Every year thousands of people are injured by garden equipment, particularly power tools. Fortunately, most of the injuries are avoidable if you take the necessary precautions when using the equipment.

Think ahead

Always take sensible steps to protect yourself when gardening. Wear thick gloves when handling rough materials and protect your eyes with goggles when pruning or working with twiggy stems.

Pruning

Move around a plant to prune it rather than stretching to your furthest reach. Use a steady ladder if you are cutting a hedge or climber over shoulder height.

Most accidents that involve a hedgetrimmer occur when the machine is in use, with lacerations, falls and electrocutions (with electric

Thorny plants, such as this rose 'Ispahan', should be pruned back from a path or a doorway to prevent the stems catching on passers-by.

models) coming top of the list. Make sure your machine has the basic safety features such as a short blade-stopping time, two-handed switches and special blade extensions that stick out beyond the reciprocating blades and prevent you cutting something accidentally.

Always use the appropriate clothing and a thick pair of gloves. Use a hedgetrimmer with care and don't try to rush the job. Keep both hands on the machine while it is in operation.

Lawnmowers

Most lawnmower accidents, on the other hand, occur when the machine is not being used. Be particularly careful while it is being cleaned, maintained or simply moved around. Check that the blade has stopped moving before removing the box, and disengage the machine from the power supply before touching the blade. Turn off the power supply to electric models and turn off the engine and disconnect the spark plug lead with petrol-driven machines. If the blades become clogged, use a stick to clear them.

Of the accidents that occur while a mower is being used, most are because the machine is being asked to do too much – either the grass is overgrown, wet or both – or is on a steep incline. If you have a steeply sloping lawn always mow across the slope rather than up and down it.

HOW TO PRUNE SAFELY

1 It is sensible to use a hedgetrimmer on a large or fast-growing hedge, but power tools such as this can be dangerous. Accidents often occur when you are in a hurry, so take your time and don't start pruning unless you know you can finish the job comfortably.

2 Pruning very tall climbers is a job that requires some care. Check that the feet of the ladder are steady on the ground. Do not attempt to reach too far above your head or stretch to the left or right. It is better to move the ladder than risk overbalancing.

Shredders

Most accidents occur either when the blades are being unblocked, or when the equipment is being used without the correct safety guards in place. Always wear eye protection and strong gloves. If you are using a shredder for a long period of time, wear ear defenders too. Never put your hand in inlets or outlets and only try to shred materials recommended by the manufacturer.

Using chemicals

If you are dealing with chemicals make sure you follow all of the manufacturer's instructions, including using protective equipment or clothing, such as waterproof gloves when handling concentrates, and washing your hands and the equipment thoroughly after spraying. Do not apply at rates not given on the packet or make chemical cocktails unless it is specifically advised in the instructions. Only apply chemicals when the prevailing weather conditions are suitable and make sure spray does not drift on to other areas of the garden. Always dispose of chemicals as directed.

ADDING BONEMEAL

It is advisable to wear protective gloves when you are adding bonemeal to the soil as there is a small risk of it harbouring disease.

USING POWER TOOLS

Always read the safety instructions supplied by the manufacturer carefully before using power tools, and follow them to the letter.

Essential tool maintenance

Having invested in a set of good quality gardening tools it makes sense to keep them in good condition. Not only will they last longer, but they will be easier and more efficient to use. Always keep bladed tools sharp so that they cut efficiently, causing as little damage to the plant tissue as possible – particularly important when pruning and propagating. It also makes sense to keep the blades of spades and hoes sharp. When storing tools make sure that all bare metal parts are clean, and have an oily rag to hand so that they can be lightly oiled before being put away. Larger tools such as border forks and spades that don't have a really sharp edge can be stood in an old bucket of oily sand when they are not needed.

Most garden cutting equipment does not require routine maintenance, other than cleaning and replacing worn blades. If you do intend to use a service centre, to service a petrol machine for example, do it at the end of the season rather than waiting until the centres are busy in the spring, when frustrating delays inevitably occur.

Power tool safety checklist

Bear in mind that most serious gardening accidents involve powered equipment, so always take extra care during its use.
• Do not attempt to use a power tool unless you are completely sure you can do so safely. Some tools, such as chainsaws, require a skilled operator.
• Read the manufacturer's instructions before you start.
• Never start a job unless you are sure you have time to finish: trying to complete work in a hurry may lead to an accident.
• Always check the equipment is in good working order.
• Ensure children and pets keep well away from the working area.
• Always use the recommended protective clothing and equipment.
• Always check that the equipment is turned off before moving it around.

Electrical equipment
• Never use in the wet.
• Always use an RCD (residual current device) or similar to help prevent electric shocks.
• Only use suitable extension cables and connectors for outside operation and for the equipment being used.
• Make sure your extension cables and connectors are in good condition and brightly coloured so they are easily seen.
• Never use a damaged cable or connector and always unplug electrical equipment before leaving it unattended.

Petrol-driven tools
• Always start petrol equipment outside or in a well-ventilated outdoor building.
• Never refuel while the machine is running.
• Store fuel in a safe and secure place, well away from heat sources.

Seasonal checklist

Many of the basic maintenance tasks required in the garden are seasonal: they depend either on a particular stage of growth or on environmental conditions to be effective. For example, it is important to choose the right time of year to prune roses otherwise you risk loosing a year's worth of flowers. It is, therefore, important to know the optimum time for each technique.

The following pages summarize the main tasks you are most likely to need throughout the year. These tasks are divided into the gardening seasons of spring; early summer; late summer; and autumn and winter, rather than the seasons of the year. The techniques are listed according to the areas of the garden they apply to. Use them as a quick guide to your gardening activities but remember that nothing in gardening is prescriptive, and the timing will depend on your garden, the weather and the time you have available.

Many gardeners enjoy the routine maintenance tasks needed throughout the year. Early preparation can pay dividends later.

Spring techniques

For many gardeners, spring is the most exciting time of the year. This is when plants begin to show signs of new life and the garden is full of promise. It isn't long before the first spring flowers make their spectacular appearance.

Beds and borders

Prune shrubs Prune early-flowering shrubs, such as forsythia, as soon as flowering is over. Prune grey-leaved shrubs, such as lavenders, to keep them compact and bushy.

Apply fertilizer After pruning shrubs apply a slow-release fertilizer on the ground during mid-spring to give them a boost.

Slugs and snails Protect emerging shoots of vulnerable plants, such as hostas, from the attention of slugs and snails.

Deadhead bulbs Remove fading blooms from bulbs but leave the foliage intact for at least a further six weeks.

Start weeding Remove weeds before they are able to flower and set seed.

Compost heap As soon as the weather warms up, turn the compost heap to ensure even composting.

Bluebells will naturalize in shady areas, providing a sweetly scented carpet in late spring.

Check equipment Make sure all garden tools and machinery are in good working order before you will be using them in earnest. Check that cutting tools are sharp and electrical equipment is safe, including cables and connectors.

New plants Mid-spring is an ideal time to plant all types of hardy plants, including deciduous and evergreen trees, shrubs and climbers and hardy herbaceous plants. Wait until late spring to plant conifers.

Lawns

First cut When the grass is dry, give the lawn its first cut. Set the cutting height of the mower to 2.5cm (1in). After a few weeks, reduce the cutting height to 2cm (¾in) for most lawns, or to 1.5cm (½in) for a fine finish.

New lawns Mid- to late spring is an ideal time to create a new lawn. Prepare the ground thoroughly as soon as weather conditions allow and either sow seed or lay turf.

Control moss Apply a moss killer in mid-spring when the grass is dry if your lawn has been colonized by moss over winter. Use a wire rake to remove the moss at least a fortnight after applying the chemical control. If you need to give your lawn a boost too, use a combined moss killer and lawn fertilizer treatment.

Make repairs Remove any large weeds using an old kitchen knife and control coarse grasses by either digging them out or weakening them by slashing them with a knife each time you mow. Any bare patches can be reseeded in mid-spring.

APPLY FERTILIZER

Apply a slow-release fertilizer around shrubs to give them an added boost.

PLANT OUT

As soon as the ground begins to warm up, plant out crops brought on in the greenhouse.

Ponds

Position pump Remove the pool heater and replace the pond pump in mid-spring.

Feed fish Start feeding fish in the pond in mid-spring, as soon as they become active.

Plant up On a warm day in late spring or early summer plant up your pond or add new plants to an existing feature. Replace tender plants that have been overwintered in a frost-free place.

Greenhouse

Start sowing Make the first sowings of summer bedding plants and vegetables. Seedlings should be pricked out as soon as they are large enough to handle.

Tender perennials Overwintered tender plants, such as fuchsias and pelargoniums, should be given more water in mid-spring to start them into growth.

Harden off plants New plants that were raised in a cosy environment indoors need to be hardened off before being planted out to face the harsher conditions outside. This should start about two weeks before you plan to plant them out.

Pest watch Stay vigilant for the first signs of pests and disease. Take appropriate action as soon as you can.

Keep cool Make sure the greenhouse does not overheat by ensuring there is adequate ventilation and shading.

Kitchen garden

Feed fruit In mid-spring apply a general fertilizer to all fruit trees, bushes and canes.

Protect blossom Protect vulnerable early blossom from late frosts by covering with a double layer of horticultural fleece, taking it off during the day to allow pollinating insects to get access.

USE CLOCHES

Particularly tender plants should be protected with glass or plastic cloches until all threat of frost has passed.

Prepare seedbed Carefully prepare the area to be used as a seedbed as soon as the weather is suitable. Cover with a sheet of clear plastic to help warm the soil and encourage weed seed to germinate. Take off the sheet and lightly hoe off the weeds before sowing.

Clear ground Once the harvesting of overwintered vegetables is complete, clear the ground of debris and weeds, and cultivate the soil ready for the next crop.

PREPARE FOR PLANTING

In the vegetable garden, break the soil down to a fine tilth and rake in some general fertilizer before planting out seedlings.

Hardy vegetables Hardy seedlings can be planted out from mid-spring as soon as they are large enough and weather conditions allow. Harden them off in a cold frame first. Plant out onion sets and shallots.

Sprout potatoes In early spring place early potato tubers in a tray or an eggbox, eyes uppermost to encourage them to sprout (chit). Wait until mid-spring for maincrop potatoes. Plant earlies in mid-spring and maincrop in late spring.

Pale yellow primroses, tiny forget-me-nots and the delicate flowers of dicentras make a lovely fresh combination for a spring border.

Early summer techniques

This is the busiest time of the gardener's year, with plenty to do in every part of the garden. Seedlings and established plants will need constant attention.

Beds and borders

Position supports Place supports around tall herbaceous plants during late spring or early summer to prevent them flopping over when in full bloom. Stake single-stemmed plants, such as delphiniums and gladioli, with canes.

Plant containers Plant up hanging baskets and summer containers with bedding plants and place outside after the threat of frost has passed.

Feed container plants About a month after planting up containers (including growing bags) start to feed with liquid feed unless you added a slow-release fertilizer at planting time. Use a balanced feed on beds and borders and a high-potash fertilizer, such as tomato feed, for flowering and fruiting plants.

Deadhead flowers Remove faded blooms from repeat-flowering plants

The hardy geraniums are one of the mainstays of the summer border. There is a wide range from which to choose.

PRUNE SHRUBS

Early flowering clematis (Group 1) should be pruned after blooming.

such as roses. Annual bedding should also be deadheaded where practical to encourage further flushes of blooms. Deadhead self-seeders, such as forget-me-nots and campanulas, to prevent them becoming a weed problem. Once flowering has finished, deadhead rhododendrons, taking care not to damage or remove the buds for next year that lie just below this year's blooms.

Pest watch Stay vigilant for the first signs of pests and disease attacks, especially aphids, which can attack plants all around the garden; take appropriate action promptly. Spray susceptible roses against blackspot, mildew and rust. Hand-pick any caterpillars and sawfly grubs.

Slugs and snails Continue to protect emerging shoots of vulnerable plants such as hostas against attacks from slugs and snails.

Water new plants Make sure new plants do not run short of water during their first growing season. Mulch after watering to help retain soil moisture and minimize competition from weeds. Also water container plants as necessary.

Prune shrubs Prune early summer-flowering shrubs, such as choisya, deutzia, kerria, lilac, philadelphus, spiraea and tamarix, as soon as the flowering is over.

Tie in climbers New growth produced by climbers should be tied into the support to keep the plant looking tidy and to avoid damage to the shoots. The stems will still be flexible and easy to manoeuvre in early summer.

Keep weeding Continue to remove weeds as they appear.

Lawns

Keep mowing Mow the lawn regularly as necessary, generally at least once a week but twice a week if the grass is growing strongly. During dry spells, growth will slow and the need for mowing will be reduced; also raise the cutting height of your mower.

Watering lawns Water new lawns throughout the summer. Established lawns rarely require watering. Even if they turn brown in summer they will soon recover following the first rains in autumn.

Lawn treatments Lawn weedkillers, moss killers and fertilizers can be applied any time the grass is growing strongly up until midsummer. If you intend to use more than one treatment, use a combined product.

Ponds

Plant up On a warm day in late spring or early summer plant up your pond or add new plants to an existing feature.

Tidy ponds This is an ideal time to refurbish overgrown or neglected ponds. Clear excessive growth of blanketweed using a rake or bamboo cane and leave it on the side for a day or two to allow any trapped pond creatures to escape back into

PLANT UP THE POND

Introduce new plants to the pond carefully. Flood the container with water and gently lower it to the appropriate depth.

This cottage garden, shown in early summer, is full of freshness and vitality as the borders begin to fill out with lush vegetation and flowers.

the water. Use a small net to remove duckweed. Divide and replant any overgrown plants.

Top up water During hot and windy spells keep the water levels topped up in ponds and in the reservoirs of all water features.

Greenhouse

Harden off plants Tender bedding plants and vegetables raised under glass need to be hardened off before planting in the harsher conditions outside. This should start about two weeks before you plan to plant out.

Keep cool Make sure the greenhouse does not overheat by providing adequate ventilation and shading. Damping down may be necessary in hot, sunny weather.

Train crops Tie in new growth on tomatoes and cucumbers and pinch out sideshoots.

Keep watering and feeding Plants that are in containers will need watering several times a day in warm weather in the greenhouse. Make your life easier by installing an automatic watering system. Feed all actively growing plants with a suitable liquid feed.

Pest watch Stay vigilant for the first signs of pests such as aphids, spider mites and whitefly and diseases such as botrytis and take appropriate action promptly.

Kitchen garden

Continue sowing Make successional sowings of salad crops to maintain a continuous supply. Thin or transplant previous sowings.

Plant tender vegetables By early summer it is safe to plant out the last of the tender vegetables, such as French (green) and runner beans. Be prepared to protect them with a double layer of horticultural fleece in colder areas if a late frost is forecast.

Protect strawberries Place a mulch layer of straw under strawberry rows to prevent the fruit touching the soil and rotting. This will also prevent mud splash in heavy rain. Cover the plants with bird-proof netting before the fruits start to ripen.

Earth up potatoes Continue to earth up around emerging shoots and cover with a double layer of fleece on cold nights to protect them from frosts. By midsummer early potatoes will be ready for harvesting.

Propagate strawberries Peg down runners from healthy plants to form new plants. Grow directly into the bed or into pots filled with moist compost sunk rim-deep into the soil.

THIN SEEDLINGS

Remove the weakest seedlings to ensure the others have enough space to grow. Check the ideal space between each plant.

EARTH UP POTATOES

When the potato shoots reach 25cm (10in) high, draw in the soil along the rows to cover the stems.

Late summer techniques

Now is the time to enjoy the garden. Beds and borders will be filled with colourful blooms, and the vegetable garden will be producing a regular supply of crops.

Beds and borders

Feed container plants Continue feeding container plants unless you added a slow-release fertilizer at planting time. Use a balanced feed for general use and a high-potash fertilizer, such as tomato feed, for flowering and fruiting plants.

Watering Water containers daily throughout the summer months. In borders, concentrate on new plants, which should not go short of water during their first growing season.

Deadhead flowers Remove faded blooms from repeat-flowering plants, such as roses. Deadhead early-flowering perennials and annual bedding where practical to encourage further flushes of blooms. Trim straggly pansies. Deadhead self-seeders such as forget-me-nots and campanulas to prevent them becoming a weed problem.

Pest watch Stay vigilant for the first signs of pest and disease attacks, especially aphids, which can attack plants all around the garden; take

Cut off a sideshoot just below a leaf joint, about 2.5–10cm (1–4in) long. Trim off the lower leaves and insert the cutting in a pot.

appropriate action promptly. Spray susceptible roses against blackspot, mildew and rust. Hand-pick any caterpillars and sawfly grubs.

Save seed Collect seed from plants you want to propagate. Cover the flower heads with paper bags and cut off when ripe.

Cut back shrubs Prune summer-flowering shrubs and hedges as soon as the display is over. Cut back fast-growing hedges and climbers, such as climbing and rambler roses. Pick lavender for drying.

Plant bulbs Plant autumn-flowering bulbs, such as sternbergia, in midsummer and spring-flowering bulbs in late summer. Also plant up winter containers.

Some edging plants, such as this poached egg plant, can spill out on to the lawn, causing bald patches. Remove completely or trim back.

Sow hardy annuals During late summer sow hardy annuals, such as calendula, candytuft and nigella, in prepared soil in the garden. During cold spells over winter, protect these with cloches or a double layer of garden fleece in cold areas.

Lawns

Keep mowing Mow when necessary, and during dry spells raise the cutting height of your mower.

Watering lawns Water new lawns throughout the summer. Established lawns should not require watering. Even if they turn brown in summer they will soon recover following the first rains in autumn.

Lawn treatments Lawn weedkillers, moss killers and fertilizers can be applied if the grass is growing strongly, up to midsummer. Use a combined product if necessary.

Ponds

Top up water During hot and windy spells keep the water levels topped up in ponds and in the reservoirs of water features.

Oxygenate the water If fish are gulping at the surface of the pond in close, thundery weather, turn on the fountain or direct a jet of water from the hose into the water to churn the surface and help oxygenate the water.

Prune rambling roses such as *Rosa* 'Bobbie James' as soon as flowering has finished in late summer. This allows plenty of time for shoots to grow, ready for next season's crop of flowers.

Deadhead aquatics Remove faded blooms from repeat-flowering marginal plants and from bog garden plants.
Thin plants Overcrowded water lily pads can be thinned out, as can overgrown submerged plants.

Greenhouse

Take cuttings Propagate tender perennials, such as pelargoniums, fuchsias and marguerites, by taking cuttings during late summer; overwinter the cuttings somewhere frost-free.
Keep cool Provide adequate shading and ventilation to prevent overheating. Damping down may be necessary on hot, sunny days.
Train crops Continue to tie in new growth on tomatoes and cucumbers and pinch out sideshoots.
Keep watering and feeding Plants in containers will need watering several times a day in hot weather; you may wish to install an automatic watering system. Feed actively growing plants.
Pest watch Continue to watch for signs of pests, such as aphids, spider mites and whitefly, and diseases such as botrytis and take appropriate action promptly.
Sow winter crops If you want to have a productive greenhouse in winter sow winter lettuce, as well as carrots and radishes for early spring.

TIE IN PLANTS

Keep an eye on plants that need support, such as tomatoes, and tie them in when necessary.

This garden, a riot of colour, shapes and textures, looks its best at the height of summer.

Kitchen garden

Keep watering Water all fruit and vegetable plants in containers as necessary. Plants with developing crops will also need watering during dry spells to prevent reduced yields. Also water potatoes and leafy vegetables, such as lettuce, during dry spells throughout the summer. Consider installing automatic watering to make the job easier.
Strawberries Prepare the ground for new fruit in autumn strawberry beds. Remove netting and mulch from fruited plants and cut back their foliage. Sever rooted strawberry runners pegged down in early summer from their parent plants.
Fruit bushes Prune blackcurrants after harvesting by removing the oldest stems.
Cane fruit Cut back canes that have fruited from summer-fruiting raspberries and tie in new canes to their support.
Harvest crops Pick fruit and vegetables as they reach the right stage of development. Some types of vegetable, including runner beans and courgettes (zucchini), need picking regularly, otherwise cropping will be reduced.

Autumn and winter techniques

This is the time to prepare the garden for bad weather. Make sure that all garden structures are sound and secure against wind and rain.

Beds and borders

Pot up tender perennials Tender perennials, such as pelargoniums, fuchsias and marguerites, should be lifted and potted up before the first frost to be overwintered in the greenhouse. If space is short, take cuttings instead.

Lift tender bulbs In colder areas, especially if the soil is heavy, tender bulbs such as gladioli should be lifted before the first frost and dried and stored somewhere frost-free. Check for rot every few weeks.

Plant bulbs There is still time to plant spring-flowering bulbs and winter containers.

Protect some shrubs Some shrubs are of borderline hardiness, depending on where you live. Protect vulnerable shrubs as well as hardy shrubs in exposed positions with a layer of windbreak netting lined with garden fleece, held taut between sturdy posts.

Tie in wall shrubs Check wall shrubs and tie in new growth as necessary. Protect not-so-hardy types such as ceanothus with a double layer of garden fleece. Tender shrubs and

Asters are one of the mainstays of the autumn garden. *Aster x frikartii* 'Mönch' flowers over a long period from summer to late autumn.

climbers will need an insulating layer of leaves or straw, held in place with fine-mesh netting.

Pruning Long whippy growth on roses in exposed sites should be cut back by about one-third to prevent wind-rock loosening the roots. Winter prune wisteria. Cut back all stems of any Group 3 clematis.

New plants The dormant season is an ideal time to plant bare-rooted trees, shrubs and hedging plants.

Protect containers Leave only frost-proof containers outside in winter. Other containers, and the tender plants growing in them, may need protecting in colder areas. Wrap pots with bubble polythene to prevent the compost (soil mix) freezing solid. Protect the plant in a double layer of garden fleece. Leave a space for evergreen plants to be watered.

Wrap conifers Protect conifer specimens from being splayed open by heavy falls of snow by wrapping fine-mesh netting or a piece of thick soft string around them. Conifer hedges should have accumulations of snow knocked off before they cause damage to the branches.

Check stakes and ties Most climbers and many trees will have ties holding them on to a support or stake. Check these in winter to ensure they are secure but not too constricting.

Protect rock plants Excessive winter wet can damage plants with woolly foliage, such as those found in the rock garden. Protect by covering them with an open-ended cloche or a sheet of glass held up on bricks.

Clear summer bedding Remove annual plants from the border and dig over the ground ready for planting in the spring.

Lawns

Lawn repairs Early autumn is the perfect time to carry out maintenance tasks such as spiking and scarifying as well as essential lawn repairs.

Final cut Make the final cut once the grass has stopped growing. Then clean and service the lawn equipment before storage.

Fallen leaves Clear fallen leaves from the lawn through autumn and early winter so they do not smother the grass. Do not walk on the lawn if it is very wet or frosted.

TIDY BORDERS

Clear summer bedding away and dig over the soil, removing large weeds. Rake the ground level so it looks neat and tidy.

PROTECT CONTAINERS

Protect vulnerable container-grown plants with a layer of insulation. Plastic bubble wrap is a good choice.

Ponds

Fallen leaves Keep fallen leaves out of ponds by covering the feature with a lightweight fine-mesh netting. Clear any leaves collected in the netting regularly to prevent them rotting and fouling the water.

Autumn tidy up Cut back marginal plants, but take care not to cut those with hollow stems too short – the cut stems should remain proud of the water surface all winter.

Prevent freezing Remove the pond pump and replace it with a pond heater in autumn. If you do not have a pond heater, keep at least one area of a pond that contains fish ice-free by melting a hole with a pan of hot water.

Greenhouse

Move tender plants Citrus trees and other tender shrubs growing in containers should be moved from their summer position on the patio to the protection of a heated greenhouse or conservatory.

Remove shading Clean shading wash from the glass or take down shading material or blinds to maximize the amount of light getting into the greenhouse in winter.

Put up insulation Fit polythene bubble insulation to the roof and walls of all the greenhouse to keep down heating costs and to help maintain an even temperature. Check that the heater is in good working condition. Unheated greenhouses also need additional insulation.

Clear crops Remove summer crops from the greenhouse and take down plant supports. Clean pots and other equipment so that they are ready for use in the spring.

Clean greenhouse On a mild day in autumn remove everything from the greenhouse and clean the structure, staging and floor with a garden disinfectant to help prevent pests and diseases overwintering successfully. Wipe pots of permanent plants and clear up all debris, such as fading flowers and yellowing leaves, to help reduce the problems of botrytis disease over winter.

Kitchen garden

Prevent problems Clear fallen fruit and leaves from under fruit crops to prevent pests and diseases from over-wintering ready to attack the crops next year. Tie grease bands around the trunks of fruit trees to trap the wingless female codling moths, which climb the trees and lay eggs.

Harvest vegetables Pick the last crops of beans and salad crops as well as squashes and tomatoes. Place cloches over tomato plants to help ripen the fruit or pick the green tomatoes and ripen in a fruit drawer containing a banana skin.

Harvest apples Late apples should be harvested when ready. Perfect fruit can be stored.

Encourage tomatoes to ripen by placing a cloche over them. If a severe frost is forecast, however, harvest the remaining fruit.

Winter digging Clear summer crops and dig over vacant heavy soil so that frost can break down large clods ready for planting next year.

Plant vegetables Plant garlic cloves, spring cabbages and broccoli in well-prepared ground.

Herbs Pot up herbs for winter use.

Pruning Complete all winter pruning of tree, bush and cane fruits.

New plants The dormant season is an ideal time to plant bare-rooted fruit trees, bushes and canes.

Prunus x *subhirtella* 'Stellata' has star-like pale pink flowers. It is an eye-catching feature in winter, flowering from late autumn to early spring, a time when the rest of the garden can appear dead.

Glossary of terms

Annual A plant that grows from seed, flowers, sets seed again and dies in one year.

Aquatic A plant that lives in water: it can be completely submerged, floating or live with its roots in the water and shoots in the air.

Bare-root A plant that is sold with no soil or compost around the roots. They are dug up from the nursery field and are ready for planting during the dormant season.

Bedding plant A plant that is raised for use in a temporary garden display; spring, summer and winter types are available.

Biennial A plant that grows from seed to form a small plant in the first year and flowers and sets seed in the following year.

Biological control The use of a pest's natural enemies to control its numbers in the garden or greenhouse.

Bog garden An area of ground that remains permanently wet and is used to grow bog plants that thrive in such conditions.

Capillary matting An absorbent material that holds a lot of water on which containers are placed and from which they can draw all the moisture they need via capillary action.

Certified stock Plants that have been inspected and declared free of specific pests and diseases. They can be used as stock plants for propagation material.

Chit A technique used to encourage a potato tuber to begin to sprout before planting.

Cloche A small structure made from glass, clear plastic or polythene that can be moved around easily to warm small areas of soil or protect vulnerable plants.

Compost (soil mix) A mixture that is used for growing plants in containers. It can be loam-based or peat-based. Peat-free versions are now available based on coir, composted bark or other organic waste material.

Compost, garden A material that has been produced from the decomposition of organic waste material in a compost bin or heap. Useful as a soil improver or planting mixture.

Cordon A trained form of tree or bush with a main stem, vertical or at an angle, and with sideshoots shortened to form fruiting spurs.

Crop covers Various porous materials used to protect plants or crops. Horticultural fleece is a woven fabric that can be used to protect plants from frost and flying insect pests; insect-proof mesh is a well-ventilated fabric, ideal for keeping out insects throughout the summer, but offers no frost protection.

Damping down Wetting surfaces in a greenhouse to raise air humidity and to help keep temperatures under control.

Deadhead To remove spent flowers to tidy the display, prevent the formation of seeds and improve future flowering performance.

Earth up To draw up soil around a plant forming a mound. Potatoes are earthed up to protect new shoots from frost and to prevent tubers from being exposed to light, which turns them green.

Espalier A trained form of tree or bush where the main stem is vertical and pairs of sideshoots are at a set spacing and trained out horizontally.

Fan A trained form of tree or bush where the main stem is vertical and pairs of sideshoots are pruned at set spacing and trained out either side to form a fan shape.

Grafted plant An ornamental plant that has been attached on to the rootstock of another, more vigorous, variety.

Ground cover plants These are densely growing, mat-forming plants that can be used to cover the ground with foliage to prevent weeds germinating.

Hardening-off A method of gradually weaning off a plant from the conditions inside to those outside without causing a check to growth.

Hardiness The amount of cold a type of plant is able to withstand. Hardy plants can tolerate frost; half-hardy and tender plants cannot.

Herbaceous plants Plants that produce sappy, green, non-woody growth. Herbaceous perennials die down in winter, but re-grow from basal shoots the following spring.

Horticultural fleece *see* crop covers.

Humus The organic residue of decayed organic matter found in soil. It improves soil fertility.

Insect-proof mesh *see* crop covers.

Leafmould A material that has been produced from the decomposition of leaves in a leaf bin or heap. Useful as a soil improver or planting mixture.

Manure A bulky organic animal waste that is rotted down and used to improve soil structure and fertility.

Mulch A material that is laid on the surface of the soil to prevent moisture loss through evaporation and suppress weed growth. Can be loose and organic, such as composted bark or garden compost, loose and inorganic, such as gravel, or a fabric, such as mulch matting or landscape fabric.

Perennial A plant that lives for more than two years. Usually applied to a hardy non-woody plant (*see* herbaceous). A tender perennial is a non-woody plant that cannot tolerate frost.

Pricking out The spacing of seedlings while still small so that they have room to grow on.

Rootball A mass of roots and compost that holds together when a plant is removed from its container.

Runner A horizontal shoot that spreads out from the plant, roots and forms another plant.

Slow-release fertilizer A specially coated inorganic fertilizer that releases its nutrients slowly.

Sucker A shoot that arises from the roots underground. The term is usually applied to shoots from the rootstock of a grafted plant that has different characteristics to the ornamental variety.

Transplanting The transfer of seedlings or young plants from a nursery bed where they were sown to their final growing position.

Windbreak A hedge, fence, wall or fabric that is used to filter the wind and reduce the damage it may cause.

Rosa 'Frühlingsgold'

Index

Pieris japonica

Rosa x *alba* 'Alba Semiplena'

Narcissus 'Tête-à-tête'

Tagetes patula 'Golden Gem'

Nymphaea 'Attraction'

Rudbeckia fulgida var. *deamii*

Acknowledgements

The publisher would like to thank
Peter McHoy for his permission to
use the following photographs:
14T; 18BL, BM and BR; 19BL, BM
and BR; 45B; 136BL, BM and BR;
137BL, BM and BR

Photography: Peter Anderson,
Jonathan Buckley, Paul Forrester,
John Freeman, Michelle Garrett,
Janine Hosegood, Andrea Jones,
Simon McBride, Marie O'Hara

Illustrations: Neil Bulpitt,
Liz Pepperell, Michael Shoebridge

Additional step-by-step text: Peter
McHoy, Richard Bird, Andrew
Mikolajski, Ted Collins, Blaise Cooke,
Christopher Grey-Wilson, Lin
Hawthorne, Jessica Houdret, Hazel
Key, Peter Robinson, Susie White